The Art of Prediction in Astrology

The Art of Prediction in Astrology

GAYATRI DEVI VASUDEV

MOTILAL BANARSIDASS PUBLISHERS
PRIVATE LIMITED • DELHI

Reprint: Delhi, 2012
First Edition: Delhi, 2008

© GAYATRI DEVI VASUDEV
All Rights Reserved

ISBN: 978-81-208-3229-9

MOTILAL BANARSIDASS

41 U.A. Bungalow Road, Jawahar Nagar, Delhi 110 007
8 Mahalaxmi Chamber, 22 Bhulabhai Desai Road, Mumbai 400 026
203 Royapettah High Road, Mylapore, Chennai 600 004
236, 9th Main III Block, Jayanagar, Bangalore 560 011
Sanas Plaza, 1302 Baji Rao Road, Pune 411 002
8 Camac Street, Kolkata 700 017
Ashok Rajpath, Patna 800 004
Chowk, Varanasi 221 001

Printed in India
By Jainendra Prakash Jain at Shri Jainendra Press,
A-44, Naraina Phase-I, New Delhi 110 028
and Published by Narendra Prakash Jain for
Motilal Banarsidass Publishers Private Limited,
Bungalow Road, Delhi 110 007

Dedicated to my beloved parents
Dr. B.V. Raman and Mrs. Rajeswari Raman

PREFACE

Astrology and interest in it have been growing at a pace that does justice to the subject as a discipline of great consequence in handling the complexities and ills of human life and existence.

Authoritative works on astrology abound in Sanskrit and several of them have been translated into English by scholars. These translations are a great boon to the diligent student and carry innumerable combinations and dicta covering almost all aspects of life. However, the difficulty lies in their actual application to horoscopes where the skills of the astrology student are challenged to the limit.

I have endeavoured in these pages to place before my readers my own experience with these dicta and their application to practical cases. I must emphasize that working under my revered father Dr. B.V. Raman for nearly 3 decades and watching him analyse astrological combinations have given me insights into the nuances of predictive astrology that no book can teach. Dr. Raman's aim was to propagate astrology methodically. I feel by sharing my experience in the subject with my readers, I would be respecting his approach and fulfilling his wish.

One of the interesting features of astrology is not only its application to individual lives but also to natural phenomena and disasters as well as the political life of a country. For instance, the terrorist attacks on the World Trade Center in the U.S. on September 11, 2001 was anticipated 11 months before based on principles of mundane astrology. It may surprise the modern scientist to learn that the tsunami that struck the Indian coastline on December 26, 2004 was not unexpected astrologically though it took him by surprise. It was anticipated in my editorial "World Trends and

Tensions" in THE ASTROLOGICAL MAGAZINE, January 2004. Likewise the drought that struck our country in 2002-2003 was also astrologically expected much before the country reeled under it. DR. RAMAN'S pioneering work in mundane astrology covering earthquakes and weather helped me further develop the methods outlined by him in making these and other predictions in my annual forecasts in THE ASTROLOGICAL MAGAZINE. I have put together these and other editorials that have earlier appeared in THE ASTROLOGICAL MAGZINE in these pages.

I would feel amply rewarded if this volume succeeds in inspiring the diligent reader to delve deeper into the subject.

I would like to express my gratitude to my husband Mr. C. Vasudev and son Mr. B.V. Omprakash for their quiet cooperation in not grudging me my long hours at astrology.

I thank Mr. R.K. Anantha Srinivas for typing the manuscript neatly, Mrs. Mahalakshmi Damodar and Mr. M. Jagadeesha for the type-setting and Mrs. S. Shylaja for reading the proof.

I express my gratefulness to Mr. J.P. Jain of Motilal Banarsidass Publishers Pvt. Ltd., for his interest in publishing this volume and his continuing support to our work in astrology.

June 30, 2006 *Gayatri Devi Vasudev*
Bangalore.

CONTENTS

Preface   *vii*

Section I: Individual Horoscopy

1. Hamsa-Gajakesari Yogas and Lasting Reputation   3
2. Tenth House Saturn and Blazing Renunciation   11
3. Ramana Maharshi's Death Experience - Astrologically Analysed   23
4. Saddam Hussein — A Study in Paisacha Yoga   33
5. Eclipses in Astrology   45
6. Treating Eclipses as Transits — I   53
7. Treating Eclipses as Transits — II   59
8. The Astrological Dissection of a Sniper Killer   71
9. The Yamaganda - Yamakantaka Conundrum   83
10. Rasi or Bhava ?   93
11. Rasi and Bhava, Not Rasi or Bhava   101
12. Moon and Human Psychology and Behaviour   113
13. Sri Jayendra Saraswati's Sanyasa Yogas   125
14. Astrological Saga of a Saint   135
15. Schizophrenic Tendencies and Lunar Nodes - I   147
16. Schizophrenic Tendencies and Lunar Nodes - II   155

Section II: Meteorology and Seismology

17. Sun and Agricultural Activity   165
18. Solar Movements and Mundane Events   177
19. Varahamihira's Law of Sunspot Activity and Events on Earth   183
20. Planets and Summer Crops   193
21. Tsunami Prediction — An Astrological Model — I   201

22. Tsunami Prediction — An Astrological Model — II 207

Section III: Political Predictions

23. Lagna Lord's Bhukti and Return to Power 221
24. Longevity of the NDA Government and Muhurta Principles 231
25. Muhurta Factors and Narendra Modi's Chief Ministership 239
26. Planets and Dynastic Ambitions 247
27. Martian Movements and *Jehad* Against America 259

SECTION I

INDIVIDUAL HOROSCOPY

HAMSA-GAJAKESARI YOGAS AND LASTING REPUTATION

1. *Lagna lord as centre of powerful Yogas gives everlasting fame.*
2. *Fifth lord conjunct powerful Venus confers prodigious talents.*
3. *Ashtama Sani can cut short even the best of careers.*

LASTING FAME

MAHA VAIDYA NATHA SIVAN was one of those dazzling stars that appeared on the firmament of Carnatic music during its golden age in the 19th century.

A musician and vocalist, the exceptionally gifted Maha Vaidya Natha Sivan's supremacy in his art was recognised by both his peers and fans. He was born with a striking combination of planets. The Lagna is Sagittarius, the sign of the archer, rooted in the ground but aiming high. It gains considerable strength by its ruler Jupiter generating a Hamsa Yoga, one of the more weightier of the Panchamahapurusha Yogas which repeats from the Chandra Lagna also supported by the Gajakesari Yoga focussing on the 10th or the house of reputation. The Moon in the 10th, free of association by conjunction, causes Amala Yoga, a Yoga for unsullied reputation and fame, both of which tagged on to Vaidya Natha Sivan in abundant measure.

MUSICAL GENIUS

Though the Lagna is Sagittarius, there is a mix of Pisces and its characteristics also due to the Lagna lord being in the latter sign, blending high ideals with deep devotion. The Lagna is aspected by Vargottama Venus, Karaka for the arts, and benefic Mars, ruler of the 5th house of creativity and inspiration. With such a brilliant array of planets, it was not unusual that the genius in Maha Vaidya Natha Sivan, who embodied the highest spirituality in his outpourings of music, came to be recognised by music lovers attracting for himself the sobriquet of one of the most brilliant singers of his period. It is said his singing was so perfect, so mesmerising and elevating he had "no peers either as a vocalist or as a musician."

* Born 26-5-1844 at 8-55-25 p.m. (IST) at 10 N 48, 79 E 09 with a balance of 4 years 0 month and 21 days of Sun Dasa at birth.

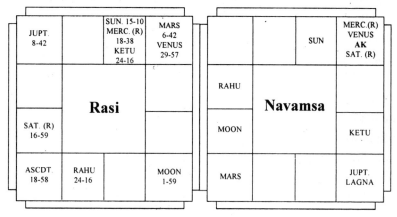

HUMBLE ORIGINS

Born in a tiny little hamlet Vaiyacheri near Tanjore in Tamil Nadu into an orthodox Brahmin family, Vaidya Natha Iyer or Maha Sivan, as he was popularly known during his times, had 3 brothers, 2 older than him. His father was a highly gifted musician, so also his mother. The Ascendant lord Jupiter in the 4th in Sukhastana gave him domestic

---

* We are indebted to Dr. N.S. Rajaram for the birth-data and biographical details.

environs in which the potential in him found support and bloomed into a gorgeous exotic flower. Though not affluent by any standards with the 8th lord Moon influencing both the Ascendant lord Jupiter as well as the 4th house and its lord, Vaidya Natha Iyer grew up in circumstances that were not indigent either. His mother, a singer herself, was a noble lady with generous instincts and delighted in feeding the poor children and Brahmin boys of the village. Jupiter as the Ascendant lord in the 4th in Matrustana, aspected by Matrukaraka Moon from the 10th, took care to give the native a pious, devout and affable mother.

Saturn is in the 2nd in his own house. Maha Sivan was a taciturn person who never or, if ever, seldom indulged in conversation for its own sake.

Deeply spiritual, thanks to Jupiter in Pisces and Jupiter's aspect on the Moon, he gave away most of his money, after he began to earn as a singer, in charity.

The Ascendant is aspected by Vargottama 11th lord Venus. His elder brother Ramaswami Sivan was a gifted composer and singer and the two brothers were said to be inseparable.

Both boys had prodigious memories. Maha Sivan was a *dwi santa grahi* or one who could remember *adverbatim* anything he heard twice. Mercury, the Karaka for memory, though in the 6th is with Vargottama 9th lord Sun and the spiritual Ketu who gets Neechabhanga. Not only that, Mercury occupies Gemini Navamsa giving the native a sharp incisive intellect and brilliant retentive brain.

VARGOTTAMA VENUS AND CREATIVITY

The aspect of the 5th lord Mars on the Ascendant joined by Vargottama Venus made him a musical genius of a very high order. As 5th lord, Mars rules creativity and his association with Venus, the Karaka for music and the other arts, made Maha Sivan compose and produce some of the best pieces of Carnatic music which could easily stand comparison with those of the Grand Trinity — Tyagaraja, Muthuswami Dikshitar and Shama Sastri of the South. The same disposition of Venus, aided by the 5th lordship of Mars who joins him and its Nakshatra Punarvasu ruled by Jupiter (the focus of Hamsa and Gajakesari Yogas), which Venus occupies, led him to compose the Mela Raga Mallika — a masterpiece which featured all the 72 major Ragas in one cycle, a feat rarely equalled.

MULTIPLE YOGAS

Maha Vaidya Natha Sivan's chart bristles with several well-known Yogas. Jupiter in a Kendra from the Moon is said to cause Gajakesari Yoga, some of the results of which are "many relations, polite and generous.... lasting reputation even long after death" all of which were evident in the great musician's life. Jupiter in a Kendra which should also happen to be his own or exaltation sign gives rise to Hamsa Yoga. Jupiter occupies Pisces, his own sign, in the 4th from Lagna and in the 7th from the Moon and generates this important Panchamahapurusha Yoga, results of which are "one will be handsome, liked by others and of a righteous disposition and pure in mind." Chatursagara Yoga with its results of "being equal to a ruler, having good children and health with lasting and wide reputation" obtains in a slightly watered form as only 3 and not 4 of the Kendras are occupied by planets as required by the Yoga. But the planets in these Kendras are all so strongly placed, they attract the results of the Yoga in ample measure — Jupiter as Lagna lord in own sign is in the 4th, Vargottama Venus and Mars are in the 7th and the Moon (unafflicted and strong) is in the 10th. Jupiter, Venus and the Moon in Kendras contribute to another favourable Yoga — Rajalakshna Yoga — which gets somewhat diluted here, as Mercury falls out of the orb of the definition. Amala Yoga, due to the 10th from the Lagna being occupied by a benefic, contributes to the high reputation Maha Vaidya Natha Sivan enjoyed both in his life-time and even after his death. Vesi, Budha-Aditya,

Lakshmi, Sankha, Bheri and many other Yogas with highly favourable results make the chart truly outstanding, their auspiciousness being amplified manifold by the strength of the Ascendant Sagittarius and its ruler Jupiter. Therefore, it comes as no surprise if Maha Vaidya Natha Sivan's name holds a hallowed place in the galaxy of the country's most illustrious singers of the last two centuries. The Atmakaraka appropriately is Venus, the Karaka for music, and it was music that was the soul of this great genius.

STRONG KARAKAMSA

The Karakamsa Gemini is influenced by as many as four planets — Jupiter, Saturn, Mercury and Mars giving birth to an extraordinarily gifted artist.

Even as his Moon Dasa progressed with the Moon in the 10th aspected by Jupiter and Mars, Maha Vaidya Natha Sivan began to be noticed and recognized as an accomplished singer. Venus Bhukti with Venus Vargottama in the 10th from the Dasa lord Moon was particularly significant in that, it was during this period that even the most critical connoisseurs of music of his times could not help but admire the confidence and effortless ease with which his voice would break out into song.

It was with the advent of Yogakaraka Mars Dasa that he was given the title *Maha* or 'great' under the suggestion of Periya Vaidya Natha Iyer, the foremost singer of that period Sivan was only 14 years old. And the title stuck to him so that more than even a century after his death, he is never referred to without the prefix *Maha*.

Maha Vaidya Natha Sivan had an usual gift, thanks to the Swakshetra Jupiter being Lagna lord and the Vargottama Venus aspecting the Lagna. It is said, he never needed practice and his voice was rich and his singing, effortless and spontaneous.

JUPITER IN PISCES AND SPIRITUALITY

He was deeply devoted to Lord Siva and a student of Advaita

consistent with the Ascendant lord being in the highly spiritual sign Pisces. The aspect of the emotional Moon put the indelible stamp of devotional spirituality on all his renditions. In fact, a lesser-known side of the great singer was as an exponent of the **Puranas** —Siva Kathas as musical recitals. He would also give Hari Kathas, though his Ishta was Lord Siva.

The 10th lord Mercury both from Lagna and Chandra Lagna in Gemini Navamsa (सौम्यांशे लिंपिगणितादिकाव्यशिल्पै:) made him a composer as well as a singer, the latter due to the exchange Mercury has with Venus, the Karaka for all arts, and his powerful aspect on the Ascendant.

To Maha Sivan, his art was an expression of his soul and its devotion to the Lord. Though famous as a musician, he spent more time in his Adhyatmic studies and practices. The 5th lord Mars strongly influences the Ascendant. The 5th rules pious practices and Upasana of which there was no dearth in his life.

The Ascendant lord Jupiter in his own sign aspecting the Moon endowed him with a pure mind, untainted by the lower emotions. Simple and straightforward, the well-placed Moon also gave him quietness and a frank nature.

Jupiter aspects the 12th house and the 12th lord aspects Lagna. His generous instincts were so strong, he never hoarded any wealth for himself, or his family. He maintained an open house where 30 to 40 people were fed daily. Jupiter in Pisces in mutual aspect with the Moon also made him tender-hearted; while he liberally gave away to others, where he himself was concerned his was a life of frugal austerity as ensured by Saturn's aspect on Jupiter.

The aspect of Venus on the Ascendant made him striking and handsome while that of Mars gave him a slim and medium build. It also made him look much younger than his age.

His wife was a devoted partner. Self-effacing and a woman of piety, she provided the perfect foil to her great husband. The 7th lord Mercury is in the 6th in a friendly sign with the 9th lord Vargottama Sun.

ADVERSE INFLUENCES—NATAL AND TRANSIT

In 1892, Maha Vaidya Natha Sivan stopped singing after an unpleasant episode when a patron of arts asked him to sing a song of the latter's choice. Maha Vaidya Natha Sivan, prompted by his elder brother, left the hall never to sing in public again. Thereafter, his singing was only for his Ishta. This event came about in Venus Bhukti of Jupiter Dasa. The two planets are mutual enemies and in Dasamsa*, Jupiter, the Dasa lord is in the 8th in Capricorn in his sign of debility. Venus, though exalted in the 10th, is eclipsed by Rahu. Venus is also the Atmakaraka and can give a shake-up to one's career.

The transits too were ominous foreshadowing the great withdrawal from singing for the public. Saturn was in Virgo on the natal Moon with the seven-and-a-half year cycle in full swing.

The end came peacefully and suddenly on 27-1-1893 under the same directional influences. Maha Vaidya Natha Sivan had a premonition the time had come for him to leave the earth. Returning home on that fateful morning after worshipping Lord Siva at the local temple, he collapsed bringing the curtains down on a life of sublime devotion and music. The Dasa lord Jupiter, though the Lagna lord, is aspected by 8th lord Moon.

From the Moon, he becomes a powerful Maraka as 7th lord in the 7th. Venus, the Bhukti lord, is in the 7th with 12th lord Mars. The 8th house Cancer is aspected by a powerful Jupiter who also aspects the 8th lord Moon. Saturn too aspects the 8th from a soft constellation Sravana. The great singer shed his body with the same quiet dignity that had marked his life and music. *(05-01)* ●

***Dasamsa** : Gemini - Ascendant and Sun; Cancer - Mercury; Leo - Mars; Virgo - Ketu; Capricorn - Jupiter and Mars; Pisces - Venus and Rahu; and Taurus - Sun.

2

TENTH HOUSE SATURN AND BLAZING RENUNCIATION

> 1. Saturn in the 10th raises one to great heights.
> 2. Saturn in the 10th makes for blazing spirituality.
> 3. Saturn in the 10th brings about abysmal fall in materialistic careers.

A DATE FOR DEPARTURE

IT WAS SLIGHTLY over hundred years ago, the Sun set on the spiritual horizon of the world when that lion among renunciates, Swami Vivekananda, the kingly Sanyasi of India who took the immortal spiritual wisdom of the country to the West, gave up his body on July 4, 1902. He was in excellent health. In fact, it had never been so good in recent months. Jupiter, the Lagna lord, aspecting the 3rd made death come, but only at his bidding when he knew his life's task had been completed and he could hearken back to those heavenly realms from where he had come.

A week before the end Swami Vivekananda had asked Swami Shuddhananda, a brother monk, to bring him the Bengali almanac. He went through it carefully. He was found to be studying the almanac keenly on several occasions later as if looking for something auspicious. Only after his passing away did it occur to his brother disciples that he was selecting an auspicious day for his departure as Sri Ramakrishna had done before him. The last day of the lunar month of Vaisakha, an

Amavasya, was current when the body was shed. The Manahkaraka Moon ruling the embodied ego or mind was fast merging and dissolving into the Sun, the Atmakaraka ruling the Universal Consciousness. And the rising sign at 9-10 p.m. when this spiritual event occurred was Pisces in Cancer Navamsa. The Ascendant lord Jupiter was Neecha with Neechabhanga in Capricorn but in the 12th Bhava as if to confirm the soul had flown to a realm of no return.

TENTH HOUSE SATURN

The outstanding feature of Swami Vivekananda's chart is the Moon-Saturn conjunction in the 10th house producing the highest levels of renunciation. Saturn in the 10th is often said to raise a native to great heights. And this has been found to occur regularly in the charts of rulers and leaders. But the same Saturn in the 10th rarely rests quietly before hurtling down the native mercilessly to abysmal depths of humiliation and defeat. This unique Yoga has not been defined in classical works really but which Dr. RAMAN identified, when dealing with the charts of nations and national

* Born 12-1-1863 at 6-33 a.m. (LMT) at 22 N 30, 88 E 20 with a balance of 3 years 3 months 27 days of Moon Dasa at birth.

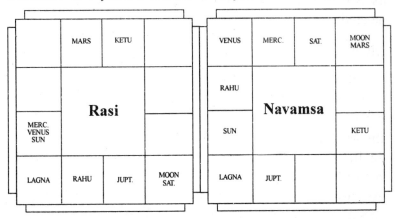

* See page 192, **Notable Horoscopes** by Dr. B.V. RAMAN.

destinies in his editorials covering world predictions, makes for leaders who often have humble beginnings but rise to the top propelled by circumstances as men of destiny. But Dr. RAMAN also had found that such men would usually leave the stage of the world humbled and humiliated. Working on this Yoga, we have since found a number of charts confirming Dr. RAMAN's findings but there have been exceptions to this general rule too.

And the exception occurs with Saturn's power to hurtle one down confined to political and materialistic careers alone. **But in the charts of those who work for the weal of humanity, Saturn in the 10th becomes an unparalleled benefic conferring his blessings endlessly.** Such natives mesmerise crowds with their spiritual strength and draw the highest respect and reverence for their blemishless renunciation. Swami Vivekananda is a good illustration of such a Saturn.

Wherever Swami Vivekananda went, he never failed to attract the masses. He left them electrified and inspired as never before with his speeches that dazzled both the illiterate as well as the intellectual. Thousands of people fell on top of one another just to get close to him and pay their respects to him. Perhaps no one in that period had such a magnetic influence on the masses as Swami Vivekananda. And Saturn in the 10th must be credited for it.

MONKHOOD CLUES

According to **Jataka Parijata** (XV-20), if Saturn or lord of the Lagna aspect the lord of the sign occupied by the Moon, one becomes a mendicant. Here, the lord of the sign occupied by the Moon, Mercury, is not aspected by Saturn or Lagna lord Jupiter. But Saturn influences Mercury deeply by the Parivartana between the two planets, fulfilling the conditions for monkhood. According to XV-40 *ibid.*, when the Moon occupies a Drekanna of Saturn and is aspected by that planet, it leads to renunciation of the world. Here, the Moon occupies the second Drekanna of

Virgo which is ruled by Saturn. Instead of being aspected by Saturn, the Moon is with him.

BRILLIANT YOUNGSTER

Born to an aristocratic but pious and noble couple, Vivekananda who was earlier known as Narendranath Datta and endearingly called as Naren and Loren, had Sagittarius rising in the Ascendant producing in him a stately soul, noble and magnanimous. Consistent with the fiery nature of Sagittarius, Naren was a brilliant, outspoken youth who impressed everyone he met with his silvery speech and piercing intellect. The 2nd house, Vakstana, has Mercury, Venus and Vargottama Sun while 2nd lord Saturn is with the Moon — an ideal combination for extraordinary eloquence.

Let us go back once more, O mind,
                 to our proper home;
Here in this foreign land of earth
Why should we wander aimlessly in
              stranger's guise ?

This song which Narendra sang before Ramakrishna Paramahamsa at their first meeting in 1882 seemed to hint at the spiritual bonding between the two souls and of a Home beyond home from whence the twosome had come. This meeting which was to change the entire course of the life of the brilliant 19th century student Narendranath Datta very appropriately occurred in Mercury Bhukti of Rahu Dasa. Mercury occupies the 2nd house in an excellent Parivartana with 2nd lord Saturn, the latter in the 10th changing the direction of the youth's life in a manner that was never expected then. Both Mercury and Saturn are connected with the 10th house; one by lordship and the other by occupation. Rahu, the Dasa lord, takes on Saturnine properties. Appropriately, the Rahu-Mercury periods triggered a major shift in the young lad's destiny.

The Moon sign provides even finer clues to the direction from which the thrust came. Saturn is the 5th lord from Chandra Lagna in exchange of signs with Mercury involving the 5th house of Poorvapunya. Some deep-rooted memory appears to have stirred in the breast of this unique lad as he asked the God intoxicated Master quite plainly and directly "Sir, Have you seen God?" And the Master's unhesitating and immediate reply "Yes, I have seen God. I see Him as I see you here, only more clearly...." impressed Narendra with explosive strength coming as it did from a man who knew nought except to speak the Truth. This meeting which took place in Dakshineswer set the tone for the young man's future mission in life, pushing worldly concerns out and replacing them with an inner longing that would soon take the world by storm. A solar eclipse had occurred in Aries on May 17, 1882. Unusually there were no lunar eclipses that year. This eclipse involving the 5th house (Aries) and the sign occupied by Lagna lord Jupiter (Libra) worked to awaken and fan the dormant spiritual embers in the youth.

RAHU AND SPIRITUAL YEARNING

The Dasa lord Rahu occupies Scorpio, his sign of debilitation, aspected powerfully by the 5th and 12th lord Mars from his own sign Aries, the highly impulsive, energetic and intrepid sign of the Zodiac. Rahu in Scorpio is no doubt Neecha to begin with and should have produced an atheist with perverted logic if the Neechattwa had not been cancelled. But in this case Rahu attains Neechabhanga by virtue of the sign-dispositors of his exaltation and debilitation signs, Venus and Mars respectively, being in mutual quadrants. As a result the Neecha results associated with Rahu are blown off without a trace and replaced by an extremely logical and rational approach to everything — from the most trivial to the most important. Rahu is in watery Scorpio in Jyeshta. This again endows the native with a deep spiritual thirst and fervour, which though not initially apparent, cannot be held down for too long but must erupt in a powerful stream just as soon as planetary conditions become favourable for it. Transit Jupiter, when this epochal meeting between Master and disciple took place, was in Aries on natal Mars in the natal 5th house aspecting natal Lagna lord Jupiter stirring in the youth's heart questions that found no answers anywhere. Saturn too was in Aries in the same sign in the 8th from natal Moon working to bring in great changes in his life, while transit Rahu was in Scorpio on natal Dasa lord Rahu.

BENEFICS IN VAKSTANA

The Ascendant lord Jupiter in the 11th, a powerful Upachaya ruling friends, associates and authority, made sure he was the soul of any gathering and the centre of attention everywhere he went. The attention was not the result of effort; rather it came unsought for his manner and demeanour, friendly, outspoken, mirthful and regal all at the same time, thanks to Venus-Mercury combining in the 2nd house. Vargottama Sun with Venus in the 2nd gifted him with a sweet voice that touched the chords of the heart of the listener whenever he broke out into song. According to the leading philosopher Dr. Brajendra Nath Seal, who was a fellow student of Naren, the latter was "Undeniably a gifted youth, sociable, free and unconventional in manners, a sweet singer, the soul of social circles, a brilliant conversationalist, somewhat bitter and caustic, piercing with the shafts of a keen wit shows and mummeries of the world, sitting in the scorner's chair but hiding the tenderest of hearts under the garb of cynicism; altogether an inspired bohemian but possessing what bohemians lack, an iron will; somewhat peremptory and absolute; speaking with accents of authority and withal possessing a strange power of the eye which could hold his listeners in thrall." All these are a clear blessing of a Vargottama Ascendant and its ruler Jupiter in the 11th house. Swami Vivekananada's greatest asset, shown by the Labhastana, was his charismatic and incisive intellect, the one shown by Lagna lord Jupiter in the 11th and the other, by 5th lord Mars in the 5th aspecting the Lagna lord from the fiery, blazing sign Aries.

The Moon in Hasta, his own constellation and a Mridu Tara, joined by Saturn, also in the same soft constellation made him kind and tender-hearted. Occurring in Virgo, in the 10th sign from the Ascendant, the Moon-Saturn-Hasta link would also one day make him experience his Oneness with all of humanity.

MUST FIND OUT FOR ONESELF

Though Rahu gave a Western education to Narendranath, it did not make him an agnostic. Well-versed in history, philosophy and literature, he held strongly the conviction nothing was to be believed without finding out for oneself. This conviction led him to question everything vigorously as only Mars in the 5th aspecting Lagna lord Jupiter in the 11th can make one do. Eager to realise the Truth, Narendra took to meditative practices, met different religious leaders, even joined the Brahmo Samaj and continued to search for the Truth that he could sense but could not lay his hands on. Rahu in the deeply spiritual sign Scorpio in a Nakshatra ruled by Mercury prodded him on in his pursuit until he met the Paramahamsa. Thereafter Narendra continued to visit the Master regularly but the strong Martian influence on his Lagna lord Jupiter and the 5th house which rules the intellect never let him accept what the Master said. He assessed every word logically and refused to be swept off his feet by the Master's deluging love for him. But as Ketu Bhukti took over, even his rational spirit could not but concede the irresistible force of the Master's blazing spirituality. For the next few years, the Master trained Narendra to carry on the mission for which he had come. The bond between the master and disciple grew stronger each day.

REVERSALS AND SETBACKS

In 1884, Narendra's father died. This was also in Ketu Bhukti of Rahu Dasa. Ketu is in the 9th from the Moon and in the 7th from Rahu. *Ashtama Sani* was in full swing, showing death-rites had to be performed. This bereavement forced a sudden change in

Narendra's status who suddenly found himself caught in heavy debt. Greedy relatives filed a suit to grab his family house. He had no job or any other source of income. The family was in dire straits and starving. All the suffering made Narendra angry with God and he began to even doubt His existence. However, he could not get out the feeling from inside him that he was not born for a temporal life revolving round money, family and fame. The Sun, the natural Atmakaraka, in his case is also the ruler of the 9th house that rules spirituality and occupies Lagna in Vargottama strength. This single factor, can to a large extent, he deemed to have made Truth the warp and woof of the fabric of the personality of the youth. He continued to visit the Master whose assurance his family would not ever be in want of necessities lifted his spirits and relieved him of his worries.

In 1885, Ramakrishna contracted cancer passing away in August 1886. By now, a band of disciples had gathered around the Master. They continued with their spiritual practices, each inspiring the other but Narendra was the unproclaimed leader.

MONASTIC VOWS

In 1887, Narendra took his monastic vows along with his brother disciples in Venus Bhukti, Rahu Dasa. Venus as 6th and 11th lord does not have the eligibility for such an event. But being with 9th lord Sun and in Uttarashada ruled by Vargottama Sun, Venus acquires solar hues. As 9th lord from Chandra Lagna, he is in the 5th with Mercury and the 12th lord Sun all of which acted merely to formalise the already burning renunciation in his heart.

In 1888, in Sun Bhukti, Narendra now known as Swami Vivekananda began his life as a wandering monk. Rahu and Sun are mutual enemies and their periods often bring about penury, wanderings and grief. In this case, Vivekananda voluntarily embraced the first two but the last could not venture to come near him. For, his Vargottama Ascendant and its lord Jupiter were so placed that wherever he went he infected everyone with the joy and peace exuding from within him. The Swami travelled widely from one end of the country to the other meeting both *runks* and *rajahs* impressing alike everyone with his spiritual fervour and renunciation.

RAJA YOGA BEGINS

As Rahu Dasa ended, several admirers of the monk, all influential people, the gift of the Lagna lord Jupiter in the 11th, requested him to attend the Parliament of Religions at Chicago in 1893. However, he did not heed this request. But in December 1892 when at Kanyakumari, sitting at the southern most tip of the Indian peninsula, he received the call from within to go to the West. Jupiter Dasa had just dawned and Jupiter is in Swati ruled by Rahu who is in the 12th in a watery sign. Transit Saturn was in Virgo on natal Moon; transit Jupiter was in Pisces aspecting the natal Moon. Both Gochara Jupiter and Saturn influencing the 10th house were about to give a big thrust to the Raja Yoga *cum* Sanyasa Yoga in the 10th house generated by Saturn and the Moon in it.

Jupiter, as Dasa lord, aspects the 10th from the Moon. So does Saturn. Jupiter, in turn, is in Swati ruled by Rahu. Rahu acts like Saturn and Saturn in turn is in the 10th from the Lagna. Saturn in the 10th house, where the desire for material success is burnt away by spiritual hunger and dispassion, paves the way for phenomenal success and popularity. This is exactly what happened to Swami Vivekananda. As soon as his wish to go abroad was known, friends and admirers raised the funds for it. And he left for the United States on 31-5-1893 reaching Chicago on 30-7-1893 just as Saturn Bhukti was commencing. He met with initial difficulties consistent with the Dwirdwadasa positions of the Dasa and Bhukti lords but these were soon overcome. And on 11-9-1893 in the opening session of the World Parliament of Religions Swami Vivekananda delivered his electrifying lecture introducing and emphasising the eternal message of Vedanta to all of the religions of the world represented there when "In the land of abundance and comfort, he spoke of renunciation as the only path to immortality;....

he proudly declared that he came from a land which not only believed in Universal toleration, but accepted all religions as true." American media and society welcomed the Swami with open arms. Saturn in a Mercury ruled sign and Mercury as Buddhikaraka brought to him many well-known Western thinkers and philosophers whose meetings with him left them greatly impressed by his redefining of religion. Jupiter as Lagna lord is a powerful planet and being in the 11th as Dasa lord showered his choicest blessings on the young Swami. He returned to Colombo on 15-1-1897 and received a royal reception. Jupiter Dasa, Saturn and Mercury Bhuktis ensured he was treated a hero wherever he went.

DASA OF LAGNA LORD

On 1-5-1897, Swami Vivekananda called a meeting of the monastic and lay devotees of Ramakrishna to discuss the establishment of his work on Vedanta on a more organised basis sowing the seed of the Ramakrishna Order — a purely spiritual and humanitarian body completely dissociated with politics. This was appropriately in Mercury Bhukti, Jupiter Dasa. Mercury is the 10th lord. Jupiter is the Lagna lord. **According to classical works and a rarely noticed dictum, any venture begun in the Dasa of a well-placed Lagna lord, can develop and grow very well.**

In Dasamsa*, Mercury is the Lagna lord in the 5th, again in Parivartana with the 5th lord Saturn. Jupiter is in the 11th therefrom. The seeds for the spiritual order were sown under these highly favourable influences. No wonder today nearly 105 years later, there are countless Ramakrishna mission centers in India and around the world inspiring people everywhere with India's great heritage of renunciation and spirituality.

---

* Virgo - Lagna, Sun and Saturn; Scorpio - Moon,. Jupiter and Venus; Capricorn - Mercury; Aquarius - Rahu; Gemini - Mars; and Leo - Ketu.

Tenth House Saturn and Blazing Renunciation

On 20-6-1899, Vivekananda left again for the West with a view to see for himself the progress of the Vedanta work he had started. Travelling to London and from there to Los Angeles (USA) he gave several lectures founding new centers in different parts of the States. From there, he moved to Paris returning to India on 9-12-1900. All these travels came about in Ketu and Venus Bhuktis.

Swami Vivekananda travelled extensively in the next few months heedless of his physical health. He kept an eye on the monks, gave regular classes in Vedanta, conducted meditation in the shrine and inspired everyone with his perennial flow of positive ideas and energy. Through every word he said and deed he did, the Swami showed that an ideal teacher is one who practises what he teaches. And in order to demonstrate this, he never even hesitated to clean the toilets himself. The association of the Moon with Saturn produced humility of the highest order and no work was below his dignity.

Swami Vivekananda passed away in Sun Bhukti, Jupiter Dasa. The Swami had said a few days before this "was make room for others . . . . the shadow of a big tree will not let the smaller trees grow" proving in death as in life that he had no identity apart from the Universal so well symbolized by the Moon-Saturn combination.

The Moon is the Manahkaraka. Saturn is the Vairagyakaraka. Together, they brought out the highest levels of Vairagya in this monk. Saturn also rules the populace, the common man and the downtrodden. And to Swami Vivekananda, his life's mission extended to the humblest of God's men though being Universal as it was, it did not exclude the princely either. *(07-02)* ●

3

RAMANA MAHARSHI'S DEATH EXPERIENCE : ASTROLOGICALLY ANALYSED

1. *A natural malefic in the 7th can generate a Sanyasa Yoga.*
2. *Full Moon in the 9th with Ketu gives blazing spirituality.*
3. *Mercury, Buddhikaraka, with Lagna lord Venus points to the path of inquiry — Who am I ?*

DEATH EXPERIENCE

RAMANA MAHARSHI was one of the greatest saints of modern India. As a boy of about 16 years, he had an unusual experience of death. The Experience was not physical but an intellectual, rational excursion into the phenomenon called death of the physical body. After this Experience, a great change came over him and about six weeks after, he left his home for Tiruvannamalai, a small town in South India, in quest of the Ultimate Truth. The date of the Experience has not been recorded but there is a record of the date he left his home-town. Piecing this information together with astrological factors, the date of the Experience can be traced. The chart of Sri Ramana Maharshi is based on birth-particulars obtained by Dr. B. V. Raman from the Maharshi's own brother, Swami Niranjanananda, and therefore, its correctness is beyond doubt.

In order to understand what this Experience was, we quote from **Self Realisation** by B. V. Narasimhaswamy who, it is said, recorded the details as narrated by Maharshi himself to him and others at different points of time.

It was about six weeks before I left Madurai for good that the great change in my life took place. It was so sudden. One day, I sat up alone on the first floor of my uncle's house. I was in my usual health. I seldom had any illness. I was a heavy sleeper. When I was in Dindigul in 1891 a huge crowd had gathered close to the room where I slept and tried to rouse me by shouting and knocking at the door, all in vain, and it was only by their getting into my room and giving me a violent shake that I was roused from my torpor. This heavy sleep was rather a proof of good health. I was also subject to fits of half-awake sleep at night. My willy playmates, afraid to trifle with me when I was awake, would go to me when I was sleep, pull me to my feet, take me all round the playground, beat me, cuff me, sport with me, and bring me back to my bed — and all the while I would put up with everything with a meekness, forgiveness and passivity unknown in my walking state. When the morning broke I had no remembrance of the night's experience. But these fits did not render me weaker or less fit for life and were hardly to be considered a disease. So on that day, as I sat alone, there was nothing wrong with my health. But a sudden and unmistakable fear of death seized me. I felt I was going to die. Why I should have so felt cannot be explained by anything felt in the body. Nor could I explain it to myself then. I did not however trouble myself to discover if the fear was well-grounded. I felt I am going to die and at once set about thinking out what I should do. I did not care to consult doctors or elders or even friends. I felt I had to solve the problem *myself* then *and there.*

The shock of death made me at once introspective or 'introverted'. I said to myself mentally, i.e., without uttering the words — 'Now, death has come. What does it mean? What is it that is dying? This body dies.' I at once dramatized the scene of death. I extended my limbs and held them rigid as though rigor-mortis had set in. I imitated a corpse to lend an air of reality to my further investigation. I held my breath and kept my mouth closed, pressing my lips tightly together so that no sound might escape. Let not the word 'I' or any other word be uttered. "Well, then", I said to myself, "this body is dead. I will be carried stiff to the burning ground and there burnt and reduced to ashes. But with the death of the body, am I dead ? Is this body I ? This body is silent and inert. But I feel the full force of my personality and even the sound I am a spirit, a thing transcending the body. The material body dies, but the spirit transcending it cannot be touched by death. I am therefore the deathless spirit." All this was not a mere intellectual process, but flashed before me vividly as living truth, something which I perceived immediately, without any argument almost. I was something real, the only real thing in that state, and all the conscious activity that was connected with my body was centered on that. Then I or self was holding the focus of attention by a powerful fascination from that time onwards. Fear of death had vanished once and forever. Absorption in the Self has continued from that moment right up to this time. Other thoughts may come and go like the various notes of a musician, but the I continues like the basic or fundamental Sruti note (drone) which accompanies and blends with other notes. Whether the body was engaged in talking, reading or anything else, I was still centered on *I*. Previous to that crisis I had no clear perception of myself and was not consciously attached to it. I had felt no direct perceptible interest in it, much less any permanent disposition to dwell upon it. The consequences of this new habit were soon noticed in my life.

JUPITER'S INDIGENCE

Ramana's father died in 1892 leaving the family in indigent circumstances. The family shifted to Madurai soon after to live with an uncle. This was in Venus Bhukti of Saturn Dasa. The 9th house is quite heavily afflicted. It is occupied by the Moon and Ketu and aspected by Pitrukaraka Sun afflicted by Rahu. The Sun as the natural significator of father is further afflicted by Saturn's aspect.

The Dasa lord Saturn is the 2nd lord from the Karaka Sun. Venus is with 7th lord Mercury, again with reference to the Karaka. The death of the father not only dealt a blow to their already modest financial circumstances but also drove them from their family home to live with relatives. Venus and Saturn in their mutual periods invariably bring in major setbacks and calamities and in this case, as the two planets are also in mutually adverse positions in Navamsa, forced the family to shift residence.

Born 29/30-12-1879 at 1 a.m. (LMT) at 9 N 50, 78 E 15 with a balance of 4 years, 1 month, 20 days of Jupiter Dasa.

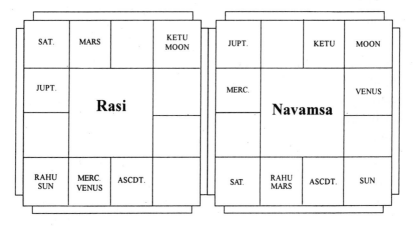

MARS AND STURDY BODY

Ramana was an intelligent boy, normal in every respect but not interested in lessons. An expert swimmer, he had an excellent memory. Mars, the planet of vitality occupies the 7th house and aspects the Ascendant. Ramana was a strong boy but consistent with the influence of Mars on both the Lagna and the Lagna lord, an element of Tamas was also present in him. Tamas is characterised by inertia, indolence, excessive sleep and lethargy. Ramana, it is said, was an abnormally heavy sleeper as a boy. In fact, once the door of the room he was sleeping in had to be broken because no amount of calling out to him could wake him up. His friends often took advantage of this abnormality. They would pull him out of his bed even as he was asleep. They would play all kinds of tricks on him, dump him somewhere and run away. Ramana had a sturdy physique for his age and his friends were scared of taunting him when he was awake. So this quality of excessive sleep was a gift from Mars, a Tamasic planet. But because of the strength of the rest of the chart, it was not a life-long feature and soon gave way to an alertness and waking state. Later on, in fact, very few devotees could ever testify to having seen the Maharshi asleep.

The family was disappointed in Ramana. They had been counting on him to do well in his studies and gain a position of influence to help their maintenance. Jupiter Dasa was on for 4 years after his birth. Jupiter is a malefic, being the 3rd and 6th lord. Jupiter exchanges signs with 5th lord Saturn which is a Dainya Yoga affecting educational performance and attainments. Saturn is the 4th lord too so that the Dainya Yoga permeates into the significations of the 4th Bhava as he had neither a home nor property of his own. Saturn Dasa deprived him of academic activity too as we shall see next.

FIRST STIRRINGS

In July 1896, a sudden fear of death overtook him as he sat alone in his uncle's house. The fear was simply overpowering. This fear turned his mind inwards, introverted. He began to tell himself: *Death has come. What does it mean? What is dying? My body is dead. Yet I am fully conscious that I am very much alive. What is this I? Who is this I? This I is spirit transcending death, beyond the body. It is eternal, deathless and I am That.*

The epochal event occurred in Saturn Dasa, Moon Bhukti. Saturn, with reference to the Moon, is the 9th lord in exchange of signs with the 10th lord Jupiter. The Moon as Bhukti lord is with Ketu which led to a fear of death preceding the *Experience*.

After the *Experience*, Ramana was normal but completely lost all interest in his studies. About six weeks later he left home leaving a note that no one should look for him and he was going to his Supreme Father Arunachala.

When he reached Arunachala, he threw away whatever little money he had — a little over Rs. 3/- in the temple tank. He never again handled money. For about two months after that he was absorbed in Samadhi in an underground vault of the temple. In May 1898, his relatives tracked him down to Arunachala. His uncle and mother pleaded with him to return but he kept silent. This was in Rahu Bhukti. Rahu is aspected by Saturn. The Moon and Sun influence Rahu. After that he moved to the hill where he remained all his life, moving to the foot after his mother's death.

This is, in brief, a description of the metamorphoses of Ramana into the Maharshi. As many as four factors — the Lagna (the Central point), Jupiter (the Gnanakaraka), the Moon (Manahkaraka) and Ketu, the Kaivalyakaraka are in airy intellectual signs pointing to the path he took as that of Gnana.

Let us take a general look at some features in the Maharshi's chart.*

SANYASA YOGA FROM MARS

Mars as a malefic, apart from his Tamas-conferring property, is good for renunciation. A malefic, natural, in the 7th is a Yoga for Sanyasa.

Mars aspects the Lagna and the Lagna lord Venus, the latter adversely. Saturn is in the 6th. From the Moon-sign Gemini, the Moon-sign lord Mercury is in the 6th adversely aspected by malefic Mars. These factors led to his cancer which ultimately was the cause of his physical death. The Maharshi always had digestive problems. He also had asthma for many years until it disappeared of its own accord. The Moon in Gemini is heavily afflicted. This probably was during most of Mercury (ruler of Gemini) and part of Ketu (who occupies Gemini) Dasas, both planets causing affliction to the sign ruling the respiratory system.

---

* For a more detailed discussion of Ramana Maharshi's chart see **Notable Horoscopes** by DR. B. V. RAMAN.

Ketu is the Kaivalyakaraka and, in the 12th from Karakamsa (the sign occupied by Atmakaraka Moon), bestows Kaivalya or Moksha.

After the *Experience* of death, a visitor to Ramana's house casually mentioned he was going to Arunachala. As soon as the word Arunachala fell on the young boy's ears, a whole new world opened up in his heart and he knew he had to go there. That was how he left for Arunachala.

The Dasa was of Saturn when this happened and Saturn is ruled by the Adi Devata Siva. Arunachala means the *pink and immovable* and the hill there is deemed to be Siva Himself and the temple of Arunachala at the base of the hill is Arunachaleshwara, in the form of a Linga. Of course, Ramana Maharshi never ever talked of an Ishta or a Mantra in his Sadhana. But he was immensely fond of the **Periapuranam**, an ancient Tamil work on great Siva Bhaktas or devotees. He loved the hill greatly.This can be attributed to the 5th lord Saturn also being the Dasa lord.

JOURNEY TO GOD BEGINS

If you take a look at the chart, the 9th house factor is all pervasive. Venus, Lagna lord, is with 9th lord Mercury. The 9th lord Mercury is in his own Nakshatra Jyeshta. The 5th lord Saturn is in Revati, ruled by 9th lord Mercury. That is why the quest that began in Saturn Dasa was not a temporary aberration. It was permanent, impactful and tremendously successful. It is said, he left Madurai on 29-8-1896 about 6 weeks after the great change in his life.

Let us try to track this date of self-illumination. Taking 29-8-1896 and going backwards by 6 weeks takes us to July 11, 1896. Let us try the planetary positions (Chart 1) for this date, mid-day for Madurai (9 N 50, 78 E 10).

The Tithi on this date would be Sukla Panchami. The previous New Moon would be on 11-7-1896, the next on 9-8-1896. The week day is Wednesday. Panchami is favoured for spiritual matters.

The Moon in Virgo, on the other hand, is hardly compatible for spiritual experiences, for spiritual occurrences of any kind.

	MARS 18-26		MERC. 15-08		MARS 15-41		SUN 28-26 MERC. 8-52 VENUS 28-54
RAHU 5-49	**Chart 1** **Rasi** 15-07-1896		SUN 2-14 JUPT. 22-59 VENUS 23-49	RAHU 5-23	**Chart 2** **Rasi** 11-7-1896		MOON 4-12 JUPT. 22-09
			KETU 5-10				KETU 5-23
		SAT. 21-23	LAGNA 28-29 MOON 0-24			SAT. (R) 21-34	LAGNA 24-32

NEW MOON AS CATALYST

Is there anything striking in this chart? The major planets remain in the same signs during the whole week. So, we are not concerned with them. What about the Moon and the Sun? Do they enjoy a special relationship to warrant such a major change in the mind of the Maharshi? Usually for major spiritual experiences, New and Full Moons become very important, especially New Moon.

Let us track the positions on the previous New Moon. Because approximately we would still be in the range of the *about six weeks* time-frame from August 29th. So, let us check the New Moon day in the vicinity of July 15 (Chart 2).

The weekday would be a Saturday and the Tithi would be Prathama by Hindu reckoning. So, we go back by 1 more lunar day to get the Amavasya (approx.). So, Chart 3 is cast for 14 hours or 2.00 p.m. (IST) on 10-7-1896 for Madurai.

This is a very interesting chart. The New Moon has occurred on the Maharshi's Moon and Atmakaraka. It has occurred in the 9th house in Punarvasu, the same Nakshatra as the Maharshi's Janma Nakshatra.

Mars is on the natal Mars. Saturn stationary is on natal Lagna and influenced by Mars. Except the Nodes all the planets are in the 9th house from the Janma Lagna — Sun, Mercury, Venus and the Moon. Jupiter in the 10th is exalted.

			VENUS 27-25 SUN 27-16 MOON 21-44 VENUS 7-11
	MARS 14-51		
RAHU 5-26	\multicolumn{2}{c|}{Chart 3 Rasi 10-7-1896}	JUPT. 21-54
			KETU 5-28
		SAT. (R) 21-35 LAGNA 23-05	

Saturn and the Moon, the Dasa and Bhukti lords, are in airy signs involving the natal Lagna — so, a great ferment began in the mind of the young lad.

If you superimpose this chart on the Maharshi's birth-chart, you find the Dasa lord is caught between transit Rahu and transit Mars. It was a tremendously scaring, cracking up, revealing, reviewing kind of experience. The transit Moon is on top of the natal Moon (who is also the Bhukti lord) and moving towards a conjunction with the natural Atmakaraka Sun. It tore him apart at the inner level — split the body and soul. The Moon being New usually brings about great restlessness and fear. The Maharshi was overtaken by both these states of mind.

There is Jupiter in Cancer in the 10th from Lagna (Janma) in a deeply spiritual sign heralding the great transformation. Jupiter is aspected by both Mars and Saturn, Mars from his Moolatrikona and Saturn from his exaltation, highlighting the epochal experience.

The experience shifts to the Moon Bhukti, to the border-line Antara of the Sun.

In the Moon Bhukti, the Moon as Atmakaraka becomes a very painful period. The Moon being in a cuspal degree assumes great significance. The Moon rules the mind and ego. Being in the 7th, from the radical Sun, the ego is dealt a death-blow by the *Experience*. The 9th house being involved, this death of the little ego is the starting or triggering point for the spiritual transformation of the native.

With Moon Bhukti, the Amavasya day assumes great importance. The Bhukti lord Moon is merging into the Sun, the *Spiritual Ego*. The Moon ruling the mind is disappearing into the Sun, the *Soul Force* not only of the individual but also of the Cosmos. The Dasa lord is Saturn and there is complete renunciation, detachment — a dis-association of the body-mind from the soul. The Maharshi from this moment ceased to identify himself with the body, with the mind and moved on to become a Seer, a witness of the little " I ". The date was 10-7-1896. *(07-96)* ●

SADDAM HUSSEIN
—A STUDY IN PAISACHA YOGA

1. *Mercury and Moon in mutual Kendras can, under certain conditions, cause insanity.*
2. *This Yoga when accompanied by Raja Yoga produces ruthless dictators.*
3. *This Yoga when with Daridra Yoga produces simple lunatics.*

HUMILIATING EXIT AND ASHTAMA SANI

WHAT A FALL it was for the Iraqi dictator Saddam Hussein when U. S. troops captured him on December 13, 2003 pulling him out from a spider hole where he was hiding. For a man who has owned 40 palaces, the ultimate in luxury and grandeur, it was indeed pathetic that he had been on the run for nearly 10 months hiding in hovels and underground cellars shifting location every 3 hours like a hounded animal until that fateful Saturday when his luck ran out. Saturn was in total command when this happened occupying the 8th house from Saddam Hussein's Janma Rasi Scorpio. A President once, today he has lost just about everything including children, property, wife, friends and power which is usually what happens when Saturn begins to transit the 8th house from the natal Moon— स्वसुतपशुसुहृद्वित्तनाशामायातिं जन्मादेष्टमानं दिशति पदवशेनार्कसूनुः क्रमेण (**Phaladeepika** XXVI — Sloka 22). Sloka 33 also attributes "danger to life itself, fall from one's position and loss of wealth (प्राणसंदेहं स्थानभ्रंशं धनक्षयम्)" to Ashtama Sani.

Saddam Hussein's time of birth is not available but it is generally accepted he was born on April 28, 1937 at a place near Tikrit in Iraq. The Ascendant as Gemini as speculated in these columns on earlier occasions appears to gain support from Saddam's ignominious capture.

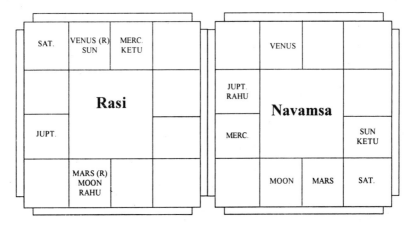

Saturn in the 10th can take one to the pinnacle of power before hurtling one down mercilessly. In 1979, Saddam assumed power as President. His first act thereafter was to launch a massive purge of the Baa'th Party to eliminate all threat to his leadership. He dragged his country into an 8 year war with Iran when millions were killed. His reign was marked by terror and ruthless vindictive acts. Saturn in the 10th does make for dictators but it is also the Moon that plays a strong role in giving shape to this Saturnine inclination.

HEAVY AFFLICTION TO MOON

The Moon is in Scorpio, the sign of his debility, with Mars, the 6th lord as also 11th lord, and Rahu. Rahu too is Neecha or debilitated. Both the Moon and Rahu get Neechabhanga individually but as this is due to retrograde Mars, it produces a mindset so Neecha or depraved, so aggrandising and so ruthless that even the devil would be put to shame. Mars and Rahu flank the Moon. The three planets in the same sign tend to concentrate the affliction. Retrograde Mars by his close proximity to the Manahkaraka Moon infests the mind with cruelty, wrath and extreme selfishness. Rahu who also afflicts the Moon makes for delusions and a greed that shoots to monstrous levels — greed for power, for adulation and money. Such a Moon can also show a frightening ruthlessness that will stop at nothing.

MOON-MERCURY YOGA

The Moon with his heavy afflictions is the center of an important Yoga which gives deep insights into the working of Saddam Hussein's mind. The Moon in Scorpio is in opposition to Mercury in Taurus which puts the Manahkaraka (significator of the mind Moon) and Buddhikaraka (significator of the intellect Mercury) in mutual Kendras giving rise to Paisacha Yoga.

बुधचन्द्रौ केन्द्रगतौ नान्यग्रहसंयुतौ न पतिदृष्टौ ।
योगोयं पैशाचस्तत्रोत्पन्नस्य सोन्मादी ॥

— **Jatakabharana** VIII-74

meaning, *if Mercury and the Moon occupy Kendra positions and be not in any way associated with any other planet nor be aspected by the lords of the said Kendra houses, the resulting Yoga is termed Paisacha. One born under it will become insane.*

Though dressed impeccably in army fatigues and always well groomed, there was never any doubt that Saddam was a mad man. And that nothing could stop him in his megalomaniac adventures as the Paisacha Yoga confirms. A question that could very appropriately be directed at this chart is as to how the Paisacha Yoga could be effective when the conditions of "not in anyway associated with any other planet nor aspected by the lords of the said Kendra houses" as required by it are not present here since Mercury is with Ketu, secondly the Moon is with Mars and Rahu and lastly, Mars aspects Mercury.

The Yoga in its purest form requires the two — the Moon and Mercury alone to be in mutual Kendras. When this happens, one is said to become mentally deranged. But before we proceed further, **let us not forget that Dr. Raman has always cautioned against categorical deductions based on any one single factor.** The Ascendant, its strength and benefic influences in the chart must all be carefully examined and judiciously weighed before branding a chart with Paisacha Yoga as of an insane person.

VARIANTS OF THE YOGA

Paisacha Yoga can be formed under 3 different conditions :-

(a) The Moon is in the 4th or the 10th house from Mercury or *vice-versa*.

(b) The Moon is in conjunction with Mercury, that is, both occupy the same sign.

(c) The Moon is in opposition to Mercury or when both occupy opposite signs.

In all these cases, the native becomes predisposed to mental illness. Though the Moon and Mercury are in the 4th and 10th from each other in mutual Kendras, the Yoga does not become a full-fledged Paisacha Yoga because in these positions, the two planets do not directly influence each other. Nevertheless there are shades of mental illness lurking in the native and even if they should surface, they do not have the strength to cause much harm and may show up as a temporary aberration that could be best handled by simply ignoring it and letting it die a natural death. But during the period of the Yoga operating, the native could indulge in mischief and devious thinking prompted by strong emotions of lust, hate, greed, infatuation, arrogance and jealousy. This version of Paisacha Yoga occurs quite commonly. In its mildest form, Paisacha Yoga produces people who are very difficult to get along with. At its worst it becomes a dangerous Yoga.

The Paisacha Yoga caused by the Moon and Mercury together in the same sign can be dangerous if the Sun is also in the same sign bringing the Moon under a Chaturdasi (14th lunar day of the dark half) or Amavasya (New Moon day). Under these conditions, the Moon becomes extremely weak and produces a fragile mind that could splinter apart under any kind of pressure — internal or external. Of course, it is important to note that though the Moon and the Sun be in the same sign, the Moon preceding the Sun makes for a stronger Yoga (more dangerous) than when the Moon is ahead of the Sun. In either case, the Moon is weak and being with the glassy Mercury generates unhealthy thinking patterns that leave the native's mind all tied up in knots. This can produce a persecution complex that easily lends justification to whatever one might do. The mind prods the intellect to produce a philosophy of righteous indignation to project itself as a martyr or wronged victim entitled to a redressal by its mad acts.

If the Moon and Mercury, in this Yoga, are very close to each other, it brings about a mindset that is vulnerable to extreme emotions but at the same time very weak also. Constantly dwelling on negative thoughts and mentally perpetrating violence against adversaries — real or imaginary, the native may end up as an incoherent babbling lunatic, not dangerous really but no longer capable of interacting normally with others. Such a native may withdraw into a shell or become suicide prone or offer little or no resistance when treated as insane or sent to a mental institution.

SUN'S PROXIMITY TO MERCURY

When Mercury and the Sun are very close, the Sun's brilliance rubs off on Mercury giving him strength to offset the weakening lunar effect on him. The Paisacha Yoga in such cases becomes defunct and the Budha Aditya Yoga takes over with its results of a strong mind and sharp intellect.

The third variant of the Yoga is caused by the Moon and Mercury occupying opposite signs. Here too, the Sun in the same sign with Mercury bringing the Moon under a Chaturdasi (14th lunar day of bright half) or Pournima (Full Moon) robs the Paisacha Yoga of much of its evil. The Budha Aditya Yoga if present again takes control of the native releasing all the blessings normally associated with a Full Moon in a birth chart.

If the Moon and Mercury are in opposite signs with the Sun separated signwise from Mercury then the Yoga becomes dangerous because it loses the stabilizing anchorage that the Sun could otherwise have provided. The danger-factor in it proceeds from the fact, the digital strength of the Moon tends to strengthen the chart as a whole endowing the native with an unusual recklessness. The native then becomes capable of wielding power and influence at different levels. Or else, one becomes strong minded (in a brutal sense and not necessarily good or pure minded) and acquires the overbearing confidence and strength needed to release one's energies in destructive channels. For such a native, *mental illness* is too generic and too mild an expression to really convey the degree of the dangerous workings of his mind. Such a native usually develops maniacal tendencies.

SIGNS INVOLVED

The Paisacha Yoga is also influenced by the sign of occupation of the Moon and Mercury, more especially of the former. In watery signs, it becomes a matter for grave concern. In fixed signs and earthy and fiery signs, it is generally weakened. In airy and common signs, the Paisacha Yoga gains some strength.

However, a pure Paisacha Yoga is not a very frequently occurring one. The Moon or Mercury or both may be subject to the influence of benefics, malefics or both. What happens then ?

EXTREMES IN BEHAVIOUR

Where benefics join the Moon-Mercury Yoga, there is still a tendency to extremes in behaviour when it can swing towards the benign. Many with such a Budha-Chandra Yoga have been known to have been deeply affected by concern for human suffering and emerged as saints and selfless Karma Yogis. At the other end of the spectrum fall such cases as belong to those capable of heinous acts of crime and brutality when malefics influence the Budha-Chandra Yoga. In such cases, Mars, Saturn and Rahu, the last named more particularly than Ketu, bring out diabolic mindsets. It is not always that such natives are raving mad or obviously lunatic. Depending upon the Raja and other Yogas present in the chart, they can be as in Saddam's case, sophisticated and refined on the exterior but with a murderous mind concealed inside. Where there are also Yogas for despotism and tyranny inbuilt into the Raja Yogas present in the chart, the natives become powerful rulers and heads of countries but always securing their power and position by unfair means such as betrayal, treachery, coups and ruthlessness.

In charts where Rekha and Preshya Yogas (Yogas for penury, servitude and dependence) are present or Daridra Yogas dominate but at the same time the Paisacha Yoga is also found, then the natives end up raving mad or suffer other kinds of serious mental illness when they can no longer relate to their environment in healthy ways or suffer complete disorientation and are found wandering aimlessly on the roads or get consigned to lunatic asylums. Other examples of this Yoga in action can be found in those suffering from neurosis, false beliefs and hallucinations that could drive them to act in utter disregard of the consequences. The mental derangement will have its roots in different kinds of obsessions depending upon the planets, houses and signs involved.

MOON'S LORDSHIP AND ROOT OF ILLNESS

The Moon's rulership can be the primary determinant of the focus of the native's mind. Or, it can be the house where the Moon is placed. If the Ascendant is Cancer, then the Moon ruling the 1st house could show narcissism and conceit. If Leo, financial difficulties, health problems and ill-will could trigger the Yoga. If Virgo, the Moon being the 11th lord the native's thoughts are focussed in sinister ways on monetary gain, friends or siblings.

If Libra is the Ascendant then career ambitions, love of limelight and political office may drive the natives to seek dangerous means to achieve their ends. With Scorpio rising religious pretension or fanaticism can fuel the Paisacha Yoga. Or, so-called religious or spiritual Gurus or Tantriks may be able to exercise their evil power on the natives and sway them to indulge in harmful activity including killing. Theoretically speaking, it would not be wrong to look for Paisacha Yoga in the charts of those who indulge in human sacrifice for gains of any kind — spiritual or temporal. Whatever the objective, such minds are very, very sick minds which receive sustenance from the mutual quadrangular positions of the Moon and Mercury, more particularly the conjunction of the two as such natives usually hail from the lowest strata of society. If Sagittarius is the Ascendant, there is an obsession with death. They could emerge as maniacal killers, serial killers and also suffer from suicidal tendencies.

If Capricorn is the Ascendant, feelings of unhealthy rivalry or sexual jealousy and possessiveness may drive the native to commit heinous acts. With Aquarius rising, there is a deep despondency and an inexplicable suffocating depression that could shatter the health of the mind. Pisces Ascendants with the Paisacha Yoga may be victims of addictions or of romantic entanglements which could propel the natives into mad acts.

With Aries, the mother syndrome or domestic unhappiness could pull the trigger on the Budha-Chandra Yoga. If Taurus, malice and hate for coborns, friends, neighbours could explode one's mind. With Gemini, greed for money or an unreasonable hatred for family members can form the core of the native's focus propelling one into dangerous routes.

The Sun if involved with the Budha-Chandra Yoga produces an inferiority complex if the Moon is New. If the Moon in such a case is waxing and Full, one has grandoise ideas of one's capabilities but which are seldom justified by reality. If the Moon is afflicted by Mars, unrealistic ambitions and greed produce inhuman, unfeeling hearts that will stop at nothing to gain their ends. If the Moon is with Saturn in the Budha-Chandra Yoga, the native becomes hypercritical and judgemental and anything that does not conform to one's idea of correctness or propriety is enough to release a frenzy of dangerous rage. The Moon with Rahu gives delusions of power and pelf. One begins to believe that these are one's as a matter of right. Naturally when reality does not support such delusions, the reaction is violent murderous anger. Any combination of Mars, Saturn and Rahu with the Budha-Chandra Yoga is a warning signal of homicidal tendencies lurking beneath a deceptive exterior. If the malefics are combust or retrograde, then the power of the Yoga for evil grows in strength.

MARS AND VIOLENT TYRANNY

In Saddam Hussein's case, the Paisacha Yoga becomes worse by coming under the influence of retrograde Mars (who is Ativakra being in extreme retrogression) which tends to release a beastial mind and an unending thirst for power.

Mercury is the planet of Buddhi or intellect or the faculty of discrimination. The Moon is the planet of emotions and reactions. When the two are in mutual Kendras, more particularly in conjunction or opposition, both reactions and the intellect get adversely affected. In Saddam's case, the Moon in watery Scorpio produces dangerous volatile emotions and Mercury, as Buddhikaraka, loses his innate ability to judge and weigh pros and cons of what might come of the unbridled flow of sick reactions.

In other words, the Budha-Chandra Yoga tends to cut one off from reality making one's obsessions balloon to dangerous proportions. In Saddam's case Mars, the planet of violence and the Karaka for greed, is in total control of both Manas and Buddhi directing the flow of mental energy into destructive channels of brutality, torture and tyranny.

Perhaps this was also why Saddam went on to invade and annex Kuwait in gross disregard of international norms. His invasion of Iran too and the 8 year war, use of chemical weapons against Kurds killing at least 5000 civilians, the ruthless killing of his sons-in-law and arrogant indifference to the Bush ultimatum of March 2003 all point to an insane dictator obsessed with power at any cost. The mass graves, the rape rooms and the torture chambers for which his reign was known testify to the dangerous strength of his Paisacha Yoga in its worst form.

The London based organisation Indict, which claims to have gathered evidence against Saddam Hussein and his associates, has published an eyewitness account of the dictator's personal behaviour which proves the degree of evil a Paisacha Yoga can generate:

"One of the president's bodyguards brought 30 prisoners out. They were Kurds. The president himself shot them one after another with a Browning pistol.

"Another 30 prisoners were brought and the process was repeated. Saddam Hussein was laughing and obviously enjoying himself. There was blood everywhere — it was like an abattoir....

"Those who were still alive were eventually finished off by the security officers."

A question not really relevant to our discussion on Paisacha Yoga but otherwise of important interest is if Saddam Hussein will be brought to justice for his crimes against humanity.

The Moon sign in the absence of the birth-time can be treated as the Ascendant to look for an answer to this question.

VIOLENT END AND EIGHT HOUSE AFFLICTIONS

Scorpio as Ascendant would have Gemini as the 8th house. The 8th lord Mercury is in the 7th aspected by retrograde Mars and Saturn. Mercury is with Ketu. Mercury is aspected by Jupiter. The 8th lord comes under mixed influences but with a tilt towards the malefic. The 8th house Gemini is adversely aspected by Mars (R) which is a heavy affliction. The 22nd Drekanna falls in the 2nd Drekanna of Gemini which is an Ayudha Drekanna. The midpoint of the 8th house falls at $13^0 \; 53'$ Gemini in Aridra Nakshatra ruled by Rahu. Rahu in turn is in Scorpio with Mars (R). According to a classical dictum, if the 5th or the 9th sign from the Moon is aspected or occupied by a malefic planet and when a Sarpa (serpent), Nigada (fetters), Pasa (noose) or Ayudha (weapon) Drekanna rises on the 8th Bhava, death is said to be brought about by hanging. Here, malefic Saturn occupies the 5th from the Moon and the 22nd Drekanna is an Ayudha Drekanna. Likewise, the 8th lord with Mars in the Ascendant is also said to show death by suicide or hanging. Here, the 8th lord Mercury is not in the Ascendant but is aspected by Mars from the Ascendant. The results cannot always be taken literally. But that does not preclude the possibility of the results sometimes materializing literally also. In other words, the conclusion would be a violent end, not natural death, for Saddam Hussein.

The Moon-sign is occupied by its own ruler Mars in Swakshetra ruling one's country of birth. Mars with the Moon in Scorpio forms a Ruchaka Yoga and is joined by Rahu who represents the international community. This could be interpreted to indicate the trial taking place in Iraq before a tribunal comprising of both Iraqi and international judges.

Transit Saturn in the 8th from Janma Rasi (Moon-sign) is a difficult transit which runs upto May 2005. Mars and Saturn conjoin in Aridra on 25-5-2004 preceded by a lunar eclipse in the same month. This may mark the beginning of a period of great vulnerability for Saddam Hussein when he may have to pay for his crimes against humanity with the "ultimate penalty".
(Written 18-1-2004) ●

ECLIPSES IN ASTROLOGY

1. Eclipses were known to be astronomical phenomena in ancient India but feared in Europe.
2. References to eclipses found in the **Srimad Ramayana and Mahabharata**.
3. Eclipses were understood as having a bearing on national and other developments.

ASTRONOMICAL PHENOMENON ONLY

EVER SINCE man began to think, eclipses have both fascinated and intrigued him. In the West, especially in Europe, eclipses, particularly of the Sun, were treated with fear. The spectacle of the skies darkening during the day seemed frightening filling man with unknown forebodings. But in India, eclipses were understood as physical phenomena being the result of the alignment of the Sun, Moon and earth in certain specific ways. At the same time this was accompanied by an awareness that they had astrological implications.

Varahamihira, in his **Brihat Samhita**, explains the phenomenon of eclipses clearly :

भूच्छायां स्वग्रहणे भास्करमर्कग्रहे प्रवशतीन्दुः।
प्रग्रहणमतः पश्चात्रेन्दोर्भानोश्च पूर्वार्द्धात् ॥

At a lunar eclipse the Moon enters the shadow of the earth, and at a solar eclipse he enters the Sun's disc. That is why the lunar eclipse does not begin at the western limb, nor the solar one at the eastern limb.

And then, he goes on to state that Rahu, the demon, is not the cause of the eclipse (*राहुरकारणमस्मिन्नित्युक्त शास्त्रद्धाव: —V-13*). He also says अनियतचार: खलु चेदुपलब्धि: संख्यया कथं तस्य ? (V-8) - *If Rahu's velocity is not fixed (amenable to calculation), how is it possible to determine his exact position?* implying to the reader that if Rahu were a demon, it would not have been possible to determine his velocity, and therefore, his position.

TRADITIONAL PRACTICES VINDICATED

Astronomy and astrology developed in ancient India as one discipline — Jyotisha — and the Indian intellect was able to perceive the connection between planetary movements in the skies and terrestrial affairs. Whether through observation, experiment, inference and verification or through intuitive flashes (which happen many a time in the case of modern scientists too), the ancient Indian thinker was able to correlate the eclipses with happenings on earth and evolve broad guidelines to ensure the safety and well-being of man much in the same way modern medical men or seismologists issue guidelines (of course, in both cases only after the worst is over) on how to prevent catching infections whenever there is no outbreak of gastro-enteritis or on the occurrence of an earthquake. The guidelines drawn for observances at eclipse time and which have, over a long period of time, taken on the force of tradition are not superstitious beliefs as scoffed at by certain sections of the "intellectuals". An outbreak of an epidemic usually finds the experts advising people to drink only boiled water and avoid eating cut-fruit or other foods sold exposed on the roadside. Many who meticulously follow such instructions are the first to go down with fevers and infections. On the other hand, numberless people across our country in spite of total indifference to such instructions, continue to enjoy excellent health. Does that make medical science a superstition, simply because of such paradoxical human body reactions and responses? Votaries of science will vehemently explain away such contradictions as being dependent on one's power of resistance and immunity. And resistance itself, which they simply cannot explain in the case of those who are gifted with it in spite of malnutrition and squalid unhygenic conditions of living, will be put down to heredity and genes. The very concept of genes should, honestly speaking, be abhorrent to the scientific mind for it is simply another word for fatalism, determinism and the sheer uselessness of human effort. Yet genetics is today being held out as providing answers to all those questions science has never been able to explain. But to the objective and open intellect, genes are simply the scientific jargon for Karma. The term Karma, to the Western clone in India, is anathema — both obscrutantist and superstitious, although its deficient equivalent in Western science — gene — never ceases to draw his endless admiration for the possibilities he imagines it promises theoretically in handling different kinds of problems. All this only goes to show the servility which is embedded in and has become an inalienable part of the "secular intellectual" of our country and which refuses to get erased awaiting some kind of certification from his overlord from the West even for the slightest shift. For all such critics who exercise their grey cells selectively and are guilty of serious intellectual dishonesty and prejudices, the practices prescribed at eclipse time appear as something to be treated with contempt. This contempt proceeds, not from intelligent awareness, but from obstinate ignorance.

ECLIPSE CAN POLLUTE DRINKING WATER

Since thousands of years traditional observances in India at eclipse time include performing remedial measures for all those born in the Rasi (Zodiacal sign) and more particularly, in the Nakshatra in which an eclipse occurs for shielding them from the untoward influences associated with the eclipse. Pregnant women as a rule are advised to avoid exposure to eclipses. An Indian medical researcher, Dr. Chari, has found that during an eclipse, a high amount of radiation of X-rays and gamma rays takes place which can cause mutations in the foetus. Likewise, pollution of edible articles, cooked foods and water is staved off by placing Kusa grass reeds on all containers during the period of an eclipse. Studies conducted during the February 16, 1980 solar eclipse at Rewa University of Madhya Pradesh (according to a *UNI* report dated 24-2-1980) have led to the following conclusions which only confirm the validity of the traditional practise.

"The belief that water exposed to a solar eclipse was unfit for human consumption was proved true in environmental and biological experiments carried out during last week's solar eclipse.

"The experiments were conducted at the environmental biology centre in collaboration with the Vikram Physics Centre of Rewa University.

"The experiments also confirmed that Kusa grass and tulasi (oscimum sanctum) leaves had a purifying effect on water, as mentioned in Indian mythology.

"The experiments, according to Dr. Rathore, dean of the life sciences department of Rewa University, show that Kusa grass was more useful than tulasi to preserve the quality of water.

"These studies, Dr. Rathore said, were conducted on the water collected from different sources and its physico-chemical properties studied."

RISE IN INFRARED RADIATION

According to the Journal of the Royal Astronomical Society *Astrophysics and Geophysics* (April 2000, Vol. 41, Issue 2),

"An experiment was performed at the Roseland Community Observatory, Cornwall, during the 11 August 1999 total solar eclipse. The main objective was to search for strong infrared coronal lines with a view to identifying candidates for subsequent coronal magnetic field measurements. In particular

we hoped to measure the intensity of the Si IX line at 3-93 u the most likely candidate line. The secondary aim of the experiment was to search for Rydberg transitions of neutral hydrogen and helium in the corona, previous observations of the infrared corona having produced evidence that cool, in coronal terms, material may co-exist in the corona with the hot (10^6 K) plasma. The experiment did not succeed in the above aims as the Sun was obscured by cloud on the morning of the eclipse at the Roseland Observatory site. However, infrared observations of the sunlight scattered through the clouds produced a remarkable result. The infrared intensity fell, precipitously 6.5 minutes before second contact and rose just as suddenly 6.5 minutes after third contact. The authors are unable to explain this result. . . . ."

It is common knowledge that infrared ray influences are of a positive nature and beneficial while ultra violet rays have dangerous implications for the human body. And an eclipse which tends to reduce infrared radiation to the earth naturally can have adverse implications for all life–forms including human.

Many of the practices associated with eclipses have valid reasons which we may have lost track of over long periods of time and were based on an understanding of the importance of solar radiation to the earth.

REFERENCES IN MAHABHARATA

Eclipses were studied and understood as also of historical importance and significance in ancient India. The earliest and the most clearest reference to the eclipses and their power to sway destinies occurs in the **Mahabharata**.

When Vyasa meets Dhritarashtra just before the epic war, he tells him a lunar eclipse is to be followed by a solar eclipse within a fortnight of 13 days and this being an unusual occurrence can be indicative of great slaughter and bloodshed. Vyasa also says (*Bheeshma Parva* - A3),

चतुर्दशीं पंचदशीं भूतपूर्वा तु षोडशी: ।
इमां तु नाभिजानेहममावास्यां त्रयोदशीं ॥
चन्द्रसूर्यावुभौ ग्रस्तावेकमासीं त्रयोदशीं ॥

meaning, *two consecutive eclipses of the Moon and the Sun occurring in pakshas or half-months (bright or dark) of 14, 15 or 16 days is not unusual but when they occur in a 13-day fortnight, it should be a matter of great concern.*

According to **Bharatiya Jyotisha Sastra** - Part I by Sankar Balakrishna Dikshit, a *paksha* or half-month of 13 days is a rare phenomenon and is never obtained if the mean positions of the Sun and Moon are taken into account but it is possible *sometimes* when their true positions are considered. This is possible when the ending moments of New or Full Moons are close to before or after sunrise. Such references to planetary phenomena and the knowledge of calculating the true positions of planets are not only a strong argument in favour of the high attainments of Indians in astronomy as early as in the **Mahabharata** period but also of their discovery of applying astronomical factors to terrestrial affairs.

LORD RAMA'S EXILE AND ECLIPSE

In the **Srimad Ramayana** which is anterior to **Mahabharata**, there is no reference to any specific eclipse. But what Dasaratha says of the affliction to his Janma Nakshatra or birth constellation from malefics is undoubtedly a veiled reference to an eclipse occurring in his Janma Rasi. Dasaratha talks of the Sun, Rahu and Mars afflicting his Janma Nakshatra to Lord Rama.

अवष्टबधम् च मे रामा नक्षत्रम् दारुणै: ग्रहै:।
आवेदयन्ति दैवज्ञा सूर्यांगारक राहुभि: ॥

(*Ayodhya Kh, Ca.* 14, *Sl.* 18)

Astrologers say that my birth star is afflicted by the strong malefics Sun, Mars and Rahu.

राजा हि मृत्युम्याप्रोति घोरमापद् मृच्छति ।

When such bad omens appear, the king would face death or a danger equivalent to death.

Dasaratha is referring to an eclipse occurring on his Moon-sign — it could be a lunar or a solar eclipse but that is not clear here but there is no denying the fact, that the eclipse occurring across his Janma Rasi and Nakshatra and its astrological implication are perturbing the old king. This incident gives a clue to the fact of astrology being an integral part of the life of the people at as early a period as the **Srimad Ramayana** (Treta Yuga) and secondly, of the awareness and understanding the people of those times had of the results associated with eclipses.

As dreaded by King Dasaratha, the tragic events that unfolded following the eclipse across his Moon-sign need little elucidation. Kaikeyi incited and manipulated by Manthara demands her pound of flesh from the poor king. Lord Rama, true to the tradition of honouring one's father's word, leaves for the forest. King Dasaratha dies pining for his beloved Rama, Bharata refuses the crown and the whole kingdom is plunged in gloom. A disaster strikes the country. A family break ups with the patriarch dying. Both results, typical of eclipses !

If only sage Valmiki had given some clue as to either Dasaratha's Janma Nakshatra or the Nakshatra in which that ominous eclipse and conjunction of Mars-Rahu-Sun occurred, it would have been possible to trace the eclipse *vis-a-vis* Lord Rama's chart and Janma Nakshatra. There could be no doubt the eclipse could have had a direct bearing on a sensitive point in Lord Rama's chart which deprived him of his kingdom and forced him into exile. *(05.03)* ●

TREATING ECLIPSES AS TRANSITS — I

1. *Eclipses aggravate transit results of the Sun and Moon.*
2. *Rahu acts like transit Saturn.*
3. *Ketu acts like transit Mars.*

KINGDOMS have been lost and regained with eclipses. Wars have broken out under their influence and whole peoples have been dislocated. Natural calamities —earthquakes, volcanoes, cyclones and floods have been unleashed by eclipses. That eclipses have a distinct impact on history and natural phenomena is an indisputable fact. A question often asked is if eclipses have no role in individual charts? Do eclipses make an impact on individual lives? Or, do they not?

Brihat Samhita deals with eclipses in great detail. But the results here are always and only associated with countries, regions, peoples, rivers, kings and leaders. But anything that can have an impact on large groups of people (who make up a nation) or big masses of land (which define geographical boundaries), goes without saying, must have some kind of, may be even stronger, influence on individuals who are much more fragile and vulnerable than when in collective groups.

Eclipses are, broadly speaking, transits, though of a different kind, and the results, if any, that can be ascribed to them can be deemed to be in accordance with the principles involved in Gochara results. But while transit rules cover single planets, eclipses involve four of the Navagrahas — Sun, Moon, Rahu and Ketu — as a unit. Can the general Gochara principles be stretched and adapted to apply to eclipses ?

When an eclipse occurs, solar or lunar, the important point to be noted is that the luminaries are overpowered by the Nodes and the results they could give —good or bad — cannot escape being influenced. Rahu and Ketu are deemed malefic and obviously, the good results become defunct; the bad, aggravate under their influence. The Nodes are in control during an eclipse and the Nakshatra in which it occurs is activated with the results being in tune with the rest of the chart understood in the context of the running Dasa and Bhukti. In keeping with astrological logic, any other sensitive point or factor in the vicinity of the eclipse defined by the Nakshatra or the sign in which the eclipse occurs or by the planets there in should generate results which could make a big difference to the tremor of the individual's life at that point of time.

Since eclipses affect the luminaries, the Sun and the Moon primarily, which are two of the 3 tripods of a chart, the other being the Ascendant, it would be logical to conclude the adverse results of the Sun (and to some extent of the Moon too whose motion is so quick that, by itself, it can be ignored) would tend to get aggravated.

The Sun's transit of houses, other than the 3rd, the 6th, the 10th and the 11th is said to produce the following results:

First: Bodily exhaustion, loss of wealth, mental irritability, disease, wearisome journey;

Second : Loss of wealth, unhappiness;

Fourth: Disease, obstruction to conjugal life and pleasures;

Fifth: Mental anxiety and loss of peace, ill-health and embarrassment in all possible ways;

Seventh: Wearisome travelling, disorders in the stomach and anus, humiliation;

Eighth: Fear and disease, quarrels, royal displeasure or trouble from government authorities and departments, excessive heat in the body;

Ninth: Danger, humiliation, separation from kith and kin and mental depression.

Twelfth: Sorrows, loss of wealth and quarrels, fever.

Rahu and Ketu, the other two factors in an eclipse, have no physical bodies and are merely geometrical points. They are therefore different from the other Grahas and so become difficult to interpret. According to some, Rahu and Ketu are not ascribed any independent influences in transits. According to others, Rahu and Ketu are said to give results similar to those of Saturn (शनिवद् राहु) and Mars (कुजवद् केतु) respectively. As an eclipse involves both Nodes, it may be deemed to give the combined results of both Mars and Saturn, adding to the intensity or magnitude of their adverse effects.

Saturn and Mars are natural malefics and the results of their transits in some of the houses are deemed good. According to **Phaladeepika** (XXIV - 8)

विक्रमायरिपुग: कुज: शुभ: स्यात्तदान्त्यसुतधर्मगै: रवगै:॥

Mars in the 3rd, 11th and 6th gives good results. So also, Saturn.

Therefore, if we opt to treat Rahu and Ketu as Saturn and Mars respectively, then, their transits of the 3rd, 6th and 11th houses should not cause concern.

Only the adverse results of their transits become relevant.

The adverse transits of Mars cover the following houses;

First : Dejection of mind, separation from one's relations, disease caused by toxins in blood, bile or heat (रक्तपित्तोष्णारोगं).

Second: Fear, angry words (with loved ones), loss of wealth.

Fourth : Loss of position, stomach disorders such as dysentery, diarrhoea, sorrow through relations.

Fifth: Fever, unnecessary desires, mental anguish through one's son or quarrels with relations.

Seventh: Misunderstanding with wife (or husband), eye disease, stomach disorders and the like.

Ninth: Humiliation through loss of wealth, gait becomes retarded through bodily weakness and wasting of the several constituents of the body.

Tenth: Failure in one's attempts, misbehaviour and exhaustion. (But Dr. RAMAN has always held this transit of Mars as favourable which line of thought we will follow).

Twelfth: Loss of wealth, disease due to excess of heat (ताप उष्णामयाद्यै:).

Likewise, Saturn's transit is not favourable in certain houses and results associated with it must be borne in mind in understanding eclipse results.

First : Wasting of the body, disease, funeral rites.

Second : Loss of wealth and children.

Fourth: Loss of wife, relations and wealth.

Fifth: Decline of wealth, loss of children, mental confusion.

Seventh: Wife (or husband) suffers danger, danger during travel.

Eighth: Loss of wealth, children, cattle, friends and disease.

Ninth: Financial loss, obstacles to good works, parental figure dies.

Tenth: Commits sinful deeds, loss of honour, disease.

Twelfth: Frustration, engaged in fruitless and worthless business, robbed of money by enemies, wife and son suffer from sickness.

Equating Rahu with Saturn and Mars with Ketu, these are the results that the Nodes can be expected to generate when moving through the respective houses but otherwise, consistent with the general pattern of the horoscope as a whole.

Most classical texts do not *per se* recognise the transits of the Nodes, although **Phaladeepika** and one or two lesser known texts, depart from this approach.

The results of Rahu's transit through the 12 houses are as follows according to **Phaladeepika** XXVI - 24 :

देहक्षयं वित्तविनाशसौख्यै
दु:खार्थनाशौ सुखनाशमृत्यून् ।
हानिं च लाभं सुभगं व्ययं च
कुर्यात्तमो जन्मगृहात्क्रमेण

from government authorities and departments, excessive heat in the body;

Ninth: Danger, humiliation, separation from kith and kin and mental depression.

Twelfth: Sorrows, loss of wealth and quarrels, fever.

Rahu and Ketu, the other two factors in an eclipse, have no physical bodies and are merely geometrical points. They are therefore different from the other Grahas and so become difficult to interpret. According to some, Rahu and Ketu are not ascribed any independent influences in transits. According to others, Rahu and Ketu are said to give results similar to those of Saturn (शनिवद् राहु) and Mars (कुजवद् केतु) respectively. As an eclipse involves both Nodes, it may be deemed to give the combined results of both Mars and Saturn, adding to the intensity or magnitude of their adverse effects.

Saturn and Mars are natural malefics and the results of their transits in some of the houses are deemed good. According to **Phaladeepika** (XXIV - 8)

विक्रमायरिपुगः कुजः शुभः स्यात्तदान्त्यसुतधर्मगैः रवगैः॥

Mars in the 3rd, 11th and 6th gives good results. So also, Saturn.

Therefore, if we opt to treat Rahu and Ketu as Saturn and Mars respectively, then, their transits of the 3rd, 6th and 11th houses should not cause concern.

Only the adverse results of their transits become relevant.

The adverse transits of Mars cover the following houses;

First : Dejection of mind, separation from one's relations, disease caused by toxins in blood, bile or heat (रक्तपित्तोष्णरोगं).

Second: Fear, angry words (with loved ones), loss of wealth.

Fourth : Loss of position, stomach disorders such as dysentery, diarrhoea, sorrow through relations.

Fifth: Fever, unnecessary desires, mental anguish through one's son or quarrels with relations.

Seventh: Misunderstanding with wife (or husband), eye disease, stomach disorders and the like.

Ninth: Humiliation through loss of wealth, gait becomes retarded through bodily weakness and wasting of the several constituents of the body.

Tenth: Failure in one's attempts, misbehaviour and exhaustion. (But Dr. RAMAN has always held this transit of Mars as favourable which line of thought we will follow).

Twelfth: Loss of wealth, disease due to excess of heat (ताप उष्णामयाद्यै:).

Likewise, Saturn's transit is not favourable in certain houses and results associated with it must be borne in mind in understanding eclipse results.

First: Wasting of the body, disease, funeral rites.
Second: Loss of wealth and children.
Fourth: Loss of wife, relations and wealth.
Fifth: Decline of wealth, loss of children, mental confusion.
Seventh: Wife (or husband) suffers danger, danger during travel.
Eighth: Loss of wealth, children, cattle, friends and disease.
Ninth: Financial loss, obstacles to good works, parental figure dies.
Tenth: Commits sinful deeds, loss of honour, disease.
Twelfth: Frustration, engaged in fruitless and worthless business, robbed of money by enemies, wife and son suffer from sickness.

Equating Rahu with Saturn and Mars with Ketu, these are the results that the Nodes can be expected to generate when moving through the respective houses but otherwise, consistent with the general pattern of the horoscope as a whole.

Most classical texts do not *per se* recognise the transits of the Nodes, although **Phaladeepika** and one or two lesser known texts, depart from this approach.

The results of Rahu's transit through the 12 houses are as follows according to **Phaladeepika** XXVI - 24 :

देहक्षयं वित्तविनाशसौख्यै
दु:खार्थनाशौ सुखनाशमृत्यून् ।
हानिं च लाभं सुभगं व्ययं च
कुर्यात्तमो जन्मगृहात्क्रमेण

First : Sickness or death or disfigurement.
Second: Loss of wealth.
Third: Happiness.
Fourth: Sorrow.
Fifth: Financial loss.
Sixth: Happiness.
Seventh: Loss.
Eighth: Danger to life.
Ninth: Loss.
Tenth: Gain.
Eleventh: Happiness.
Twelfth: Expenditure.

Broadly, the pattern displayed here is the same as Saturn's.

Rahu's transit is downplayed as of negligible or no consequence by itself but getting activated only at eclipse time. *5.03* ●

7

TREATING ECLIPSES AS TRANSITS — II

> 1. Dasa or Bhukti of the Sun or Moon or of a Node coinciding with an eclipse can show mishaps.
> 2. Eclipses on the Ascendant or the Moon-sign or Janma Nakshatra coinciding with a Maraka period can indicate death.
> 3. Eclipses on the Ascendant or the Moon-sign coinciding with Dasa-chidra can point to humiliation, violence or loss of honour.

ECLIPSES IN combination with adverse natal factors call for great caution and vigilance against major mishaps.

Chart 1 is of a distinguished sociologist. The total solar eclipse of 11-8-1999 took place in Cancer in Aslesha Nakshatra, the native's Janma Rasi and Nakshatra. The eclipse touched the natal Nakshatra, natal Moon, natal Rahu and also natal Saturn who, in this case, is also the Bhukti lord. Rahu in the 1st sign is said to cause *Dehakshayam* or sickness or death. The Dasa was of Jupiter who, though 6th and 9th lord, is aspected by Maraka Saturn, the 7th and 8th lord both from Lagna (Ascendant) and Chandra Lagna and becomes a Maraka himself. What started off as a simple cold two weeks earlier ended fatally on 4-11-1999 as bronchial pneumonia.

Many years earlier on 24-4-1970, a fire started by arsonists reduced the native's study at Standford's Centre for Advanced Study in Behavioural Sciences in the U.S.A. to ashes. All the 3 copies of his field work notes processed over a period of 18 years were destroyed in this bizarre fire. The Dasa was of the Moon, the Ascendant lord who, though well placed in his own sign in the 1st house, is afflicted by Rahu and malefic Saturn showing danger from arson, anti-social elements etc. The Bhukti was of Ketu, similarly afflicted. The eclipses of 1970 were spread over Leo and Aquarius with Rahu in Aquarius. On March 7, 1970, there was a total solar eclipse with a partial lunar eclipse on August 17, 1970 involving the 8th and 2nd houses respectively. But more importantly the eclipse coincided with the Dasa of the Moon, who as Dasa lord was afflicted by the eclipse very strongly. This coinciding with an adverse Dasa-Bhukti resulted in tragic loss of the native's painstaking work in the field of his study — a calamity of dire proportions.

But in this incident, the Dasa was of a heavily afflicted but well-placed Moon. The eclipses directly involved the Dasa lord Moon but as the chart was not of Madhyayu, there was no harm to longevity. But in 1999, the chart was under a Maraka Dasa and Bhukti and had also moved into the appropriate Ayurdaya — Purnayu when the eclipse occurring on Janma Rasi and Janma Lagna triggered the fatal planetary stroke.

Chart 1 : Born 16-11-1916 at 23h.20m. at 13 N, 77 E 35 with a balance of 12 years 7 months 18 days of Mercury Dasa at birth.

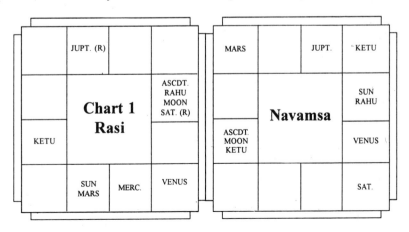

Chart 1: Arson: Dasa of Moon, Bhukti of Ketu, Dasa lord afflicted by Nodes and Saturn *plus* eclipses in the 2nd and 8th.

Death: Maraka Dasa (Jupiter) and Maraka Bhukti (Saturn) *plus* eclipses on the Ascendant, Janma Rasi, Janma Nakshatra and Bhukti lord.

An eclipse occurring when the Dasa or Bhukti, more specially the former, is of the Sun or the Moon renders the chart more vulnerable to mishaps as in such cases, the eclipse involving the luminaries directly affects the Dasa lord.

Chart 2 is of a young girl whose dress caught fire from the lamps in the puja room when she was saying her prayers. The accident occurred round 10 0' clock in the morning on 30-4-1978.

Chart 2: Born 4-11-1959 at 15h.57m. at 11 N 18, 75 E 48 with a balance of 2 years, 7 months and 12 days of Ketu Dasa at birth.

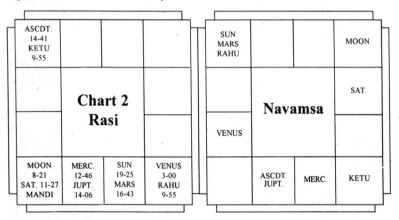

The accident took place in Saturn Bhukti, Venus Dasa. Both Venus and Saturn are powerful malefics for this chart as they do not own any good houses either from the Lagna or the Chandra Lagna. Venus is debilitated and is with Rahu in a Maraka house, both planets in Uttaraphalguni ruled by the 6th lord Sun who is with Mars in the 8th. Saturn is the lord of the sign occupied by Mandi in a Nakshatra ruled by Ketu (akin to Mars) and becomes more malefic. He also aspects both Dasa lord Venus and natal Rahu.

Transit Rahu was moving over natal Venus (Dasa lord) as well as over natal Rahu. Transit Ketu was in the Ascendant and on natal Ketu.

The eclipses of March and April 1978 were spread over Virgo and Pisces respectively. In fact, the lunar eclipse of 24-3-1978 had Ketu at 14^0 4' Pisces very close to the girl's Ascendant point. Saturn Bhukti was due to end in July 1978. The accident occurred about 5 weeks after the March eclipse.

The focus of the eclipse shifts on the Ascendant (Pisces) and the Dasa lord Venus and aggravates the natal Nodal affliction centered on the Ascendant.

Chart 2: Fire Accident: Dasa of the 8th lord Venus and Bhukti of malefic Saturn *plus* eclipses on the Ascendant, natal Rahu and Ketu and the Dasa lord Venus.

If the eclipse occurs on the Janma Rasi where the chart does not indicate death or calamity at that time, then it can be safely ignored. If the chart shows a Maraka period and termination of life, then death. If the chart shows a difficult phase, the eclipse can show an event, mishap, accident, dangerous situation or involvement that could have a calamitous effect on the native's life and turn it upside down.

When an eclipse occurs on the Janma Nakshatra, it has a strong influence and therefore, it is best such natives stay indoors and avoid any kind of travel and movement and keep off alterations of any kind. Likewise, eclipses occurring in the signs occupied by natal Rahu and Ketu are also important, as evidenced in both Charts 1 and 2.

A shooting rampage by 2 schoolboys, Dylan Klebold and Eric Harris in April 1999, led to the killing of 13 people at Columbine High School in Colorado, U.S.A. The killer boys later turned the guns on themselves fatally. The nation was shocked as parents reeled under the impact of what had happened in the least likely place.

The charts of one of the boys which is available provides interesting insights into the catalytic influence of an eclipse.

The trigger to this homicidal rampage came from the Nodes and the eclipses of January and February 1999. The potential killer was already there in the chart of the boy and we will not go into these details. All that we will focus on will be the sudden madness that overtook the boy leading to the wild and senseless killings of his friends and a teacher.

Chart 3: Dylan Klebold: Born 11-9-1981 at 9h.11m. (MDT) at 39 N 44, 104 W 59 with a balance of 8 years 3 months 6 days of Mars Dasa at birth.

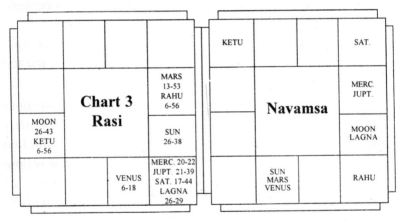

The Moon is in Capricorn (Chart 3) in conjunction with Ketu in the 5th house which rules emotions. The Moon and Ketu are aspected by debilitated 8th lord Mars, himself afflicted by Rahu. The mind, coming under the Moon, under such planetary positions, gets deeply influenced by the Martian traits of hate, malice and selfishness which, in turn, lead to strong prejudices aided by the Nodal influences.

The Moon is in Dhanishta ruled by the malevolent malefic Mars. The Dasa of Mars at birth created a mindset made morbid by sick emotions. The Dasa after Mars is of Rahu and Rahu is equally afflicted. The Ascendant, no doubt has benefics Mercury, Jupiter and Saturn–good features for psychological health-but these are blocked by the fact of the Dasas running ruled by powerful malefics and which influence the native's Moon and so, his mind powerfully. Therefore, Dylan's mind was one of violence right from birth, whether it expressed itself or not for others to notice. The Dasa of Rahu was running with the Bhukti of Ketu on between June 1998 and July 1999 when the shooting incident occurred. Both Rahu and Ketu are afflicted by the 8th lord Mars and in turn afflict the mind or the Moon. The eclipses of 1999 fell in the Cancer-Capricorn axis. The annular solar eclipse of February 16, 1999 touched the natal Nodes — the Dasa and Bhukti lords — and the eclipse fell exactly on Dhanishta, the boy's Janma Nakshatra.

The natal afflictions revolving round the Moon (mind), Mars (violence and death as well as heinous acts) and the 5th house were stimulated and forced out in the form of a mindless blood splattering shoot-out by the eclipse touching the Janma Nakshatra. The eclipses involving the Janma Rasi, Janma Nakshatra, the Dasa and Bhukti lords not only drove the lad into an imbecile rage against others but also against himself triggering an event or situation that could never be reversed or set right — the shooting of his classmates and then, himself.

Chart 3: Killings and Death: Rahu Dasa, Ketu Bhukti *plus* eclipses on Janma Nakshatra, Janma Rasi, natal Rahu, natal Ketu. Eclipse involves both the Dasa and Bhukti lords.

Eclipses occurring on a heavily afflicted Moon generate self-destructive energies.

An excellent illustration of the triggering effect of eclipses is to be found in John F. Kennedy Jr's chart.

The Ascendant Leo (Chart 4) has Rahu with the 12th lord Moon in the 7th joined by Ketu. The solar eclipse of February 16, 1999 occurred in Dhanishta Nakshatra in Kumbha or Aquarius which is also the Janma Rasi of Kennedy Jr. This eclipse led to a tragic air-crash on 16-7-1999 at Martha's Vineyard, which not only killed the handsome young man but also left the nation numb with shock.

The chart has only malefics in Kendras which tends to afflict longevity adversely. The Dasa was of the 7th (and 6th) lord Saturn

Chart 4 : Born 16-11-1916 at 23h.20m. at 13 N, 77 E 35 with a balance of 12 years 7 months 18 days of Mercury Dasa at birth.

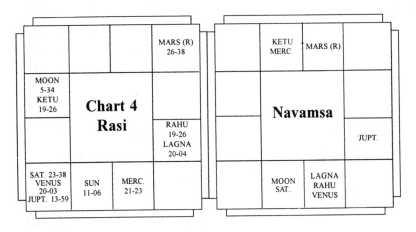

and the Bhukti of the 2nd (and the 11th) lord Mercury. The chart coming under a Maraka period and the eclipse affecting the Lagna and the Moon resulted in physical danger and death to the native.

Chart 4: Accident and Death: Maraka Dasa (Saturn), Maraka Bhukti (Mercury) *plus* eclipses on Janma Nakshatra, Janma Rasi and Ascendant.

Eclipses occurring on natal Moon and Janma Nakshatra when Maraka Dasa and Bhukti are running and the longevity coming under threat in terms of Ayurdaya lead to death.

Chart 5 is of a girl who was found missing on 1-10-1993. She was kidnapped at knife point from home while her mother slept in an adjoining room. On 4-12-1993, the girl's body was discovered on the West coast.

The Dasa and Bhukti when this happened were both of Ketu. Ketu is with exalted Mars in the 12th house aspected by Jupiter. Jupiter did not help. It is generally noticed that when the Nodes are in the 12th afflicting it and joined by malefics, one gets caught in sordid situations indicating pain, suffering, confinement, assault, molestation and other perversions from anti-social elements especially if the Dasa is also of a planet related to such a 12th house.

Chart 5 : Born 3-1-1961 at 10h.41m. (ZST) at 37 N 47,122 W 25.

					VENUS MARS	ASCDT	JUPT. SAT.	KETU
ASCDT	Chart 5 Rasi AM-07-95-565		RAHU			Navamsa	
KETU MARS					MOON		
SUN MERC.	MOON VENUS		JUPT. SAT.		RAHU	MERC.	SUN

In this case, the Dasa was of the 12th occupant Ketu. The Bhukti also was of Ketu. The Nodes in transit were in Scorpio and Taurus respectively. A total lunar eclipse occurred on 4-6-1993 in Jyeshta Nakshatra involving the Janma Rasi and Nakshatra of the unfortunate girl.

Chart 5: Kidnapping and Death: Ketu Dasa, Ketu Bhukti *plus* eclipse on Janma Nakshatra, Janma Rasi. Eclipse involves both the Dasa and Bhukti lords.

In this case (Chart 6), the girl set out for a ride on her bicycle (while visiting her grandparents) on 5-8-1993. She never returned and a frantic search by neighbours and the police led to her bicycle on the roadside. Later, her body was recovered on 23-10-1993.

The girl was found missing in Rahu Bhukti, Saturn Dasa. Saturn, the Dasa lord, is a malefic (Badhaka) and occupies a Maraka house (the 7th) in Swati, ruled by Rahu. Rahu, the Bhukti lord, is in the 3rd, also in a Rahu ruled Nakshatra. These periods of Rahu and Saturn are always to be approached with great caution and often lead to death and disaster. Rahu Bhukti began in January 1993. She disappeared a few weeks before the solar eclipse of 13-11-1993 which occurred in the Aries-Libra axis across the Ascendant and the Dasa lord Saturn, the only eclipse to occur during that year in these two signs.

Chart 6 : Born 19-1-1983 at 10h.45m. (EST) at 42 N 16, 71 W 48 with a balance of 14 years 4 months 16 days of Saturn Dasa.

MOON 6-36	ASCDT 0-31		RAHU 10-42
MARS 9-29	Chart 6 Rasi		
VENUS 25-15 SUN 6-50			
MERC. 28-50 KETU 10-42	JUPT. 12-23	SAT. 12-08	

	ASCDT		KETU
SUN	Navamsa		
SAT.			MOON VENUS
MERC. MARS RAHU		JUPT.	

Chart 6: Missing and Death: Maraka Dasa (Saturn), Rahu Bhukti *plus* eclipses on Ascendant and Dasa lord.

A solar eclipse occurring on 13-11-1993 fell across Libra and Aries housing her Ascendant and Dasa lord respectively. Here, the kidnapping and death occurred just before the eclipse.

A Maraka Dasa and Bhukti or Dasa-Chidra or Dasa Bhukti of Badhaka or of a malefic or Node coinciding with an eclipse across the Ascendant point to grave physical danger such as kidnapping, assault and molestation.

In Chart 7, the native, a bank employee was returning home on her scooter after a party with friends to celebrate a promotion when she was waylaid by 2 serial-killers in a deserted vacant plot just adjoining her house. They stopped her, pulled her off her scooter, gagged her with waste rags, hit her head with an iron rod, smashed her face with bricks and then dumped her body in a trench by the side of the plot. The murder, for petty gain, took place on 19-2-1998 in Jupiter Bhukti of Saturn Dasa in the Dasa-chidra period. The Dasa Bhukti lords are in Shashtashtaka which makes the chart highly vulnerable to danger. Jupiter is the 7th lord and Maraka. Saturn, as 8th lord, is in the 11th debilitated. The Janma Rasi is Aquarius with the Moon in Poorvabhadrapada. The last eclipse of 1997 that occurred on 16-9-1997 was a total lunar eclipse and in Pisces in Poorvabhadrapada on the girl's Janma Nakshatra. The next eclipse thereafter was of the Sun and took place on 26-2-1998 in Aquarius on her Janma Rasi. These two eclipses relating to her Janma Nakshatra and Janma Rasi cover a period of 6 months approximately coinciding with the Dasa-chidra period as well bringing the chart under extremely treacherous influences.

Chart 7 : Born 1-8-1969 at 3-10 a.m. (IST) at 11 N 28, 77 E 27 with a balance of 9 years 11 months 23 days of Jupiter Dasa at birth.

RAHU 1-24	SAT. 16-36		ASCDT. 5-06 VENUS 5-24
MOON 25-01	**Chart 7** **Rasi**		SUN 16-30 MERC. 26-30
	MARS 13-20		JUPT. 10-29 KETU 1-24

	JUPT.	MOON	
MERC.	**Navamsa**		RAHU
			SAT.
	ASCDT. SUN MARS VENUS		

Chart 7: Violent Death: Dasa - chidra of mutually adversely placed 8th lord (Saturn) and Maraka (Jupiter) *plus* eclipses on Janma Nakshatra and Janma Rasi.

One of the best examples for the malevolent influence of eclipses on individual charts is of our late Prime Minister Rajiv Gandhi (Chart 8).

Rajiv Gandhi (Chart 8) was assassinated by a suicide-killer in a bomb blast on 21-5-1991. This was in Venus Bhukti of Rahu Dasa which began in April 1991 and was a Maraka period according to commonly known principles of astrology. A malefic Venus in Rahu Dasa acquires killing powers in his Bhukti.

The eclipse of 15-1-1991 (solar) took place in Capricorn with the Rahu-Ketu axis across Capricorn and Cancer, the latter being occupied by Dasa lord Rahu. The next eclipse, a lunar eclipse, was on 30-1-1991 again, across the same signs. Therefore, the period of approximately 6 months from these eclipses and especially coming under Venus Bhukti of Rahu Dasa had to be watched out for with great care. It was these planetary phenomena that promted us to indicate in an editorial *Planets* and *Mid-term Polls* dated 10-4-1991 and appearing in the June 1991 issue of THE ASTROLOGICAL MAGAZINE while discussing the charts of prime-ministerial aspirants during the May 1991 Lok Sabha election campaign that Rajiv Gandhi had no Yogas *again* for prime-ministership and which also was the

Chart 8 : Born 20-8-1944 at 8h.11m. (WT) at 18 N 50, 72 E 50 with a balance of 12 years 1 month 6 days of Venus Dasa at birth.

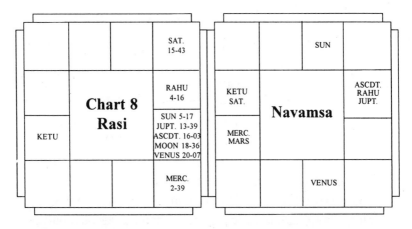

basis of a cyrptic forecast "The Rajiv Era is Over" we made in a lecture delivered on 16-3-1991 at the Indian Institute of World Culture, B. P. Wadia Road, Bangalore and of which a report appeared in THE ASTROLOGICAL MAGAZINE, June 1991, page 535 and which was on the stands in the second week of May itself.

Chart 8: Assassination: Maraka Dasa (Rahu) and Maraka Bhukti (Venus) *plus* eclipse on natal Rahu and Ketu and on Dasa lord Rahu.

Eclipses are closely connected with catastrophic events and in charts which become vulnerable due to specific Yogas as well as Dasa-Bhukti periods around the time of an eclipse falling in a sensitive part of the chart, warn against impending calamities, including death.

The eclipses occurring on any one of the following points in a horoscope tend to indicate an event of serious consequence before the next set of the eclipses of the year (or within the next 6 months approximately), the exact time of the crisis depending upon the Dasa and Bhukti and the predisposition of the chart to such an event:
1. The Janma Rasi.
2. The Janma Nakshatra.
3. Natal Rahu and Ketu in the chart and more so, if the Dasa is of Rahu or Ketu. The Bhukti also of a Node aggravates the intensity of the blow.
4. The Ascendant.
5. Any sign with a multi-planet group. If this group involves Rahu or Ketu also, the effect can be more severe.
6. Mars, Ketu, Rahu or Saturn in the 12th severally or jointly and the Dasa-Bhukti of any of these planets *plus* the eclipse influencing the Moon — assault, abduction, molestation, victim of violence.
7. Janma Rasi or Janma Lagna and if Saturn-Rahu periods are on — assault, attack, violence.
8. Janma Rasi or Nakshatra with Rahu or Ketu Dasa running.
9. Janma Rasi or Ascendant combined with Dasa-chidra period — intense humiliation, violence, loss of honour, serious charges.
10. The Dasa or Bhukti or both of the Sun or the Moon or of both, more so, if the eclipses occur across the signs they occupy.

When these planetary situations obtain, it can show a crisis in life when death or a major accident or violent attack or health crisis can throw life completely out of gear.

Eclipses are phenomena one must guard against. But there is no reason to panic everytime there is an eclipse since several factors have to fall in place before it can make an impact on the native. *(10-03)* ●

THE ASTROLOGICAL DISSECTION OF A SNIPER KILLER

> 1. Heavy malefic influences on Lagna show a life of reversals and setbacks.
> 2. Lagna lord combust destroys the positive traits of the rising sign.
> 3. Yogas for homicide work only in Killer Dasas; otherwise not.

CREEPY KILLINGS

OCTOBER 2002 was a creepy month for Americans. Fourteen shots from an unknown sniper took away 10 lives. The shootings made such a chilling impact on the nation that even President Bush could not avoid mentioning the killings while the FBI kept hoping his words would not "goad the shooter again". Even the White House began to think in terms of opening up safety zones for children in suburban parking lots.

The shootings began on October 2, 2002 with gunfire crackling the window of a store in Maryland but with none hurt. This was at 5-20 p.m. Within an hour at 6-04 p.m., in the same town, a 55 year old man was shot dead by an unseen shooter in a parking lot. And with this killing, the sniper having savoured the thrill of killing, much like a maneater thirsting for more blood, went on a horrifying rampage shooting indiscriminately at innocent passers-by from a cleverly designed perch in a Cheverlot trunk. With each killing, he seemed to have got bolder and bolder until the early hours of October 24, 2002, when federal agents crept up to the car where the killer was sleeping and dragged him out with a teenage accomplice. And with these arrests, the grisly killings came to an end.

ASCENDANT HEAVILY AFFLICTED

A friend from the United States sends in the birth particulars of this deadly sniper John Allen Muhammed.

The Ascendant Sagittarius though occupied by its ruler Jupiter is heavily afflicted by malefics Mars and Saturn in opposition across the 1st and 7th houses in Chart 1. Jupiter, the Lagna lord, is combust. The Ascendant and its occupants are aspected powerfully by a retrograde Mars.

Chart 1: John Allen Muhammed: Born December 31, 1960 at 6-12 a.m. (CST) 29 N 55, 90 W 05 with a balance of 2 years 5 months 4 days of Mars Dasa at birth.

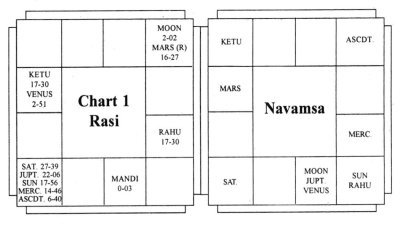

Moving on to the Moon-sign Gemini, it is joined by 6th and 11th lord Mars (R). This in itself is an extremely violent combination involving as it does the Manahkaraka Moon. "The real disposition of Mars is anger, violence and apparently an eager wish to be in quarrels and mischief, the countenance is extremely vicious and unbending, rude, unkind, ferocious and bitter. They expect and exact universal submission and although often generous and magnanimous, they are never kind or even sociable. Such dispositions, however, are seldom seen, as the aspects of other planets alter it materially...." Mars influencing the mind also makes one "active, furious and contentious". Though Mars confers an incisive intellect, it is easily prejudiced more by rashness than solid judgement. It also makes for one who "is possessed of great mechanical skill, high courage, having a contempt for death, impatience of control or submission and but little respect for social or moral laws when they interfere with his liberty of action." Such natives can also be crafty, violent, dangerous and are likely to die violent deaths.

PAISACHA YOGA

The 7th house from the Moon-sign is occupied by 7th lord Jupiter who is combust, Vargottama 2nd and 3rd lord Saturn and Mercury, himself afflicted by malefic factors. And as if this were not bad enough, there is a Moon-Mercury opposition involving the Lagna and the Moon-sign generating a Paisacha Yoga or combination for insanity (**Jatakadeshamarga** VIII-74).

बुधचन्द्रौ केन्द्रगतौ नान्यग्रहसंयुतौ न पतिदृष्टौ ।
योगोयं पैशाचस्तत्रोत्पन्नस्य सौन्मादी ॥

This Yoga requires Mercury and the Moon in mutual Kendras (quadrants). They should not be joined by any other planet or be aspected by their sign dispositors. The result is insanity.

We have seen that when there are malefic influences involved in this Budha-Chandra Yoga, then such natives develop highly aggressive and malevolent behaviour patterns though apparently sociable. In other words, such a Yoga can produce a psychopath. When the Yoga conditions are fulfilled in toto, then it becomes a case of plain insanity that cannot be hidden.

In this case, the Yoga is intensified and aggravated by the Mars(R)-Saturn opposition involving the constellations Aridra of incendiary Rahu and Uttarashada of fiery Sun respectively across the Lagna and the Moon-sign.

Whatever the specific details of such a nativity, **the conglomeration of heavy malefic influences shows a general life pattern spotted with turbulence, marital discord, career reversals, frustration and violence rendered worse by a dangerously egoistic and cruel devilish disposition.**

EARLY YEARS

John Allen Muhammed was initially known as John Allen Williams. He was a football player, thanks to the strong Martian influence on the chart as a whole. His life began under the Dasa of Mars after which it moved into that of Rahu next. Rahu in the 9th is quite well-placed and in the constellation of a benefic 5th lord Venus. Rahu is aspected by Lagna lord Jupiter whose influence though feeble is not defunct. Rahu is also aspected by Vargottama 5th lord Venus. All of these factors saw him through school and college. He is remembered as a good team member. Rahu in the 3rd from the Moon helped his love for sport. In 1978 when he graduated from school, he was in Sun Bhukti of Rahu Dasa. He then enlisted in the Louisiana Army National Guard in Moon Bhukti. The Moon is with Mars. And this drew him into the security services.

In 1981, about three years later, John Williams married a high school date. A son was born soon after. Jupiter Dasa had just begun. Jupiter as Lagna lord is in the 1st aspecting the 7th and 5th houses. He is joined by 7th lord Mercury and 9th lord Sun. John Williams' cup of life seemed to be full and brimming with joy. As Lagna lord, Jupiter is a first rate benefic to begin with. John Williams was often described as charming which he undoubtedly could be thanks to the Moon in the 7th and Jupiter-Mercury and the Sun in the 1st. **He could have continued to be just that had it not been for the dreadful Mars-Saturn opposition working on his Lagna and the Moon, with Lagna lord Jupiter too getting afflicted by combustion by his proximity to the Sun.** Adding fuel to these inflammable factors was the Paisacha Yoga involving the Moon and Mercury. As a result, beneath the bewitching smile he was famous for with his friends, deep-seated volcanic emotions were waiting to germinate. **Only the weather had to be just right for these diabolic sprouts to splinter through his psychological frame before ripping it apart. And as we all know, it is the Dasas and Bhuktis that decide on the weather.**

JUPITER'S BENEFICENCE DISSOLVES

Mars as 5th lord is with the Moon and such a Mars focussing on the Ascendant in full Chestabala (retrograde strength) in tandem with Saturn acted like a powder keg waiting for the spark to ignite and blast John Williams' entire personality. In 1982, failing to show up for duty he was fined heavily and demoted by one rank. In 1983 as Saturn Bhukti of Jupiter Dasa took over, he was pulled up for assaulting an officer. Jupiter as Dasa and Saturn as Bhukti lords are aspected by Mars (R) from Gemini. Such an aspect, if also influencing the Ascendant and the 10th house, leads to frequent changes of residence and employment and generally proves unfortunate. It also makes one ingenious but fickle. Suddenly, John Williams seemed to be going out gear, losing control over himself for no reason. **The combustion was beginning to bear results shovelling Jupiter, the benefic, aside and with it overpowering whatever positive features it had given him.**

1985 deepened the fissures in John Williams' personality and the cracks began to hurt his life. He separated from his wife. The 7th house has the Moon and Mars, the latter's maleficence rendered worse by his retrogression. Jupiter aspects Mars but himself is rendered weak by his proximity to the Sun. The 7th lord Mercury, though with Jupiter, is in a common sign with two other malefics. From Chandra Lagna too, the 7th house with four planets in it is in a common sign Sagittarius aspected by 11th lord Mars, again from another common sign Gemini, making the marriage fragile and vulnerable to break-up. Further, the multiple influences and dual signs involved clearly indicate more than one marriage. It was not unusual therefore that the first marriage fell apart.

APOSTACY AND COMBUSTION

A major event in 1985 in Jupiter Dasa, Saturn Bhukti was John Williams' conversion to Islam. One of the Yogas for apostacy is the combustion of Devaguru Jupiter or of the Lagna lord. Both conditions are fulfilled in this case. In the same period, he quit his job as a national security guard and joined the army, again a vocation coming under Mars who aspects the 10th house and the 10th lord Mercury as also both Dasa and Bhukti lords.

In 1988, John Muhammed married a second time. This was in Ketu Bhukti of Jupiter Dasa. Ketu with Venus is pre-eminently qualified to bring about this event.

John Muhammed was sent abroad to Germany and the Middle-East between 1990 and 1992 as part of a combat engineer unit. It was in the military that his hidden talent for precise aim came to light. He was soon at "expert level" for his marksmanship. This can be attributed to the close Martian influence on Mercury. While this was the positive side of Mars showing up, the negative side of an overpowering restlessness was not far behind driving him to give up his army job in 1994. This was in Mars Bhukti with retrograde Mars in conjunction with the Manahkaraka Moon and aspecting Lagna lord Jupiter, Buddhikaraka Mercury who is also the 10th lord (Karmastanadhipati) as well as malefic Saturn resulting in extreme frustration. Mars and Jupiter in opposition involving the Lagna and 7th houses produce a Yoga for lunacy according to **Jataka Tattwa**, C-151 (इज्येड्डे कुजेसे उन्मादी). And as John Muhammed moved into Rahu Bhukti, he began to drift aimlessly. He started a Karate school which never took off. He began to get dangerously aggressive in his behaviour. Mohammed was now caught in litigation with his first wife over his children and as he found he was losing control, his behaviour turned more and more menacing and violent.

Juipter Dasa though it began well could not consolidate the good results of his own Bhukti after which the downslide and in a way, the disintegration of the man accelerated with the Sun Bhukti robbing Jupiter of all his benevolence. By the time Jupiter Dasa came to its end, the disintegration and the overcoming of the man by the beast was near complete. **It is the Sun who is responsible for Jupiter's combustion and therefore it was only appropriate their mutual periods should have led to a total breakdown of the man and whatever good and sane was left in him.**

EXPLOSIVE SATURN DASA

Saturn Dasa, Saturn Bhukti started in April 1997. Muhammed's second wife began proceedings against him for divorce in 1999 unable to put up with his violence and threats. The Mars-Saturn opposition is a dangerous combination for any relationship and involving the 7th house did not let the second marriage also survive.

2001 saw the annihilating of all of what Jupiter as a benefic could stand for in John Muhammed's life and personality. The courts cut off even his visitation rights to the children (from both marriages). This judicial ruling devastated the man. The frustration levels that a combust Jupiter as Lagna lord generated reached such a pitch that the only outlet for his pent up rage and chaotic mind was to turn to violence.

Saturn Dasa, Saturn Bhukti made him a lonely man, bereft of children, wife, home, job — everything. It was in may be 2001 that he first met his teenage accomplice, a runaway from home, called Malvo. Malvo was not known to be violent but once under the influence of John Muhammed was totally dominated by him emotionally and began carrying out his biddings without question.

Mercury Bhukti of Saturn Dasa had begun. Jupiter, though it wiped out the man, was better in that it did not bring out the homicide in him. **It was only Saturn as Dasa lord influenced by the opposition from Mars (R) that made John Muhammed's Paisacha Yoga come alive.**

KILLER YOGAS, KILLER DASAS

According to **Jataka Tattwa** (L-152), जीवार्कारयोगे ब्रह्महत्या or, if Jupiter conjoins the Sun and Mars, one becomes guilty of Brahmahatya or the killing of a *brahmin*. According to L-151 *ibid*, यमार्कारयोगे ब्रम्हहत्या or if Saturn, Sun and Mars conjoin one kills a *brahmin*. And the term *brahmin,* in this context, can be interpreted to mean innocent victims who are killed without provocation. Both the Yogas are applicable to John Muhammed's chart where Jupiter is with the Sun, combust. Jupiter is not joined by Mars but aspected by him which meets with the requirements of the Yoga. Likewise, the Sun and Saturn are in conjunction aspected by Mars instead of all three being together as literally required by the second Yoga. The interesting point is, the affliction to Jupiter needed to produce a killer took all of Jupiter Dasa to prepare the ground for such a propensity to ripen and emerge simply because Jupiter as Lagna lord rules the total personality of the native. The afflictions to the Lagna lord produced a morbid personality. Saturn, the next Dasa lord, is with the 10th lord Mercury and aspects him which provides the needed impetus to perpetuate crime which is translating the thought (or potential for homicide) into act (Karma). **What this highlights is even if the potential for homicide is present in a chart, unless the right Dasas operate, the native may never resort to killing. For killer Yogas, killer Dasas are very important. In other words, Dasas that aid the translation of the killer Yogas into actual acts must run and also receive active support from transits at the same time for the native to actually kill.**

An interesting insight into the Paisacha Yoga and its operation is provided by the Moon's lordship in John Mohammed's chart. The Moon is the 8th lord and the Moon rules death. And so it was, he became obsessed with killing. The Moon is with Mars who rules firearms. And the tool the sniper employed was a rifle.

There was no real motive for the murders for all the victims were randomly picked except that the sniper was trying to say, he had lost everything and it no longer mattered who lived or who died. It was the working of a sick mind rendered worse by the fact there was no shoulder for him to lean on and cry his heart out. He was angry, not with anyone. He was angry with society, with the world,

The Astrological Dissection of a Sniper Killer

with all those men and women in the streets who went about their work with bright faces as if his grief and frustration did not matter. Such a callous world, such unfeeling people did not deserve to live. They were better off dead. And the game he was to play snuffing out lives would give him respite from his frustrations. It would bring excitement into his otherwise empty world. And so began the mindless shootings from October 2, 2001 just as transit Saturn in his Janma Nakshatra was beginning to slow down to a standstill before assuming retrograde motion on October 12, 2002.

ECLIPSE STIMULUS

Saturn, the Dasa lord and Mercury, the Bhukti lord, had already been sufficiently stimulated to blow up the man's mind as early as in June 2002 when the solar eclipse in Taurus (Chart 2) occurred involving these two planets. Saturn was combust in the eclipsed Sun and was joined by Mercury in Taurus, all three in Mrigasira Nakshatra, John Muhammed's Janma Nakshatra. Mars was exactly atop natal Mars in the 17th degree of Gemini setting the stage for the bizarre splurge of violence that was to follow shortly.

Chart 2: Solar Eclipse: June 10, 2002 at 20h. 53m. (UT) at 38 N 50, 77 W 00.

Chart 2 Rasi			
	MERC. 9-06 RAHU 25-24 SAT. 26-12 MOON 25-54 SUN 27-22	MARS 16-21 JUPT. 26-08	
ASCDT. 6-58	KETU 25-24		

Navamsa			
MERC. MARS	JUPT.	ASCDT.	
KETU			VENUS
			RAHU MOON SAT.
			SUN

All the killings occurred in Saturn Antara, Mercury Bhukti, Saturn Dasa. Transit Saturn was in Gemini on natal Moon aspecting the Dasa-Bhukti lords as well as the Antara lord. Transit Saturn in Gemini and transit Mercury in Virgo were both afflicted by natal Mars. The Dasa lord Saturn was moving into retrogression when the killings began.

VIOLENT END

John Muhammed was charged with murder, apart from several other lesser charges. The 8th lord Moon in the 7th is afflicted by powerful malefics Mars (R) and Saturn. Such a combination generally indicates an unnatural end. There is also a special combination according to which if malefics be in the 4th and the 10th or the trines and the 8th lord combines with Mars in Lagna, then death is due to hanging. It can be self-inflicted or otherwise

---

The Killings

October 2: *A 55 year old man was shot dead near a grocery store.*

October 3: *A 35 year old taxi driver was killed at a gas station. Hardly 25 minutes later, the sniper's bullet hit a 30 plus women sitting on a bench. And slightly over an hour later, a young woman was killed at another gas station. The same evening a 72 year old man fell victim to the sniper's wild killings.*

October 4: *A 43 year old woman was shot at (but who survived with serious wounds) in a parking lot.*

October 7: *A 13 year old youngster was shot at as he walked to school.*

October 9: *A man in his fifties was shot dead at a gas station.*

October 11: *Another 53 year old man was shot dead at a gas station.*

October 14: *A woman was killed by bullet shots in a parking lot.*

October 19 and 21: *Two men were killed in sniper attacks. The total tally of victims came to a gruesome 10.*

also as when one is sentenced to death. Here, the 4th and 10th are not occupied by malefics; it is the 1st and the 7th Kendras that get afflicted by malefic occupation. Additionally, Rahu is in the 9th, a trine. These factors which point to violent death combined with the fact of transit Saturn crossing natal Moon bringing the chart under *sadesathe* carry ominous signs for a quick conviction and death sentence. *(03-03)* (Written on *24-1-2003*). ●

THE YAMAGANDA - YAMAKANTAKA CONUNDRUM

> 1. Yamagandam covers a 90-minute period.
> 2. Yamakantaka refers to a specific point of time.
> 3. Yamagandam is inauspicious. Yamakantaka is auspicious.

AMBIGUOUS TERMS

Yamagandam, like rahukalam, is also based on the diurnal motion of the earth. It is akin to Rahukalam in that it is also a period of 90 minutes, differing in its starting time for different weekdays as follows :

Sunday 12-30 p.m. to 1-30 p.m.; Monday 10-30 a.m. to 12 noon; Tuesday 9-00 a.m. to 10-30 a.m.; Wednesday 7-30 a.m. to 9-00 a.m.; Thursday 6-00 a.m. to 7-30 a.m; Friday 3-00 p.m. to 4-30 p.m; and Saturday 1-30 p.m. to 3-00 p.m.

Yamagandam too is generally deemed inauspicious for venturing on any kind of activity. However, compared to Rahukalam, Yamagandakalam does not carry the same intensity of evil and is not as widely followed as the former. All said and done, neither Rahukalam nor Yamagandakalam is a Mahadosha or major affliction as defined in classical works and does not merit the importance it is being given in certain parts of the country.

Soon after these views appeared in THE ASTROLOGICAL MAGAZINE sometime back, a spate of letters came which expressed confusion on the relatively little understood factor of Yamagandam, its method of determination and its applicability. Another point of ambiguity raised in this context and apparently under even greater confusion in these letters was the Yamakantaka factor and how it differed from Yamagandam. Going through the methods of determination of Yamakantaka as given in classical works only made the situation even more confusing when it was found that the time intervals given for it coincided with those shown against Yamagandam in almanacs leading to the question if both were one and the same factor and why then was there a difference in their nomenclature.

Kalaprakasika is a standard work on Muhurta or electional astrology and is attributed to Narasimha whose date it is difficult to fix. In Chapter XXXIII, Sloka 65, Narasimha says,

अर्धप्रहारं कालञ्च यमगण्डकमेव च ।
शुभकर्मसु यत्नेन वर्जयेत्सर्वदा नर: ॥

Or, *the three periods of Ardhapraharam, Yamagandam* (यमगण्डं) *and Kala **should be rejected as inauspicious**.* That is, Yamagandam is deemed to be an unfavourable factor.

DEFINITION

Yamagandam is defined as the 5th period (of 8) of Sunday, the 4th of Monday, the 3rd of Tuesday, the 2nd of Wednesday, the 7th of Friday and the 6th of Saturday. In other words, it is the part coming under the rulership of Jupiter for a day birth, when the duration of day is divided into 8 equal parts, the first part being ruled by the weekday lord in question followed by the successive weekday lords. For a night birth also, the duration of night is divided into 8 equal parts but the first part now is ruled by the ruler of the 5th day from the weekday in question followed successively by the other weekday lords in order, the part ruled by Jupiter being Yamagandam.

But in **Jataka Parijata**, which its author Vaidyanatha Dikshitar says is an abridged version of **Saravali**, it says in Chapter II, Sloka 6, listing the Upagrahas, that

क्रमश: कालपरिधिधूमार्द्धप्रहराह्वया: ।
यमकंटककोदण्डमान्दिपातोपकेतव: ॥

Or, *Kala, Paridhi, Dhuma, Ardhaprahara, Yama-kantaka* (यमकण्टक), *Kodanda, Mandi, Patha and Upaketu are Upagrahas.*

Earlier in Sloka 5, it says,

उपग्रह भानुमुखग्रहांश कालदय: कष्टफलप्रदा: स्यु: ॥

Minor planets Kala and others (enumerated in Sloka 6) are portions belonging to Ravi (Sun) and other planets (respectively) and produce painful consequences.

And Yamakantaka is given as Jupiter's Upagraha or minor planet. That is, according to **Jataka Parijata** and **Saravali**, which treat exclusively of Jataka or predictive astrology and not Muhurta, Yamakantaka may be deemed to be productive of evil in a birth chart.

Are They the Same ?

Yamakantaka's periods given in **Phaladeepika** which the translator V. Subramanya Sastri reproduces in his *Notes* under Sloka 6 of **Jataka Parijata** are the same as those given for Yamagandam in **Kalaprakasika**.

Therefore, judging by the timings given for Yamagandam and Yamakantaka on each weekday, it may not be incorrect to presume they are the same factor in a general sense. However, Yamagandakalam for Muhurta purposes is deemed evil as observed in practice and is generally avoided by the majority of people. Yamakantaka according to these texts is also said to be evil and to be interpreted accordingly in natal horoscopy. The whole confusion appears to revolve around the use of the terms Yamagandam (यमगण्डं) and Yamakantaka (यमकण्टक) for defining apparently the same astrological factor in different classical texts.

According to **Brihat Parasara Hora Sastram** (Chapter 4, Sloka 13), translated by Pandit Devachandra Jha and published by Chowkhamba,

शन्यंशो गुलिक: प्रोक्तो गुर्वंशो यमघण्टक: ।

Or, *that part coming under Saturn is called Gulika while that coming under Jupiter is Yamagantaka* (यमघण्डक).
But Parasara does not label either as evil or capable of evil. But we notice, Parasara uses the term यमघण्टक, not यमकण्टक as other texts would have it. What difference would that make is a question only Sanskrit scholars well versed in astrology can answer.

In **Phaladeepika**, a work on predictive astrology again and much later than **Brihat Parasara Hora**, the Upagrahas receive more detailed treatment. According to Chapter XXV, Sloka 18,

गुलिकस्य तु संयोगे दोषान्त्सर्वत्र निर्दिशेत् ।
यमकण्टकसंयोगे सर्वत्र कथयेच्छुभम् ॥

Wherever Gulika is in conjunction (with a planet), in all those (instances), evil has to be predicted. Whenever Yamakantaka is associated, good has to be expected.

KARAKATTWA INFLUENCED

Gulika's association with different planets is said to give bad results. When Gulika is with the Sun, one is said to kill one's father; if with the Moon, one will cause pain (suffering) to one's mother; if with Mars, one may lose a brother and if with Mercury, one can turn insane. With Jupiter, one becomes a blashphemous heretic; if with Venus, one seeks the company of low and base members of the opposite sex; with Saturn, one will be short-lived and afflicted with leprosy. With Rahu, Gulika is said to make one suffer from विषरोग or toxins in the body and if with Ketu, faces danger of fire accidents. So, when in the same strain classical works say that Yamakantaka is Jupiter's son and by implication said to give good results, it would mean he acts as a benefic influence on a natal planet. From the results given for Gulika it would appear, his association primarily blemishes the Karakattwa or the natural signification of the planet involved. Therefore, it implies Yamakantaka in contrast promotes the Karakattwa of the planet he joins. With the Sun, Yamakantaka can therefore be said to promote relationship with father; with the Moon, one becomes kind and affectionate towards the mother. With

Mars it helps ties with brothers and with Mercury, it sharpens the intellect. With Venus, it brings in restraint in one's sexual conduct and with Saturn, longevity finds support. Yamakantaka with Jupiter leads to spiritual aspirations. With Rahu, the body is in good health. Ketu with Yamakantaka renders the native safe from fire hazards. The next verse, Sloka 9 says,

दोषप्रदाने गुलिको बलीयान् शुभप्रदाने यमकण्टक: स्यात् ॥

According to it, *Gulika becomes powerful in causing evil while Yamakantaka becomes strong in generating good.*

AKIN TO JUPITER

Phaladeepika does not stop with this demarcation between Gulika and Yamakantaka as bad and good respectively, but goes on to emphasise these contrasting properties of the two Upagrahas by comparing Gulika to Saturn (शनिवद्गुलिके) and Yamakantaka to Jupiter (गुरूवद्यमकण्टक) in Sloka 20. Again in Sloka 21, Gulika is shown to bring on death (गुलिकस्तु मृत्यु:) while Yamakantaka is said to be of an invigorating nature or productive of good results (जीवातुक: स्याद्यमकण्टकोपि).

Since Yamakantaka is equated with Jupiter in terms of results, the following can be attributed to Yamakantaka occupying different Bhavas on the analogy of Jupiter.

Yamakantaka in Lagna can make one good looking, noble, fortunate, long-lived and blessed with children.

In the 2nd House : One is a good speaker, enjoys good food, has a beaming face, is learned and affluent.

In the 3rd House : One becomes niggardly, does not command respect, will be wicked in nature but have good brothers.

In the 4th House : One lives with (or takes care of) one's mother, has a lot of friends, good servants, son, wife, prosperity and is happy.

In the 5th House : One suffers on account of one's children but is intelligent and highly placed in service.

In the 6th House : One is indolent, is treated shabbily by others but can overcome his adversaries.

In the 7th House : One is amicable, generous and has a good wife and sons.

In the 8th House : One is indigent and earns his livelihood as a menial, commits sins but has a long life.

In the 9th House : One becomes an influential personage, will have children, be wealthy and intent on doing virtuous deeds.

In the 10th House : One will be upright and ethical, will be known for his integrity, is rich and has contacts with the authorities and those in high positions.

In the 11th House : One will be wealthy, fearless, have few children, will have conveyances and a long life.

In the 12th House : One antagonises others, will be foul-tongued, will have no children, will be sinful, idle and a menial.

However, **Jataka Parijata** (XIV-II) makes a sweeping generalization regarding the 7th house when it says "When the 7th Bhava is occupied by an Upagraha, the wife will be wicked (पापप्रकाशसंयुक्ते कलत्रे दुष्टचारिणी)". Perhaps, this is an exception ? We leave it to our learned readers to draw their own conclusions.

THURSDAY BAR

In all cases of conflicting views, that given in **Brihat Parasara Hora** is generally accepted as final. But in this instance, the **Hora** is silent on the point. It may not be out of place to recall what DR. RAMAN says in answer to *Question No. 91* (page 69) in his book **A Catechism of Astrology,**

Yamakantaka is a very auspicious Upagraha and anything done at that time ends only in good. But on Thursdays, it is observed as inauspicious because he is believed to be the illegitimate son of Jupiter. Still if birth happens in his rising time, it is considered as most fortunate on all days.

DR. RAMAN does not draw a very rigid line between Yamakantaka's role in electional astrology and natal astrology but concludes Yamakantaka may generally be treated as good. The only exception he recognises is Thursdays when Yamakantaka rising in Muhurta Lagna can be deemed as an adverse factor.

Yamakantaka is said to rise at the end of the period associated with it. In the case of the weekday being Thursday for a 12 hour day with sunrise at 6-00 a.m. Yamakantaka rises at 7-30 a.m. A Muhurta Lagna for 7-30 a.m. in this case is to be avoided, according to Dr. Raman. But at the same time, since he endorses its favourable nature for a birth chart, a birth occurring at 7-30 a.m. could be deemed to benefit by Yamakantaka's presence in the rising sign.

A simple example will clarify the difference between Yamagandam and Yamakantaka. Taking the date 28th October 2002 which is a Monday, Yamagandam is between 10-30 a.m. to 12-00 noon. This holds good for a 12 hour day when sunrise is at 6-00 a.m. But on the date in question, sunrise is at 6-15 a.m. (IST) and sunset is at 5-51 p.m. (IST) at Bangalore making the duration of day 11 hours 36 minutes.

90 mins. : 12 h. : c : 11 h. 36 mins.

$$c = \frac{90 \times 11h. 36m.}{12h.}$$

$$c = \frac{90 \times 11.6}{12}$$

$$= 87 \text{ min.}$$

$$= 1 \text{ hour } 27 \text{ mins.}$$

Therefore, the duration of Yamagandam on 28-10-2002 at Bangalore is for a period of 1 hour 27 minutes. On Mondays, Yamaganda is the 4th of 8 equal parts of daytime which means the Yamagandakalam would be between 10-36 a.m. and 12-03 p.m.

Yamakantaka is said to rise at the end of this 4th period or at 12-03 p.m. The rising degree at 12-03 p.m. on 28-10-2002 would be at $2^0 43'$ of Capricorn. If a birth occurs at 12-03 p.m. on 28-10-2002 at Bangalore, the following chart would give the planetary positions, including Yamakantaka.

Therefore, any birth on 28-10-2002 with Capricorn rising can be deemed to benefit by Yamakantaka's presence in the Ascendant. So also, if other Muhurta requisites are satisfactory Yamakantaka in Capricorn Lagna can be said to be good for an election. But the period 10-36 a.m. to 12-03 p.m. being Yamagandam cannot be treated as favourable for any activity in the same way as Rahukalam is tabooed.

Sagittarius 11^0 52' would be rising at 10-36 a.m. when Yamagandam begins and Capricorn 2^0 43' when it ends at 12-03 p.m. Except for the specific point of time of 12-03 p.m. the stretch of time coming under Yamagandakalam is to be avoided on the date in question.

		RAHU 16-44	SAT. 6-24
YAMA KANTAKA 2-43 ASCDT. 2-43	Rasi		MOON 0-33 JUPT. 23-35
	KETU 16-46	MERC. 1-26 VENUS 17-23	SUN 12-13 MARS 15-34

VENUS	SUN	MARS	RAHU
JUPT.	Navamsa		MOON
Y.K. ASCDT.			
KETU	SAT.	MERC.	

DIFFERENCES BETWEEN THE TWO

Therefore the differences between Yamagandakalam and Yamakantaka in this example can be noted as follows :

(1) Yamagandakalam stretches from 10-36 a.m. to 12-03 p.m. while Yamakantaka is confined to the specific point of time of 12-03 p.m.

(2) Yamagandakalam covers part of Sagittarius and part of Capricorn signs. While Sagittarius does not get the benefit of the Yamakantaka factor, Capricorn gains by its presence as Ascendant, whether in a birth chart or a Muhurta chart.

(3) Yamagandakalam stretching over part of Sagittarius and part of Capricorn cannot be assessed in terms of Shadvarga or Shodasavarga strength. Yamakantaka rising at 2^0 43' Capricorn is

in Vargottama Navamsa and its other Vargas can also be determined.

Therefore, in the ultimate analysis what we find is that :

(1) while Yamagandam covers the 90 minute period (for a 12 hour day with sunrise at 6 a.m.), Yamakantaka may be understood as rising at the end of this 90 minute interval.

(2) yamagandam can be limited to one sign or stretch over two signs but Yamakantaka is confined to a specific *degree* of a sign.

(3) therefore, though Yamagandam cannot be assessed on Shadvarga or Shodasavarga strength, Yamakantaka can be judged not only on its Rasi and Navamsa positions but also in all the sub-divisional charts.

(4) while Yamagandam is taken cognisance of in Muhurta or electional astrology, Yamakantaka is a factor primarily relevant to predictive astrology and to a lesser extent in Muhurta where it can be deemed favourable.

(5) though Yamaganda is to be treated akin to Rahukalam and generally avoided for venturing on any constructive activity, but being a relatively minor Dosha, it can be balanced by a powerful Muhurta chart that is free of Maha Doshas. On the other hand, apart from avoiding Yamakantaka in the rising sign in a Muhurta Lagna on Thursdays only, its presence in the Muhurta or birth Ascendant specified by longitude and sign on other weekdays can be deemed favourable and interpreted accordingly.

(6) Yamakantaka, being an Upagraha, though benefic in nature, must perforce be treated as influencing the chart favourably only in a secondary sense. And its results may broadly be deemed to reflect Jupiter's just as Ketu reflects Martian and Rahu, Saturnine influences. But unlike Rahu and Ketu, to a lesser degree.

These views are not the final word on this conundrum and are open to review and revision. It is for our readers to take our humble views for what they are worth. *(12-02)* ●

RASI OR BHAVA ?

> 1. *Rasi and Bhava charts are quite different in concept.*
> 2. *Bhava positions can differ from Rasi positions.*
> 3. *A planet shifting in Bhava chart retains the characteristics of its sign of occupation.*

THE HOROSCOPE IN its simplest form is the map of the positions of the planets and the Zodiacal sign rising on the eastern horizon and is called Rasi. The term Rasi (राशि) signifies a heap, a collective set of things or articles or an aggregate of several factors. In this sense, the Rasi chart is exactly that and once pried open carries a mine of astrological technical data such as the Shadvargas (6 divisional charts), Saptavargas (7 divisional charts), Dasavargas (10 divisional charts) and the Shodasavargas (16 divisional charts). The details of the Nakshatras and specific Padas occupied by each planet, the balance of Dasa at birth and even the Nadiamsa classification can also be computed from the Rasi chart. Until a few decades ago until computers appeared on the scene, the horoscope meant the following astrological data — Rasi, Navamsa, Nakshatra Padas occupied by the planets, the longitudes of the planets and the balance of Vimshottari Dasa at birth apart from the calendric details of birth. In some parts of the country, particularly the North, it could sometimes include details of Ashtottari Dasa as also the Saptavargas. But many a time, there would also be another horoscopic chart included, namely, the Bhava chart. The Bhava (भाव) chart is conventionally accepted as integral to the Parasari system which forms the basis and bedrock of Jyotisha.

The Bhava chart is not quite the same as the Rasi chart in concept. The Rasi chart is an exact representation of the skies for the time of birth. It carries the Nirayana longitudes of the planets obtaining at that moment showing the rising sign and the planets occupying different positions in the Zodiac of 12 signs or Rasis. The Bhava chart on the other hand is a representation of the same planets and the Ascendant in terms of houses or Bhavas. What is a Bhava?

The Zodiac is divided into 12 signs of 30^0 each from Aries to Pisces, each sign having its distinct characteristics. It starts with the first point of Aries. The Zodiac when represented as a horoscope has its initial point shift to the Udaya Lagna or the sign rising on the eastern horizon. Though the entire sign is taken as the Ascendant, it is the exact degree of the rising sign that is deemed the actual and exact Ascendant for the horoscope in question. The Bhava chart proceeds from a division of the Zodiac into 12 parts starting from this point of the Ascendant as the central point of reference for the chart. Each part is called Bhava or house and is defined as having governance over certain areas of human life and parts of the human body.

According to **Brihat Parasara Hora** Chapter VII, Sloka 37,

तनुर्धनं च सहजो बन्धुपुत्रारयस्तथा ।
युवतीरन्ध्रधर्मारव्यकर्मलाभव्यया: क्रमात् ॥

The body, wealth, brothers, relatives, progeny, enemy, wife, evil (adversity), virtue, livelihood, gain and loss are respectively the significations of the first to the twelfth Bhavas.

According to **Brihat Parasara Hora** Chapter V, Slokas 4-5,

शीर्षानने तथा बाहू हत्कोडवस्तय: ।
गुह्योरुयुगले जानुयुगमे वै जङ्के तथा ॥
चरणौ द्वौ तथोजादेर्ज्ञेया: शीर्षादय: क्रमात् ॥

The head, face, two shoulders, heart, stomach, waist, lower belly, genitals, buttocks, thighs, calves and the two feet come under the 12 Rasis (from Aries to Pisces) respectively.

The different parts of the body assigned to different Rasis or signs can also be incorporated into the 12 Bhavas.

Each Bhava need not necessarily synchronise with the sign or Rasi. The rising sign and its longitude define the starting and closing points of the first house successfully followed by the other houses in like manner.

There are several systems of Bhava or house-divisions evolved mostly by western astrologers. In India, it is the Equal House System that is in vogue throughout the country. In fact, this appears perfectly valid for births in India where all births occur at not too distant a latitude *visavis* the equator. The longitude of the Ascendant is taken as the centre or midpoint of the first house or Bhava. Its extent is defined by extending the *arc* 15^0 backwards and 15^0 forwards from the midpoint. This becomes the first house. A simple illustration should make it clear.

Chart 1 shows the planetary positions for the given time with reference to the signs of the Zodiac. That is, Rahu is in Pisces, Saturn and the Moon are in Taurus, the Sun is in Cancer, Venus, Mercury and Mars are in Leo, Ketu is in Virgo and Jupiter is in Scorpio. This is the Rasi chart.

In the Bhava chart for Chart 1, the exact longitude signwise of the Lagna or 12^0 Aquarius is taken as the midpoint of the first house. Extending the arc of 15^0 forwards and backwards, we get 27^0 Capricorn as the starting point and 27^0 Aquarius as the ending point. The first house therefore begins not in Aquarius but at 27^0 Capricorn. It ends not at 30^0 Aquarius but 27^0 Aquarius. Any planet beyond 27^0 Capricorn though appearing to be in the 12th in the Rasi chart would actually be in the first house. In Chart 1, all the planets continue to occupy the same houses as in Rasi. The Rasi and Bhava charts are identical for Chart 1.

Chart 1 : Born 8-8-1912 at 7h. 23m. (IST) at 13 N, 77 E 35 with a balance of 6 years 10 days of Mars Dasa at birth.

	SAT. 11-35 MOON 25-11		
RAHU 24-12			
ASCDT. 12	Chart 1 Rasi	SUN 24-25	
		VENUS 3-43 MERC. 15-26 MARS 22-50	
	JUPT. 14-26	KETU 24-12	

	SAT.	VENUS	
SUN RAHU	Navamsa		
ASCDT.			MERC. MOON KETU
	JUPT.	MARS	

Chart 1 Bhava

	RAHU	SAT. MOON	
ASCDT.			SUN
			RAHU MOON SAT.
	JUPT.		KETU

In Chart 2, the Ascendant is 27° 12' Aquarius. Extending the arc on either side by 15°, we get the starting point of the first house as 12° 12' Aquarius (27° 12' Aquarius *minus* 15°) and the ending point as 12° 12' Pisces (27° 12' Aquarius *plus* 15°). The first house in Chart 2 therefore extends from 12° 12' Aquarius to 12° 12' Pisces. Therefore, if a planet be at 6° Aquarius in this case, it would not be taken as occupying the 1st house but only the 12th house. The Bhava chart for Chart 2 would be quite different from the Rasi. Mars at 6° 48' Makha would not be in the 7th house but regress into the 6th house; likewise the Sun at 8° 58' Libra would not be in

Rasi or Bhava ?

the 9th house but would be in the 8th house. Jupiter at 2° 37' Pisces would be in the 11th Bhava, not the 12th as shown in the Rasi. The Bhava and Rasi charts differ for Chart 2.

Chart 2: Born 24-10-1949 at 15h. 23m. (IST) at 13 N, 77 E 35 with a balance of 2 years 3 months 10 days of Saturn Dasa at birth.

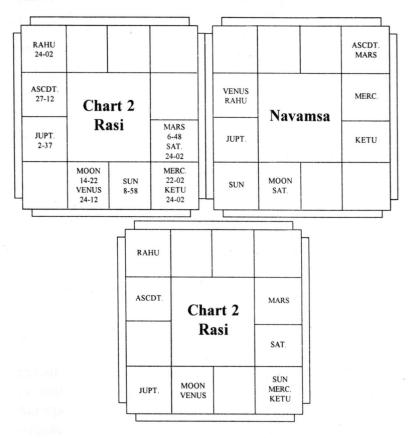

Dr. RAMAN has never overlooked the importance of the Bhava chart. Though there have been no regular or frequent references to the Bhava chart in his writings, he has invariably taken it **also** into account before coming to a conclusion. The fact, he says "Predictions according to Hindu Astrology are invariably to be based on Bhava Chakra and therefore, the longitudes (Sphutas) of all these are absolutely necessary to get a correct Bhava Chakras"* highlights the need to look at the Bhava chart also in interpreting results.

The Bhava and Rasi charts are totally different from each other in concept. It is quite possible the Bhava and Rasi charts can be identical. They can also be dissimilar depending upon the longitudes of the Ascendant and planets signwise.

Chart 3 is of Indira Gandhi. The Bhava chart shows some difference from the Rasi chart. The Ascendant lord Moon is in Capricorn at 7^0 04' in the 7th in Rasi. The Ascendant being at 29^0 16' Cancer, the 7th house extends from 14^0 16' Capricorn to 14^0 16' Aquarius and cannot hold the Moon at 7^0 04' Capricorn and who therefore gets relegated to the 6th Bhava. We must note here that while the Ascendant lord retains the characteristics associated with the sign Capricorn such as capriciousness, domination, organisational skills and others, he also takes on the significations of the 6th house. In other words, the Ascendant lord's position cannot be interpreted only in the sense of being in the 7th house as shown in the Rasi chart.

We should be clear that the 6th house does not mean Sagittarius in this context, but only such properties and significations as are by definition attributed to the 6th house. Likewise, the Sun in Scorpio at 5^0 34' shifts to the 4th Bhava. As 2nd lord, the Sun takes on the characteristics of the sign Scorpio together with those of the 4th house. The 4th sign is Libra but when interpreting results, the Sun is to be treated as occupying the 4th house in Scorpio sign.

The view that the length of each Bhava is 30^0 extending to 15^0 on either side of the ascending degree is held by the vast majority of astrological savants. But there is also another view prevailing which does not accept the Equal House System as scientific as it does not consider the relationship between the ecliptic and the equator which

---

* *Preface* to First Edition: **Nirayana Table of Houses** by Bangalore Venkata Raman and R. V. Vaidya.

Rasi or Bhava ?

Chart 3: Born 19-11-1917 at 23h. 13m. (IST) at 25 N 27, 81 E 51 with a balance of 1 year 3 months 26 days of Dasa at birth.

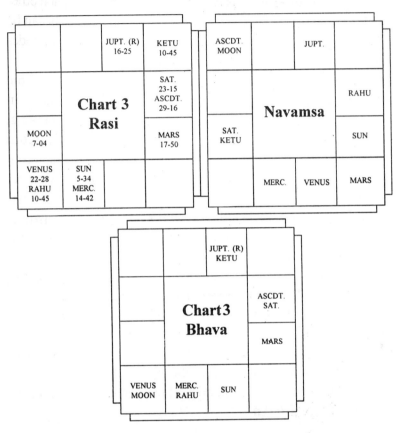

is deemed as important in determining the extent of the Bhavas. This system given by the classical writer Sripati and also known as the Porphyry System of House Division, had found wide acceptance amongst western astrologers where mathematical precision was given more importance until the last two decades. According to it, the point where the ecliptic cuts the horizon in the east is known as the Rising Sign (Lagna). The point where the ecliptic cuts the horizon in the west is known as the Setting Sign (Lagna). The points where the meridian of the place cut the ecliptic are known as the Zenith

Lagna and the Nadir Lagna*. Accordingly, a Bhava becomes one-third of the *arc* of the ecliptic intercepted between any two adjacent angles, namely, the Udaya (rising), Patala (Nadir), Asta (West) and Madhya (Zenith) Lagnas. The points of trisection of the ecliptic *arc* are what are called Bhava Madhyas or midpoints of Bhavas.

But Dr. Raman in explaining these methods also cautions the student against relying too heavily on the mathematics of a chart : "I must warn the zealous reader that while mathematical astrology is important in its own way upto a certain stage as an aid to successful predictions, too much indulgence in it is harmful as marring one's power of intuition, the proper development of which is absolutely necessary."**

Endorsing the Equal House System, Dr. Raman says "In our humble experience.... the Equal House System appears to yield more satisfactory results."

Now that we have seen the difference between the Rasi and the Bhava charts, the moot question before us is — should the interpretation be on the Rasi positions or the Bhava chart. Or, should both Rasi and Bhava charts be analysed separately and the results fused into a single conclusion. How far does the Rasi chart influence the interpretation and where does the Bhava chart come in ? We shall deal with these all important questions of predictive astrology at a later date.(*03-04*) ●

---

* **A Manual of Hindu Astrology** by Dr. B. V. Raman.
** See **Graha and Bhava Balas** by Dr. B. V. Raman.

RASI AND BHAVA, NOT RASI OR BHAVA

> 1. Yogas are applicable to the Rasi chart.
> 2. Aspects work only in the Rasi chart.
> 3. Rasi chart shows the surface; Bhava depicts the reality underneath.

ASPECTS AND YOGAS

A COMMON question one often encounters in the context of the Rasi-Bhava issue is whether Yogas, have to be examined with reference to the Rasis or the Bhavas? For instance, Gajakesari Yoga is said to result when Jupiter and the Moon are in mutual Kendras. Is the reference to the mutual Kendra positions of the two planets in the Rasi chart or the Bhava chart?

RAHU 24-12		SAT 11-35 MOON 25-11		RAHU		SAT MOON	
ASCDT	Chart 1 Rasi		SUN	ASCDT	Bhava		SUN
			VEN 3-43 MERC 15-26 MARS 22-50				VEN MERC
	JUPT 14-26		KETU 24-12		JUPT		KETU

What about aspects? Are they to be reckoned by the exact longitudes of the planets involved or by their Rasi positions or the Bhavas they shift to?

On prepage in Chart 1, the Ascendant Aquarius may be said to be aspected by as many as four planets — Saturn, Venus, Mars and Mercury — these planets being in Kendra signs from the Ascendant and such signs coming within the definition of the 10th house aspect for Saturn and of the 7th house aspect for the remaining planets.

RAHU 24-02				RAHU			
ASCDT 27-12	Chart 2 Rasi			ASCDT	Bhava		MARS
JUPT 2-37			MARS 6-48 SAT 24-02				SAT
	MOON 14-22 VEN 24-12	SUN 8-58	MERC 22-02 KETU 24-02	JUPT	MOON VEN		SUN MERC KETU

The Bhava chart sees no change from the Rasi positions. There is total synergy between Rasi and Bhava positions.

In Chart 2 which serves as a better illustration since some of the planets shift in the Bhava chart, let us examine the aspects received by the Ascendant in the Rasi chart.

Mars and Saturn aspect Aquarius from Leo and the aspect involved for both planets is the 7th house aspect. If the Bhava chart is taken, then Mars shifts to the 6th house while Saturn remains in the 7th house. How would one reckon the aspects now?

ASPECTS FROM RASI CHART

For all practical purposes and this is based on our humble experience and therefore can lay no claim to being the last word on the issue, the aspects are to be taken only according to the Rasi chart. In other words, Mars and Saturn aspect the Ascendant by their 7th house aspect. Mars does not aspect the Ascendant by the 8th house aspect from his 6th Bhava position. But when it comes to judgement of Bhavas, Mars behaves in part as if in the 6th Bhava and in part as if in the 7th while Saturn acts only as being in the 7th house.

The Ascendant shows one's total personality while the 7th shows partners and the 6th adversaries. As for the lordships, Saturn is the Ascendant and 12th lord while Mars is the 3rd and 10th lord.

Mars as the 10th lord in the 7th aspecting the Ascendant and joining the Ascendant lord, the main result would be a work-oriented personality. As 3rd lord Mars is also the 10th lord he shows teammates working with the native. But as 3rd lord in the 6th, such participation tends to afflict the native's work rather than support it. The 3rd house lordship brings in inimical elements into play in this area influencing the native's Karmastana adversely. The Mars-Saturn combination in Rasi shows what the world sees while the Bhava position explains the actual position, the true position, which may not always be obvious. The appearance is shown by Rasi, the reality by the Bhava position.

Moving on to the other planets that show a difference in the Bhava chart from the Rasi, the 7th lord Sun is in the 9th Rasi but in the 8th Bhava. The results of the 7th lord in the 8th are of a delayed marriage which was the case, the native marrying in the 30th year.

The Sun aspects the 3rd house in Rasi and his position in a Rahu-ruled Nakshatra has influenced results of the 3rd house. The results of such an aspect are extreme hostility and lack of cordiality from the significations of the 3rd house. The aspect of the Sun has shown up on 3rd house. Its Bhava position in the 8th has not affected the results in the sense of an aspect on the 2nd house in that its significations (Dhana, Kutumba) have not shown any related results.

The 11th lord Jupiter is in the 12th Rasi but 11th Bhava. The 7th house is therefore not aspected Rasi-wise by Jupiter. Results such as those normally associated with Mars and Saturn acting on the 7th house bereft of the Jupiterean influence have been seen.

YOGAS EMBEDDED IN RASI

The Rasi 7th house itself has no Papakartari Yoga. But the shifting of Mars into the 6th and Mercury-Ketu-Sun to the 8th would seem to generate a Papakartari Yoga on the 7th house. But the results of such a Yoga have not been felt on 7th house matters.

Jupiter in Capricorn and Moon-Venus in Scorpio flank the 11th house in Rasi producing a Subhakartari Yoga while in Bhava, this Yoga is absent. The results of the Subhakartari Yoga on the 11th house have been amply demonstrated *visavis* significations of the 11th house, though the shift in Bhava position by Jupiter would seem to break the Yoga.

Such cases seem to indicate that Yogas are to be interpreted from and applied to the Rasi chart, not the Bhava chart.

In Chart 3, the Rasi shows the Ascendant Cancer with 7th lord Saturn in it while the Ascendant lord Moon is in the 7th in Capricorn. In the Bhava chart, the 7th lord Saturn remains in the Ascendant while the 1st lord Moon shifts into the 6th Bhava. Is there or is there not a Parivartana Yoga in this case? The Parivartana Yoga is indeed present as seen in the Rasi chart. Despite the Parivartana between the Ascendant lord and 7th lord, the native lacked in understanding with the spouse. The Bhava chart explains clearly this lacuna in the native's life. The Ascendant lord and 7th lord are in Shashtashtaka

		JUP(R) 16-25	KETU 10-45			JUPT KETU	
	Chart 3 Rasi		SAT 23-15 ASCDT 29-16		**Bhava**		ASCDT SAT
MON 7-04			MARS 17-50				MARS
VEN 22-28 RAHU 10-45	SUN 5-34 MERC 14-42			VEN MOON	MERC RAHU	SUN	

or mutually adverse positions Bhava-wise being in the 6th and 8th from each other. Marital life was marked by endless conflict and friction though to all appearances it was a love marriage.

This is a case of Mahabhagya Yoga also which is caused by the Ascendant, Moon and the Sun occupying even signs in the case of female natives and odd signs in the case of male natives. Though the Moon's position changes in Bhava, it does not affect the Yoga formed in the Rasi chart.

Gajakesari Yoga as given in **300 Important Combinations** by Dr. B.V. Raman, is formed by Jupiter being in a Kendra from the Moon, In other words the Yoga is produced by the Moon and Jupiter being in mutual Kendras. Does this definition work only in the Rasi chart or will it work for the Bhava chart too?

In Chart 1, the Moon and Jupiter are in Kendras from each other in the 7th from each other occupying Taurus and Scorpio respectively producing a Gajakesari Yoga. The Bhava chart also shows the Moon and Jupiter in the 7th from each other; there is no confusion here, therefore, as to the presence of the Gajakesari Yoga.

Take a case (Chart 4) with Gajakesari Yoga where the Ascendant (Lagna) is Aquarius 4^0 55'. The Moon is at 28^0 49' Libra. Jupiter is at 9^0 7' Libra. In Bhava, Jupiter continues to remain in the 9th Bhava while the Moon shifts to the 10th Bhava. Irrespective of the shift in Bhava positions, the Yoga may be deemed to be operative. However for an Aquarius Ascendant rising case (Chart 5) with Lagna at 5^0, the Moon at 25^0 Cancer and Jupiter at 5^0 Leo, there is no Gajakesari Yoga *perse*. In the Bhava chart, the Moon shifts to the 7th Bhava where Jupiter is situated. Does this generate a Gajakesari Yoga? A Yoga that is not found in the Rasi chart cannot be said to be produced in the Bhava chart by a change of Bhavas or houses. The results of the Yoga can be experienced only if the Yoga occurs in the Rasi chart. Its so-called presence in the Bhava chart does not produce the Yoga results.

In Chart 6, the distance from the Moon to Jupiter is 275^0. Signwise, Jupiter is in the 10th from the Moon. But in the Bhava,

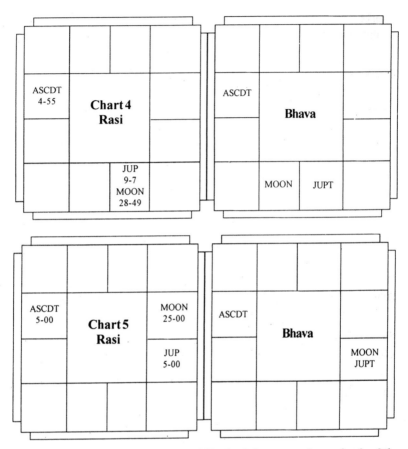

Jupiter shifts to the 7th Bhava while the Moon continues in the 9th thereby losing apparently the mutual Kendra disposition with the latter. The Gajakesari Yoga present in the Rasi chart is not disturbed by the change in Bhava positions. The shifting of Jupiter into the 7th house would make a qualitative difference to married life, enchancing it against the position of Mars-Rahu in it and the aspect of Saturn on it.

Likewise, the 10th house in Rasi which comes under the aspect of Jupiter, Saturn and Mars will reflect their combined influence and will not be deprived of Jupiter's or Saturn's influence because of their displacement in the Bhava chart. The influence of Venus in the 10tn is not that of sole occupant of the house. The Sun and Mercury

Rasi and Bhava, Not Rasi or Bhava 107

Chart 6: Born August 14, 1928 at 12h. 30m (IST) at 14 N 42, 79 E 59 with a balance of 4 years 9 months 18 days of Saturn Dasa at birth.

	JUPT 18-45	MARS 11-51 RAHU 14-15				JUPT MARS RAHU	
	Chart 6 Rasi		MOON 13-18 MERC 27-47 SUN 29-48		Bhava		MOON
			VEN 11-52				SUN MERC VEN
	ASCDT 3-14 KETU 14-15 SAT 21-08			SAT	ASCDT KETU		

who move into the 10th house also add their influence on career matters.

Benefic planets in Kendras from the Ascendant are said to strengthen it. Again does this apply to the Rasi chart or the Bhava chart ? In any case where the Kendras are fortified in the Rasi chart, the shift in Bhava to non-Kendra positions does not detract from the strength of the chart. Conversely, malefics in Kendras are said to show a life of sorrow and suffering and can even adversely affect longevity. A change in the Bhava chart of malefics to non-Kendra Bhavas does not help longevity or the quality of life otherwise.

KUJA DOSHA

Another moot issue is that of Kuja Dosha. This Dosha basically is a Yoga that centers round the position of Mars and the results attributed to it are adverse such as separation from or loss of spouse. Being a Yoga in the sense of being formed by specific planetary positions, it is the Rasi chart that counts, not the Bhava chart.

Chart 3 has Kuja Dosha with Mars occupying the 8th from the Moon-sign Capricorn in Rasi. In Bhava, the Moon shifts to the 6th Bhava while Mars continuing in the same Bhava as in Rasi appears to have lost control in generating Kuja Dosha. The native lost her husband quite early in life. The absence of the Dosha in the Bhava chart did not invalidate it in the Rasi chart. The Yoga in the Rasi chart worked, not its absence in the Bhava chart.

Rahu associating with a Kendra or Trikona lord is said to produce Ashtalakshmi Yoga, a Yoga for fabulous riches. The 4th lord Venus is with Rahu in the 6th in chart 3. In Bhava, the two planets move into different houses so that they cease to be in conjunction. The Bhava result did not show. The Yoga is the Rasi chart bestowed the native with fabulous riches by birth in the Nehru family.

Chart 7: Born November 6, 1973 at 0h. 28m. at 12 N 59, 77 E 40 with a balance of 3 years 24 days of Rahu Dasa at birth.

	MARS(R) 5-58		KETU 8-50 SAT(R) 12-27	MARS(R)		KETU	SAT(R)
MOON 19-45	Chart 7 Rasi		ASCDT 26-03	MOON	Bhava		ASCDT
JUPT 12-27				JUPT			
VEN 8-5 RAHU 8-50	MERC(R) 1-27	SUN 21-11			VEN RAHU	SUN MERC	

The Rasi (Chart 7) shows Mars in Aries in the 10th from the Ascendant Cancer. Mars in a Kendra from the Ascendant in his own sign or sign of exaltation is said to produce Ruchaka Yoga. Does Mars generate the Yoga in this chart? Yes, this is indeed a case of Ruchaka Yoga though Mars shifts from the 10th sign to the 9th house in Bhava. In other words, career matters coming under the 10th lose greatly the Martian influence while 9th Bhava significations partake of the Martian effect. Mars in the 10th generally tends to give a career connected with the armed forces or the police. In this case, it has not happened as the native could not make it to the defence forces. Mars shifting into the 9th house (Bhava) ruling religion, preceptor and guide and Guru as 10th lord has given the native a flair for counselling and an inclination towards philosophy. The Ruchaka Yoga however is not diffused in toto by the change in Bhava; its results may be evidenced in later years conferring on the native a leadership role in his vocational life.

Another Yoga that can be found in this chart is the Ashtalakshmi Yoga formed by Rahu being with 4th lord Venus in Libra, the 5th sign from the Ascendant. In the Bhava, both planets shift into the 6th; this in no way detracts from the merits of the Yoga though the Yoga may get coloured by the 5th house significations.

Another planet which changes position in the Bhava chart is Ketu. In the 12th Ketu is said to register spiritual progress. But in the 11th, both the pace and degree of spiritual growth get affected. Instead, Ketu produces more the results normally associated with his occupation of the 11th house.

NEED TO COMBINE RASI-BHAVA

The best illustrations for understanding any principle of astrology are of those whose lives and events are well known.

Chart 8 of Adolf Hitler would be a good illustration to understand the Bhava-Rasi question. Several Yogas can be identified in the Rasi chart.

Chart 8: Adolf Hitler Born April 20, 1889 at 18h. 30m (LMT) at 48 N, 13 E with a balance of 16 years 4 months 6 days of Venus Dasa.

	SUN 9-56 MERC 4-48 VEN 25-50 MARS 25-31		RAHU 25-06
	Chart 8 **Rasi**	SAT 22-35	
MOON 15-46 JUPT 17-23 KETU 25-06		ASCDT 0-54	

	SUN MERC	VEN MARS	
	Bhava		RAHU
KETU JUPT			SAT
	MOON	ASCDT	

Ruchaka: Mars occupies his own sign Aries identical with a Kendra.

Lakshmi Yoga: The Ascendant lord Venus and 9th lord Mercury combine in a Kendra.

Mahabhagya: The Sun, Moon and Ascendant occupy odd signs Aries, Sagittarius and Libra respectively.

Gajakesari: The Moon and Jupiter occupy the same sign Sagittarius, that is, Jupiter is in a quadrant from the Moon.

Parijatha Yoga: (a) The sign-dispositor of the Ascendant lord namely, Mars, is in a quadrant in own sign Aries. (b) The ruler of the Navamsa occupied by the sign-dispositor of the Ascendant lord, Mars again, is in own sign in a quadrant.

All these Yogas are present in the Rasi chart but they break up in the Bhava chart with Mars, Venus, Rahu, Jupiter and Ketu changing positions. Their presence in the Rasi chart is what counts for the results of these specific Yogas are now part of history. The Ruchaka Yoga made him an aggressive leader with a great following. Gajakesari Yoga resulted in the hypnotic spell he cast on his audiences. Lakshmi Yoga and Parijatha Yoga brought him wealth and power respectively. Mahabhagya Yoga made Hitler one of the most powerful leaders of his time with limitless power at his command. The fact Mars moves into the 8th Bhava or Venus and Mercury occupy different Bhavas or that the Moon moves into the next Bhava did not deprive the native of the results of the Yogas.

Moving on to aspects, both Hitler's build and demeanour (which are to be judged from the Ascendant) carried the imprint of the combined aspects of Mars, Venus, Mercury and the Sun from Aries on Libra. The aspect of Mars on the 10th distinctly showed up in his military career although, initially he began as an architect's draftsman. The Gajakesari Yoga tainted by Ketu resulted in fanatical hatred for a whole race. That is, the Moon-Jupiter Yoga which started as Gajakesari was converted into a Guru Chandala Yoga due to Ketu's presence. The fact, the Moon in Bhava is free of the Ketu-Jupiter association did not redeem the Chandala Yoga.

Going by both Bhava and Rasi charts, either taking the Sun-Mercury combination alone in the 7th Bhava or of all the four planets in the 7th Rasi, the many ugly details in his appetites and private life are only too well known.

Coming to Saturn in the 10th, this disposition is generally associated with a spectacular rise in career followed by an equally disgraceful termination to it. But Saturn shifts to the 11th house. How is one to explain Hitler's rise and final fall? This is where we must reiterate, isolated combinations are not always the best way of looking at a chart. Reading them in combination with other factors against the background of the entire chart would be a better way to pry open a chart. Mars and Saturn in mutual aspect involve the 10th house which is why Hitler's life ended the way it did, in ignominy, in tragedy.

Summing up,

1. Rasi and Bhava charts are not to be read in isolation but interpreted in a judicious manner with the results of both being blended in understanding the results.

2. Planets which see a change from Rasi to Bhava charts generate a difference in results which tilt more towards the Bhava positions. In fact, the Rasi chart may be said to reflect what the external world sees. The Bhava chart may be said to portray the actual state of affairs, which may seldom be obvious. However, in interpretation, the results may overlap with the results of the Bhava position taking the upperhand.

3. Yogas may be taken to operate from their Rasi positions. Changes in the Bhava chart which could break the Yogas do not materially affect the working of the Yogas.

4. Kuja Dosha, a Dosha of much controversy, may be said to operate only if present in the Rasi chart.

5. Aspects are best judged from the Rasi positions, not the Bhava positions of planets. ●

MOON AND HUMAN PSYCHOLOGY AND BEHAVIOUR

> 1. Benefics — natural and functional — influencing the Moon show good mental attitudes.
> 2. Natural malefics when also functional malefics harm mental health.
> 3. Heavy afflictions to Moon show mental disorder.

THE HUMAN personality as a mind-body complex has been analysed in great depth by Charaka, the ancient Indian master of Ayurveda. In tracing disease, whether of the body or mind, Charaka says, the causes can be sought and identified in the proportion of the three Gunas of Sattwa, Rajas and Tamas operating in the individual. On the same basis of the Gunas, Charaka divides the mind into three types. Sattwa predominating produces a Suddha Manas or pure mind whose activities will be conducive to the good of both the individual and society. Such a mind is called Kalyanamsa Visishta (preponderance of the beneficial elements). When Rajas becomes the predominating Guna, activities of the mind take the form of anger and hate and come under Roshamsa Vishishta (element of wrath in control). When the mind comes under Tamas, the activities take on the shape of senseless ones coming under what is known as Mohamsa Vishishta with the elements of ignorance and inertia predominating.

Human nature is thus classified into three categories by Charaka who further elaborates on the characteristics showing up in the human psyche under the influence of each of the Gunas. According to him, Sattwa Guna is seen in the following classes of people.

Brahma type : Intellectual and moral, scientific or philosophical scholarship, truthful, not overpowered by emotions and lower cravings, senses under control.

Arya type : Keen perception, power of persuasion, inclination for religious observances or Sastric rites, hospitable, emotions and senses under control.

Aindra type : Powerful, great energy, given to religious, economic and pleasure giving activity.

Yamya type : Attentive to secular duties, presence of mind, persevering, strong memory, control over senses and emotions.

Varuna type : Calm, courageous, clean, great energy, patronising the deserving, discriminate show of anger and resentment.

Kaubera type : Fond of family life, given to performance of religious and secular duties, favouring or punishing according to merit or demerit.

Gandharva type : Fond of music, dance, arts, cosmetics but within legitimate channels.

Rajasic predominant human nature is divided into the following types :-

Asura type : Physical prowess, anger, self-conceit, gluttony, fondness for riches.

Rakshasa type : Enduring anger, aggressive, cruel, malicious, tough.

Paisacha type : Lethargic, unclean, cowardly, intimidative.

Sarpa type : Heroic when angry but generally cowardly, strong likes and dislikes, sensual cravings.

Praitya type : Gluttonous, unpleasant nature, envious of others' success, intolerant, greedy, slothy.

Sakuna type : Fond of sensual pleasures, fickle, ruthless, extravagant.

Those in whom Tamas predominates are classified into the following types :-

Pasaya type : Shabbily dressed and unclean, ignoble in dealings, fond of sensual pleasure, rejecting everything.

Matsya type : Cowardly, stupid, gluttonous, wrathful and malicious, restless and fond of movement, fond of water and liquids.

Vanaspatya type : Indolent, inactive, lethargic, gluttonous, total absence of intellectual inclination.

In astrology too, the Gunas are associated with different planets as follows :

सात्विक भानुचन्द्रेज्या राजसौ सोम्यभार्गवौ ।
तामसौ कुजमऐ तु ज्ञेया विद्धद्वरै: सदा ।

Brihat Parasara Hora III - 23

The Sun, Moon and Jupiter rule Sattwa, Mercury and Venus rule Rajas and Mars and Saturn, Tamas.

While these Grahas are clearly ascribed specific Gunas, Rahu and Ketu find no mention. How are we to classify them ?

In **Phaladeepika**, Chapter II, Sloka 26, it says, आदित्यद्विड्गुलिकशिखिनस्तस्य पीडाकरा: स्यु: । meaning, *the enemies of the Sun, namely, Rahu, Gulika and Ketu cause trouble to the body and soul.*

Rahu and Ketu, as inimical to the Sun who rules Sattwa, cannot therefore come under Sattwa. Elsewhere in classical works, Rahu and Ketu are said to imitate or behave like Saturn and Mars respectively (*sanivad rahu kujavad ketu*). Therefore the Nodes can be said to reflect the same Gunas that Saturn and Mars rule. In other words, the Guna of Tamas can be ascribed to Rahu and Ketu.

These and such other clues that are found in astrology make it an effective tool of foreknowledge that can not only be applied to handling life and its problems more intelligently but also in gaining insights into the psychology of an individual.

Matching of charts is one of the best known uses of Jyotisha and is often thought to ensure the perfect marriage. While this to some extent is not debatable, the role of matching charts is more pronounced in preventing unhappy marriages or marriages that can breakdown for a variety of reasons. Such reasons can relate to physical health, mental illness or calamitous adversity and are not necessarily limited to temperamental incompatability. But few realize that temperamental incompatability itself does not necessarily sprout from mismatched temperaments so much as it does from psychological complexes and kinks in human nature.

Mental sickness in easily the hardest to find out while finalising a match. There can be absolutely no clue on the mental state or health of the proposed marital alliance except, of course, in cases of obvious lunacy where in the first place a match is never considered. Otherwise, many mentally sick people who can be dangerous for marital peace pass off as highly eligible candidates on the basis of appearance, academic, financial and family status and the largely deceptive angle of social demeanour.

Many marriages end in tragedy for the reason an otherwise eligible spouse has been found to be suffering from a state of mind so morbid and sick and so incorrigibly immature, life becomes impossible. It is for this reason the Janma Nakshatra and the Janma Rasi are given importance in marital counselling in astrology.

Janma Rasi is the sign occupied by the Moon at birth while Janma Nakshatra is the Nakshatra occupied by him at birth. The emphasis on Janma Rasi springs from the fact the Moon is ascribed governance of the individual psyche or the mind in classical works.

दिवाकरो हि विश्वात्मा मन: कुमुदबान्धल्लः ।
सत्वं कुजो बुधो वाणीदायको विबुधै: स्मृत: ॥
देवेज्यो ज्ञानसुखदौ भृगुवीर्यप्रदायक: ।
क्रूरग् विबुधैरूतच्छायासूनुश्च दु:खद: ॥

Brihat Parasara Hora - I - 13, 14

The Sun is the universal soul, the Moon mind, Mars strength, Mercury speech, Jupiter wisdom, Venus virility and Saturn sorrow and suffering.

It is from an assessment of the Moon that a picture of the mental disposition and health of a native can be had. Afflictions to the Moon, as they do for the body in the case of the Ascendant, affect the mental health of a native. Benefic association by aspect or conjunction contributes to mental well-being and positive attitudes. Malefic influences, in any way, disturb mental health.

When the planets ruling Sattwa, Rajas and Tamas influence the Moon by association or aspect, they pass on their characteristic Guna to the native influencing his psychology accordingly. When Jupiter or the Sun influences the Moon strongly, the characteristics under Sattwa types described by Charaka manifest in the native. Likewise, when an unafflicted Mercury or Venus join the Moon, the Rajasic characteristics may show up. When Saturn or Mars influence the Moon, the Tamasic type of mental disposition arises.

The Moon rules Sattwa. If the Moon in the natal chart is free of the influences of any planet, a preponderance of Sattwa Guna manifests.

Sri Ramakrishna Paramahamsa was the personification of Sattwa Guna. The Moon in his horoscope is in Aquarius with the Sun and Mercury trinally aspected by Jupiter. The Moon is therefore totally under the influence of the Sattwa planets Sun and Jupiter. Though Mercury has been ascribed Rajas, it is a well-known principle of astrology that this planet is totally influenced by the planet he associates with. Here Jupiter and Sun, Sattwapradana Grahas, make him Sattwic too.

An excellent example of Jupiter's Sattwa Guna influence on the Moon of the Brahma and Yamya types is of the President of India Dr. A. P. J. Abdul Kalam. The Moon occupies Scorpio and is aspected trinally by an exalted Jupiter. Not only is the President an intellectual and moral giant but also attracts all the other qualities listed by Charaka under this type of Sattwa Guna. Jupiter's exaltation (supported further by his occupation of his own sign Pisces in Navamsa) brings out the finest kind of Sattwa Guna in his influence on the Moon.

A strong contrast is found in Chart 2, though here also the Moon is in Scorpio. The Moon is Neecha with Neechabhanga and joined by Rahu and Mars (R) aspected by Mercury. The retrogression of Mars and the Rahu-association with the Moon make Saddam Hussein

Chart 1: A. P. J. Abdul Kalam : Born 15-10-1931 at 9 N 18, 79 E 18.

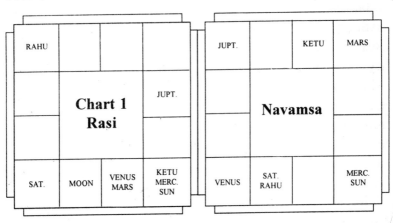

a good example of Rajas-Tamas mix and coming under Asura *cum* Rakshasa *cum* Matsya types. Mercury takes on the malefic influence of retrograde Mars-Ketu-Rahu and reflects their maleficence in influencing the Moon.

These are, however, extremely broad generalisations and undergo modification based on the rest of the chart, primarily on the basis of the lordships and houses involved. If for example Jupiter, Venus and Mercury are the Ascendant or 9th lords, the Sattwa characteristics

Chart 2: Saddam Hussein : Born 28-4-1937 at Tikrit.

SAT.	VENUS (R) SUN	MERC. KETU			VENUS		
				JUPT. RAHU			
JUPT.	Chart 2 Rasi			MERC	Navamsa		SUN KETU
	MARS MOON RAHU				MOON	MARS	SAT.

predominate. If they are Kendra lords, it gives a Rajasic *cum* Sattwic orientation to the mental disposition. If they are rulers of Dustanas, the Tamasic *cum* Sattwic angle gets highlighted. Likewise, if Mars and Saturn become benefic lords, their association with the Moon takes on Sattwic qualities coloured somewhat by the Tamasic. If they are malefics, Rajasic and Tamasic attributes predominate.

However, a large number of cases have shown that the natural benefics, irrespective of their functional lordship, retain a large proportion of the Sattwic content and contribute to the mental well-being of the native. Jupiter as 9th lord (for Aries Ascendant) or 6th lord (for Libra Ascendant) with the Moon gives a good mental disposition, the degree of well-being defined by the lordship. The 9th lordship native may score over the 6th lordship native in Jupiterean traits, but basically both are good. The same applies to Venus where the Rajasic tilts towards Sattwa and so also with a well-placed Mercury.

When a natural malefic influences the Moon, however, a slight shift in interpretation becomes necessary. If it is Mars or Saturn as the Ascendant lord or a benefic lord or sign-dispositor, the Sattwa Guna predominates and gives a good mindset. But the Sattwa manifestation may be flavoured by the natural characteristic of the planet. For Libra, for example, if Saturn influences the Moon favourably, the native acquires a predominance of Sattwa. His external demeanour may be seen as reserved and taciturn though he may not mean it that way. The same applies to Mars who for Leo or Cancer or Aries or Scorpio Ascendant if favourably influencing the Moon, can give a Sattwic nature but its expression may be harsh in comparison to that of a native with a Jupiter influenced Moon. In such cases, there is Sattwasamshuddhih (honesty of purpose) though its expression may not be gentle.

Chart 3 is of the famed classical singer Mrs. Subbalakshmi whose performances have dazzled music connossiers by their uplifting quality. A gentle soul, religious minded and highly charitable, the Moon with Jupiter made the native out and out Sattwic by nature.

Chart 3 : Mrs. Subbalakshmi: Born 16-9-1916 at 9h. 30m. at 13 N 05, 80 E 18 with a balance of 5 years 10 months 9 days of Sun Dasa at birth.

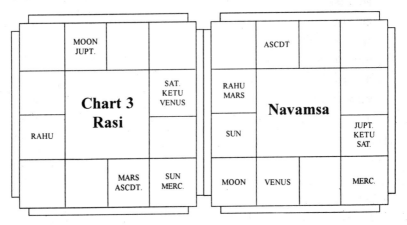

The aspect of Mars on the Moon loses its Tamasic quality by virtue of his being the Moon-sign dispositor and gives rises to Sattwic qualities. So also the aspect of Saturn as that of a Yogakaraka or functional benefic. This horoscope is also a good example of the Kaubera *cum* Gandharva type of Sattwa Guna.

If Mars or Saturn is a malefic lord or is not a benefic lord (Ascendant or 9th lord or Yogakaraka or Moon-sign lord, the last under certain circumstances only), the mind becomes prone to sickness. That does not necessarily imply an unsound mind or lunacy but gives a predeliction to wrong thinking habits and patterns. Depending upon the intensity of the affliction, the negative traits coming under Rajas and Tamas such as avarice, malice, jealousy, self-pity, lethargy, extreme selfishness, indolence, lack of motivation take possession of the native driving him to say and do things that not only disturb his own mental peace but also injure and hurt others. The afflictions can come from Mars, Saturn and an afflicted Mercury.

These traits, positive or negative, coming from the planetary influence on the Moon result in peace or pain, not only to others, but to the native himself. Another way of looking at the picture is to interpret benefics as contributing to what lord Krishna describes as *daiva sampat* or virtuous traits or mental attributes in Chapter XVI (Slokas 1-3) of the **Srimad Bhagavad Gita** :

अभयं सत्व संशुद्धि: ज्ञानयोगव्य वस्थिति: ।
दानं दमश्च यज्ञश्च स्वाध्यायस्तप आर्जवम् ॥
अहिंसा सत्यमक्रोधस्त्याग: शन्तिरपैशुनम् ।
दया भूतेष्वलोलुप्त्वं मार्दवं ह्रीरचापलम् ॥
तेज: क्षमा धृति: शौचमद्रोहो नातिमानिता ।
भवन्ति सम्पदं दैवीमभिजातस्य भारत ॥

Fearlessness, purity of heart, steadfastness in knowledge and Yoga; charity, self-restraint and worship, study of scriptures, austerity, uprightness. Harmlessness, truth, absence of anger, renunciation or spirit of sacrifice, absence of calumny, compassion to creatures, non-covetousness, gentleness, modesty, fickleness.

Energy, forgiveness, fortitude, purity, absence of hatred, absence of pride — these belong to one born for a divine lot, Oh! Bharata.

Afflictions to the Moon from malefics — natural *cum* functional only leads to *asuric sampat* or demonical nature as described in the same chapter, Slokas 4 and 8-18.

The result of *daivia sampat* is said to be liberation. This liberation is freedom from the agonies that are brought on from a mind caught in the play of misguided and untramelled emotions and passions, for as the Upanishads say मन एव मनुष्याणां कारणं बन्धमोक्षयो: ।

This is also borne out by the fact that the demoniac qualities listed in the **Srimad Bhagavad Gita** and said to lead to bondage cause more suffering to the one harbouring them than those against whom they are directed when the Lord says निबन्धायासुरी मता ॥

The *asuric* mind is fettered and bound in chains generated by itself destroying all peace of mind. How can then such a mind lay claim to freedom whose thoughts are forever dictated by how to harm, hurt or ruin others ?

These qualities of the *asuri* type listed by Lord Krishna include "greed, avarice, ostentation, harshness, malice, arrogance, envy, anger, insolence and are said to fill one with insatiable desires, hypocrisy, pride and unwholesome views through delusion ...." and inflict suffering on oneself and on others as well. Affliction to the Moon holds the key to what constitutes *daiva sampat* and what produces *asuri sampat*.

Most people are a mix of both kinds of nature — divine and demonical and the degree of these traits is such as to, at the worst, bringing in little tensions, friction, misunderstandings, quarrels, dissentions, anger or irritation in day to day life. But when the factors afflicting the Moon get aggravated, the *asuri* traits predominate and assume dangerous tones. Afflictions from Mars or Saturn or Rahu-Ketu individually or in combination produce either Rajasic (externalization) or Tamasic (introversion) responses from the native.

Chart 4 : Born 19-5-1952 at 7h. 00m. with a balance of 12 years 5 months 27 days of Saturn Dasa at birth.

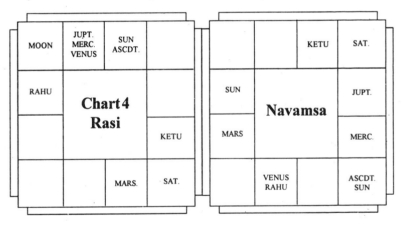

The Moon in the 11th is directly aspected by Saturn, a natural malefic but functional benefic as a Yogakaraka for the Ascendant Taurus in Chart 4. But Saturn is retrograde and afflicted by a Papakartari Yoga which makes his aspect on the Moon of the nature of an affliction. The native is a victim of chronic depression and self-pity.

In another case of Gemini Ascendant, with the Moon in the 8th in a Dustana aspected by combust Saturn from the 11th, greed, malice, self-pity, deceit and craftiness constantly made the native indulge in manipulative tactics leading to constant friction and misunderstandings amongst family members.

When the *asuric* symptoms assume difficult proportions as a result of heavy afflictions to the Moon, then the ground is laid for mental disorder. *(09-04))* ●

SRI JAYENDRA SARASWATI'S SANYASA YOGAS

> 1. Dasa chidra periods carry traumatic developments in life.
> 2. Predominantly benefic influences on the Moon add to the strength of Sanyasa Yogas.
> 3. Badhaka planet in the 10th casts a shadow on reputation.

THE ARREST OF the Kanchi Acharya Sri Jayendra Saraswati on Diwali day in November 2004 left countless devotees and followers numb with shock and anger. The anguish of millions of devotees went unnoticed with large sections of an insensitive media pouring venom on the monk and working overtime to churn out sleazy details from every conceivable angle. Such outrageous and out of the ordinary events in one's life as the pontiff's arrest and incarceration are closely connected with adverse Dasas and Bhuktis. Transits, one or more, may also turn unhelpful at such times. Yet no matter how adverse a Dasa or transit, certain acts and circumstances as severe as those alleged in this case are possible only if the chart itself meets with certain planetary conditions. And these conditions would involve certain specific Yogas — some good, some not good.

The Sanyasa Yogas, first. The term *sanyasa* in Indian philosophy is derived from a combination of the two words *samyag* and *nyasah* meaning "giving up or renouncing in a virtuous way." What is emphasized here is the fact of not only renunciation but also that it is not a result of frustration. It is used to describe a state of being where a withdrawal from mundane aspirations and objectives takes place following a deep understanding of the ephemeral and transitory nature of worldly life and its lures. This transformation within one's innermost being results invariably in a reorientation of one's goals and priorities with all of one's energies being directed at efforts to perceive and experience the one and only source of perennial happiness or Parabrahman. This change in one's personality is a quiet happening and not necessarily perceived externally though the general tradition in India has been to announce it through the donning of *gerrua* or ochre robes. But not all ochre-robed people are true *sanyasis* for the majority of whom, it is only *Udaranimittam Bahukrita Veshah*. An astrological examination of a chart can, with a fair degree of accuracy, help in identifying true *sanyasa*. Most classical works devote an entire chapter to Pravrajya Yogas which in essence mean Yogas for renunciation. Charts where these Yogas are present show the *sanyasa* mindset. Such combinations if afflicted by malefic influences can produce those who though professing *sanyasa* are a shame to their order being vulnerable to the baser instincts and swayed by morbid emotions. Where the Sanyasa Yoga is generated by benefic planets in dignity, the result is an evolutionary elevation of the total personality and a sublimation of primeval urges.

One of the strongest types of Sanyasa Yoga requires four or more powerful planets in any one single Bhava or house. This is a rather infrequently occurring Yoga and the best example for it is of Gautama, the Buddha, who had as many as five planets in the 10th house. Other Yogas are more generic in definition. Sanyasa Yoga can occur in the following circumstances :-

1. When the Ascendant lord is not aspected by other planets but aspects Saturn.

2. When Saturn aspects the weak Ascendant lord.

3. When the Moon is in a Drekanna (decanate) ruled by Saturn and occupies a Navamsa ruled by Mars or Saturn and is aspected by Saturn.

4. When the Moon is in a Navamsa ruled by Mars and is aspected by Saturn.

According to **Phaladeepika** under Chapter XXVII entitled "Pravrajyayogah", Slokas 6 and 7,

अतिशयबलयुक्त: शीतगु: शुक्लपक्षे
बलविरहितमेनं प्रेक्षते लग्ननाथ: ।
यदि भवति तपस्वी दु:खित: शोकतप्तो
धनजनपरिहीन: कृच्छ्रलब्धान्नपान: ॥६॥

The Moon becomes exceedingly powerful in the bright half of the month. If the lord of the Ascendant should aspect the Moon when he is devoid of strength (waning Moon or otherwise), the person will become a miserable ascetic, engaged in the practise of rigorous penance, distressed and wretched, without wealth or helpmate and getting his food and drink with great difficulty.

प्रकथितमुनियोमे राजयोगो यदि स्या-
दशुभफलविपाकं सर्वमुन्मूल्य पश्चात् ।
जनयति पृथिवीशं दीक्षितं साधुशीलं
प्रणतनृपशिरोभि: स्पृष्टपादाब्ज्युग्मम् ॥७॥

If in the ascetic Yoga alluded to in the previous Sloka, if there should exist a Raja Yoga, it will pull up by the roots all the bad effects and then make him a lord of the earth initiated into asceticism and virtuously inclined, at whose feet other kings make salutations with their head bent.

Therefore, in order the Sanyasa Yoga is both enduring and of a high order, the Moon should be strong. If there are other Yogas that are in the nature of Raja Yogas, then it shows a renunciate who commands the respect of all and possibly occupies a formal position as well in society.

Three out of four Yogas obtain in Sri Jayendra Saraswati's chart. The first two are inbuilt in the combination involving the Ascendant lord himself. The third combination too is present but with a small modification, in that the Moon in a Saturn ruled Drekanna is *not aspected by* but *conjunct* Saturn and occupies a Martian Navamsa. The presence of these Sanyasa Yogas testifies astrologically to the

Sri Jayendra Saraswati : Born July 18, 1935 at 19h. 00m.(IST) 10 N 40, 79 E 26 with a balance of 4 months 2 days of Mars Dasa at birth.

```
┌─────────────────────────────────────┐  ┌─────────────────────────────┐
│         │       │       │ MERC      │  │ ASCDT  │ JUPT.│      │      │
│         │       │       │ 13-29     │  │ SAT.   │      │      │      │
├─────────┼───────┴───────┼───────────┤  ├────────┼──────┴──────┼──────┤
│ SAT.(R) │               │ KETU 0-13 │  │        │             │      │
│ 18-07   │               │ SUN 3-28  │  │ MERC.  │             │ KETU │
│ MOON    │     Rasi      ├───────────┤  │        │   Navamsa   │      │
│ 6-00    │               │           │  ├────────┤             ├──────┤
├─────────┤               │ VENUS     │  │        │             │      │
│ ASCDT.  │               │ 17-26     │  │ RAHU   │             │ SUN  │
│ 9-42    │               │           │  │        │             │      │
│ RAHU    │               │           │  │        │             │      │
│ 0-13    │               │           │  │        │             │      │
├─────────┴───┬───────────┼───────────┤  ├────────┼──────┬──────┼──────┤
│             │ MARS 2-40 │           │  │        │      │      │      │
│             │ JUPT.     │           │  │        │ MOON │ MARS │ VENUS│
│             │ 21-59     │           │  │        │      │      │      │
└─────────────┴───────────┴───────────┘  └────────┴──────┴──────┴──────┘
```

highly evolved personality of the monk. Specific Yogas as these are important but not necessarily conclusive. An analysis of the Manahkaraka or the natural significator of the mind Moon against the general disposition of the chart and the functional roles of planets can help arrive at confirmatory clues.

The Moon in Sri Jayendra Saraswati's case is in Aquarius at 6^0 in a Drekanna ruled by Saturn and associated with him. The birth having occurred on Krishna Triteeya (the 3rd lunar day of the dark fortnight), the Moon may be deemed to be strong with digital strength. Saturn as a natural malefic shows Tamas but, in this case, is a benefic as the Ascendant lord and occupies Aquarius, his Moolatrikona sign. Therefore Saturn is in great dignity. It is such a Sattwic Saturn who influences the Moon through association directly by both sign-occupation as well as Drekanna-occupation.

The Moon is also aspected directly by Venus as well as trinally by Jupiter. Venus though Rajasic in nature becomes Sattwic by virtue of his lordship of benefic houses both from the Ascendant and the

Moon-sign (Chandra Lagna). From both Ascendants, he has simultaneous quadrangular and trinal lordships. Considering the trinal lordship from the Ascendant, Venus is a Yogakaraka with rulership of the 5th or Poorvapunyastana while from the Moon-sign, as 9th lord he is Dharmastanadhipati. Indian philosophy ascribes virtuous propensities (*samskaras*) to Poorvapunya and regressive tendencies and inclinations (*vasanas*) to Poorvajanmapapa. In this context as 5th lord Venus aspecting the Moon promotes pious tendencies, not vicious passions. The 9th lordship of Venus as Dharmastanadhipati, likewise, generates a proclivity for righteousness, not its opposite. In these astrological circumstances, both Saturn and Venus add to the Sattwa Guna content of the native's mind produced by Jupiter who is naturally Sattwic. Therefore, the mindset of the native is overwhelmingly Sattwic contributing to the high quality of the Sanyasa Yoga in the chart. This in turn is unlikely to qualify the native to possess the mindset needed to perpetrate heinous acts of any kind. Sick and morbid emotions, be they for a fraction of a second or for longer periods, that can drag one into acts which the Dharma Sastras define as evil, can therefore be deemed absent in a horoscope such as this.

Heinous acts such as murder, felony, assault, molestation etc. themselves are a relatively little touched topic in astrological literature, save for one or two references in most classical works. **Jataka Tattwa** defines some combinations for such acts as follows :

1. The signs Aries, Leo or Aquarius aspected by Mars and the Sun.

2. The Sun, Mars and Saturn in conjunction.

3. The Sun, Mars and Jupiter together.

4. The Moon in Aries, Leo or Aquarius aspected by the Sun, Saturn and Mars.

5. The lord of the Ascendant and Mars conjoined in Rasi and in the same Navamsa.

However, apart from such specific Yogas which do not obtain here, heavy afflictions to the Moon ruling Manas (emotions) or

Mercury ruling Buddhi (faculty of discrimination) or the 4th house (mind) or the 5th house (thinking) jointly or severally could generate the psychological material for vicious acts which in the ultimate analysis begin in the mind and then only manifest externally.

The Moon or Manahkaraka is in the 2nd in Aquarius with Ascendant lord Saturn. The Moon being with the Ascendant lord Saturn is not a damning situation as for as the Karakattwa of Manastithi (mental state) is concerned. That Saturn is retrograde makes for some difference but both the Moon and Saturn come under the trinal benefic influence of Jupiter who is quite well placed in the 10th.

The Buddhikaraka Mercury occupies Gemini, his own sign. Jupiter aspects Mercury trinally and becomes a beneficial influence on the planet and the Karakattwa coming under him.

Where in a case, the Moon is afflicted heavily enough to give homicidal tendencies, if Mercury is well placed and free of affliction, then whatever the mindset and the inner turbulence one may experience, the unblemished Mercury ensures the emotions do not run wild and translate into destructive acts — direct or indirect. Where the Moon is free of afflictions as in this case and Mercury is also untainted, frenzied emotions or of their translation into destructive acts can be ruled out. Also to be noted are the mutually trinal positions of the Moon and Mercury and the trinal influence of Jupiter on both.

The 4th house from the Ascendant is aspected by its ruler Mars, Ascendant lord Saturn and Jupiter. Jupiter's influence on Mars is benign and protects the 4th house. The 5th house is aspected adversely by Mars which could have been an affliction if the power of Mars to harm had not been reined in by Jupiter. The 4th and 5th houses are congenially placed as to rule out heinous acts of any kind.

Venus is the Kalatrakaraka and rules, among other things, बहुवधूसंङ्ग विलासं मन्दं (**Phaladeepika II-**6) or *addictions to many women, pleasure pursuits and lasciviousness*. His disposition in a chart can either add to or detract from the merits of Sanyasa Yoga.

Venus is in his own Nakshatra Poorvaphalguni. He is aspected by the Ascendant lord Saturn (R) almost to the exact degree. The 7th lord Moon also aspects Venus. Both the Moon and Saturn, in turn, are aspected by Jupiter. This combination is helpful for a life of celibacy, the 7th lordship of the Moon fading before the strength of the master renunciate which Saturn can become if placed as he is in his Moolatrikona. Such a Saturn-Moon combination aspects Kalatrakaraka Venus which devitalizes the sensuality normally associated with the latter. Further, Venus is in the Navamsa of Kanya or Virgo, the sign of the virgin, and in the 7th house here is aspected again by the ascetic abstinent Saturn who is in Pisces, the Moksha Rasi of the Zodiac.

Considering the 7th house from the Ascendant, the Sun and Ketu occupy it, the latter being Vargottama. As 8th lord, the Sun in the 7th can blight 7th house matters but being with Kaivalyakaraka Ketu can help sublimate cravings. The fact Ketu occupies Punarvasu ruled by Jupiter, the 12th lord, is also significant. Add to that the Subhakartari Yoga enfolding the 7th house and its occupants and what emerges is a planetary disposition that is congenially placed for a celibate life.

The arrest and the continuing build up of charges against the monk have occurred in the Dasa-chidra of Saturn Bhukti in Mercury Dasa. The Dasa and Bhukti lords are in Rahu-ruled Nakshatras which brings in an element of suspicion, intrigue, deceit, manipulation and can also cast a shadow on the native's reputation.

Mercury is the 6th lord from Lagna placed in the 6th. Saturn is with the 6th lord Moon with reference to Chandra Lagna or the Moon-sign Aquarius. Both planets related to the 6th house have not withheld the results of incarceration coming under this Bhava. According to Dr. B. V. Raman in his **Hindu Predictive Astrology**, Saturn Bhukti of Mercury Dasa can show "Bad luck, stranger to success and happiness, severe reversal, enmity, pain in the part governed by Saturn, downfall or disgrace to relatives, mind full of evil forebodings and distress, fear from diseases... destruction of family, scandals ..." and these are already being amply demonstrated in this case.

The shifting of transit Saturn into Cancer finally in June 2005 and of transit Jupiter into Libra in September 2005 could indicate developments and fresh facts coming to light that could help stem the adverse indications of Dasa chidra.

Five planets occupy Kendras while three are in great strength due to their Vargottama positions. The Moon with Lagna lord Saturn in Aquarius generates a Sasa Yoga. Venus in the 7th from the Moon forms a partial Adhi Yoga. All these contribute, as Raja Yogas, to the stature of the monk. Additionally, the position of Mars in the 10th with Digbala with Jupiter is a factor that can generate Raja Yoga in the form of Guru-Mangala Yoga. But as it involves the 12th lord Jupiter, such a disposition can sometimes indicate abdication.

Mars as a Badhaka lord for the Ascendant Capricorn placed in the 10th and aspecting the Ascendant appears to be a major drawback in the chart. Capricorn rising gives a nature that seeks to cling to and exercise control over the minutest of details. This trait can get toned down or aggravated depending upon the influences on the Ascendant and its ruler. While the ruler himself Saturn in this case is well placed signwise and by aspect and association, the Ascendant comes under the aspect of Badhaka Mars and of the Ketu-associated Sun. While the latter influence is enobling, that of Mars produces a weakness for power and authority, the house from where this aspect is generated being the 10th. Though a positive Mars produces good managers and organisers, as Badhakadhipati he carries to an extreme level the urge to retain control over everything and which can finally prove to be one's undoing. The position of Mars here as the Bhumikaraka and Badhaka prompted the hoary Advaita Math to shift focus from *tapas* and the propagation of Vedic Dharma to running a vast empire of trusts and educational institutions. The dominant position of malefic Mars in the 10th and the occupation of Rahu-ruled Nakshatras by both the Dasa and Bhukti lords together with the October 28th eclipse in 2004 occurring in Libra and transit Saturn turning retrograde on November 8, 2004 all combined to trigger the midnight drama of November 11, 2004.

Ketu Dasa will take over by the end of 2005. The Subhakartari Yoga that Ketu as Kaivalyakaraka comes under may see the pontiff return to a life of prayer and distance himself from temporal engagement. Ketu is in Cancer, a sign associated with religious and holy places, and can show like surroundings, rather than the cold and impersonal confines of prison walls.

The fact the next Dasa lord Ketu is flanked by benefics, natural as well as functional, raises hopes of the decline that has apparently set in the Math fading away as the Dasa unfolds. Fears that the reputation of the Math has been permanently tarnished may not last through this Dasa.

When exactly the clouds hovering over the Math will be blown away will also depend upon the horoscope of the junior pontiff of the Kanchi Math Sri Vijayendra Saraswati. *(02-05) 18-12-04.* ●

ASTROLOGICAL SAGA OF A SAINT

> 1. *Affliction-free Sun and Moon conjunction can show strong spiritual tendencies.*
> 2. *The Ascendant lord, Jupiter and Mercury influencing Ascendant strengthen it.*
> 3. *Dasa of 5th lord taps spiritual potential.*

SPIRITUAL PLANETS

THE SUN and the Moon are two important factors, apart from the Lagna, in any chart but more especially so in those that belong to spiritually advanced souls. The Sun is the natural significator of the soul or Atmakaraka ruling the Supreme Self. The Moon on the other hand, which receives identity from reflecting the solar brilliance, is the Manahkaraka or natural significator of the mind or the ego which is the cause of all duality and therefore takes the soul away from its true nature.

In most charts with spiritual potential, the Sun and Moon therefore occupy pivotal points or houses indicating thereby the potential for the Higher Self to overcome the lower self or individual ego of the native.

The Moon or mind controls one at every moment of one's life and in the process tends to lead one away from one's true Self, the Atma, symbolised by the Sun. The Moon leads one to a false identification with thoughts from which the mind derives its strength.

Sans thoughts there is no mind. *Sans* thought the True Self reveals Itself. The death or fading away of the mind leads to comprehension of one's true Self.

The Sun and Moon together or moving towards a conjunction, therefore, is one of the best combinations for spirituality under certain other planetary conditions. Such a birth, described as occurring on or about an Amavasya, in common parlance is treated with fear as showing a life devoid of success, happiness and health. Such charts are usually written off as of failures in life. Though true to a large extent, such a combination where supported by other planetary factors can indeed release unusual levels of spirituality where the natives, though losers in a grossly materialistic sense, are truly winners conquering themselves and progressing to a state of eternal happiness beyond the ken of materialistic values. The Moon, when moving towards a conjunction of the Sun, is seen to disappear from sight in the haze of solar brilliance and splendour. In other words, the Manas coming under the Moon can be said to dissolve in the Atma (ruled by the Sun) where it loses its puny individuality to become one with the Universal Cosmic Soul.

SELF-REALIZED SOUL

An excellent example of such a combination is that of the Jagadguru Sankaracharya Sri Abhinava Vidya Teertha, the 35th pontiff in the spiritual lineage of the Sringeri Peetam founded by Bhagavatpada Adi Sankaracharya.

The Moon in this case is the 9th lord. The 9th house is the Dharmastana which rules one's sense of right and wrong. As 9th lord the Moon occupies the 12th or Mokshastana emphasising the orientation of the chart with Dharma being directed towards Moksha. The Sun who is the Atmakaraka is also the 10th lord, ruler of one's main activity or Karma in life. Such a 10th lord is in the 12th in Mokshastana which makes Moksha the main objective of the native's Karma or activity.

Astrological Saga of A Saint

The Acharya's main goal in life was Moksha but it was not to be in an isolated sense far from the madding crowd. Right in the midst of the world and its teeming troubled souls, the Acharya had to not only pursue the goal himself but also guide and lead his lesser brethren towards it. It is therefore natural for such a leader of spiritual matters to enjoy Raja Yogas for otherwise, how can one be the pontiff of the ancient most seat of Advaita philosophy, the hoary Sringeri Sarada Peetam.

The Sun and Moon together act as the 9th and 10th lords to generate a Raja Yoga, Dharmakarmadhipati Yoga, welding temporal duties with spiritual tasks.

STRENGTH OF ASCENDANT

According to Varahamihira,

होरास्वामिगुरूज्ञवीक्षितयुता नान्यैश्च वीर्योल्कटा ।

Brihat Jataka I-19

The Ascendant lord, Jupiter or Mercury in the Ascendant make it extremely powerful. If planets other than these aspect or occupy the Ascendant, the results are not so.

Chart 1: Born 13-11-1917 at 8h. 30m. (IST) at 12 N 58, 77 E 35 with a balance of 13 years 11 months 11 days of Rahu Dasa at birth.

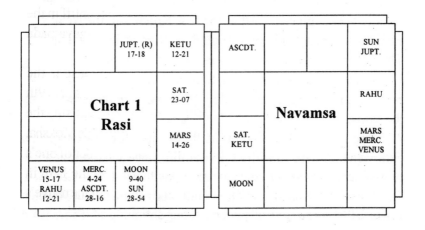

The Ascendant is the main pillar of a chart and its strength or otherwise can alter its entire scope. The Ascendant Scorpio is aspected by its lord Mars from the 10th, the most powerful Kendra. Mercury occupies the Ascendant itself while Jupiter aspects it from another Kendra. All the three conditions given by Varahamihira obtaining simultaneously make the Ascendant unusually powerful.

SCORPIO RISING

The sign rising on the Ascendant is Scorpio, the most spiritual as well as the most beastial sign, as described in astrological texts. Scorpio afflicted makes a beast of a man — crude, vulgar, indolent with brute apetites and an animal in human form. Symbolised by the deadly scorpion which is known to sting itself to death, this sign often produces renegade souls who court misery and self destruction caught in unbridled passions and excessive levels of attachment and hate with scant regard for humaneness. In dignity, Scorpio is known to produce the highest levels of spirituality where love of humanity and concern for the suffering supercede all considerations. As the 8th sign of the Kalapurusha (Zodiac) ruling life, a well-placed Scorpio bestows regenerative strength on its natives who can cut through the limitations of the body and mind to embrace all humanity as their own selves.

The Ascendant in this case is further strengthened by the fact, its ruler Mars occupies the 10th, the best Kendra, in the royal sign Leo. Mars here not only gets Vargottama strength but also Digbala. The Ascendant point rises in Pisces Navamsa, the sign symbolising Liberation. As a result, the sign Scorpio becomes predominently positive unleashing the tremendous potential it has in spiritualizing the native.

Mercury in the Ascendant as the Karaka for *vak* or speech endowed the Acharya with a bright smiling face and a strong sense of humour and who was quick to repartee with wit shorn of sarcasm.

Jupiter is the Karaka for Sattwa Guna, the natural fallout of which is peace that *surpassath* all understanding springing as it does from an unending fount of bliss from within. Jupiter's aspect on the Ascendant endowed the Acharya even as a little boy with a rare tranquility and compassion.

Mars, the Lagna lord, is in the 10th, with Digbala where he becomes exceedingly powerful in conferring the highest office one can enjoy in one's vocational life. Being Vargottama his blessings multiply manifold. Since the 10th house is instricately connected with the Ascendant through its lord, the pontificate came to him very early in his life even as he stepped into his teenage years.

The 5th lord in the 7th is not conducive to marital life. In this case as a first rate benefic, the 2nd and 5th lord, Jupiter in the 7th aspected by Mercury resulted in a life of unsullied brahmacharya, one of the pre-requisites for not only qualifying for office under this order but also for attaining the ultimate in spiritual life.

Venus, the 7th lord, is in the 2nd in Sagittarius in exchange of signs with the 2nd lord Jupiter. This combination by itself could have led to a happy family life but Rahu with Venus would not let it be. Both Venus and Rahu occupy Moola Nakshatra ruled by Ketu who, in turn, in the 8th, a Mokshatrikona, is extremely comfortably placed to attract the native to the pursuit of spiritual truths. Moola is particularly associated with Saraswati, the goddess of learning, but being subtly influenced by the Jupiterean significations as a result of the exchange of signs between Venus and Jupiter transmutes learning into Gnana or spiritual wisdom.

JUPITER, THE SOFT-HEARTED

Birth occurred in a traditional Vedic Brahmana family of Advaita scholars in Rahu Dasa. Rahu in the 2nd does not help finances. Worse, he is with 12th lord Venus. Circumstances were indigent, as it usually happens in families which place spiritual goals above all else letting go mundane considerations. Saturn in the 9th though excellent for spiritual propensities rarely supports Bhagya or material prosperity. The father was a humble school teacher and the mother, a simple housewife.

Mercury is in the Ascendant aspected by benefic Jupiter. These two influences on the Ascendant made the Acharya a soft hearted pleasant natured child who never got into fights that are part of the growing up years of boys. Always willing to help, he even took on the harsh punishment meted out to a playmate as he could not bear to see the friend in pain. However, Mars as Lagna lord in the 10th aspecting the Ascendant makes for boldness and grit and great physical energy. The Acharya seldom tolerated bullies and would take them on easily if only to protect his meeker friends. A considerate child, he never failed to lend a helping hand to his mother in her chores. This is basically traceable to the influence of Jupiter who as a Sattwic planet, if unsullied, generously bestows Sattwic qualities on the native.

Jupiter's powerful influence on the chart saw the Upanayanam of the Acharya take place in unusual circumstances on May 4, 1930. It so happened the senior Acharya of the Sarada Peetam was looking for a suitable successor when the young Acharya's horoscope was brought to him by a devotee as a possible choice. Perhaps the chart appealed to the master for a senior attendant of the Math immediately took upon himself the responsibility of arranging for the boy's Upanayanam at Sringeri. It was an unsought blessing descending on the Acharya's family. Transit Jupiter was in Taurus influencing natal Jupiter, the 2nd and 5th lord, the 5th standing for Mantra Diksha. This event came about in Moon Bhukti of Rahu Dasa in Sun Antar. Rahu in the 2nd is in Sagittarius reflecting the results of his sign-dispositor Jupiter. He is in Moola Nakshatra ruled by the Kaivalyakaraka Ketu who very significantly is placed in the 8th house of mysticism and esoteric knowledge. The Moon as 9th lord in the 12th is always supportive of auspicious events. The Antara lord Sun is of course the deity propitiated by the Gayatri Mantra one receives at one's Upanayanam. Once at Sringeri, the young Acharya decided he would stay on there to learn Sanskrit, rather than go back to school which would only equip him to find a job for a living.

PURVAPUNYASTANA AND SANYASA

The next major event came a year later on May 22, 1931 when the Acharya was initiated into Sanyasa and annointed as the 35th pontiff of the Peetam. Jupiter Dasa was about to begin. The Dasa was of Rahu who in the 2nd should reflect Jupiter's results. The Bhukti of Mars was on. Mars as Lagna lord is in the 10th with Digbala and has obtained Vargottama Navamsa. In the 10th as Lagna lord, he becomes capable of conferring Raja Yoga carrying authority and power, both of which vested in him the moment the anointment took place.

A diligent student, the Acharya never complained of any inconvenience. He devoted himself heart and soul to the study of scriptural works. Even as he progressed at lighting speed in his studies, his spiritual advancement kept pace with it. Jupiter as Dasa lord provided the right conditions and opportunities for Vidya. As a benefic 5th lord, he conferred on the young initiate not only the rare advantage of the tutelage of an illumined master but also the benefit of training under some of the best traditional scholars of the day.

ENLIGHTENMENT

The aspect of Mars on Mercury, both being placed in quadrants individually as well as mutually, and Mercury benefitting also from the aspect of Mars as his sign dispositor, made the young Acharya a past master in Tarka Sastra or the science of logic.

The week between 10-12-1935 and 17-12-1935 was a highly significant one when the Acharya's spiritual efforts culminated in reaching the highest state of enlightenment and which state continued throughout the rest of his life. This period coincides with Jupiter Dasa, Saturn Bhukti both planets, by ownership and occupation respectively, predominantly suited for such an event. Transit Jupiter (Chart 2) was on natal Lagna in Scorpio aspecting both Dasa and Bhukti lords. Transit Mercury too was in Lagna in Scorpio during this eventful period. Venus was in Libra, Lagna lord

Mars was exalted, Rahu and Ketu were across the natal Nodes while Saturn was in Aquarius, his Moolatrikona sign. This unusual positioning of planets in favourable signs both individually and in relation to natal positions acted as a trigger facilitating the unique Experience in the teenage seeker.

Chart 2: Experience : 10-12-1935 at 13 N 25, 75 E 19.

		MOON 23-30	KETU 22-34
SAT. 12-53	**Chart 2 Rasi**		
MARS 10-39			
RAHU 22-34	SUN 25-28 MERC. 25-17 JUPT. 15-21	VENUS 10-01	

	MARS KETU		
SUN MERC.	**Navamsa**		
VENUS SAT.			MOON
	JUPT.	RAHU	

FIFTH LORD FOR SPIRITUAL CULMINATION

A spiritually potent chart generally finds its potential surface in the Dasa of the 5th lord. And this upsurge continues to get strengthened as the Dasa unfolds. If such a Dasa does not operate in one's life time, then though there may be streaks of spirituality, it is unlikely to predominate or take control of one's life. In this case, Jupiter Dasa which began just as the Acharya was stepping into his teens unlocked the great store of spirituality hidden within. The position of the 5th lord in a Kendra aspected by Mercury added to the spirituality dormant in the native. In fact this Experience was so powerful that according to authentic sources, the young Acharya touched the pinnacle of spiritual pursuit within less than 2 years after coming into the fold of the senior pontiff. Interestingly, this occurred on Margasira Pournami in the lunar year Yuva on 10-12-1935 with the

Sun in Scorpio and the Moon in Taurus. The Moon as 9th lord was not only exalted but in full digital strength in Taurus in all brilliance when the Acharya plunged into this Ultimate Experience which, it is said, never left him thereafter. The Moon is aspected by the excellent benefic Gnanakaraka Jupiter. The weekday is a Tuesday ruled by Lagna lord benefic Mars, exalted in transit, and being placed in the 10th house of achievements in Chart 1 signals the attainment of the Highest. The eclipses in 1935 occurred across the natal Nodal axis. Usually eclipses occurring on natal Rahu or Ketu, natal Sun or natal Moon tend to mark epochal stages in the lives of spiritual people. The planets on this date are all in great dignity as if contributing to the Experience, each in its own way.

The epochal Experience came about in the periods of Jupiter and of Saturn, the latter occupying the 9th.

There are very few specific Yogas for spirituality and renunciation in this chart. But the individual dispositions of the planets are such as to point to the great spirituality of the native, starting with those of the Atmakaraka and Manahkaraka, the Sun and Moon respectively in the 12th from the Ascendant.

RAJA YOGA TOO

According to Varahamihira,

नवमभवनसंस्थे मन्दगेन्यैरदृष्टे भवति नरपयोगे दीक्षितं पार्थिवेन्द्र : ।

Brihat Jataka X-4

Or, if the 9th is occupied by any planet, the person becomes a Dikshita (initiate) when he is born in Raja Yoga.

According to **Jataka Parijata** XV 13

ज्ञानव्योमाधिवासासस्तनुज्ञगुरुदशमस्थानपा:षड्बलाढ्या
जात: षट्शास्त्रवेत्ता निखिलनिगमविद् ज्ञानदीक्षामुपैति ।
धर्मव्यापारलग्नाधिपबुधविबुधाचार्यपाकापहारे
सत्कर्माचारसर्वर्ऋतुफलनिगमज्ञानविद्याकर: स्यात् ॥

JP XV -13

If the occupants of the ज्ञान *(Gnana - 5th, 4th and 2nd) and the 10th Bhavas as well as the lords of the 1st, 9th, 10th be* *possessed of abundant six-fold strength (Shadbala), the person born will be conversant with the six sciences and know all the **Vedas** and will receive initiation in the sacred knowledge.* In the पाक and अपहार *of the lords of the 9th, 10th and 1st Bhavas, or Mercury and of Jupiter, he will become a mine of sacred knowledge and science securing to him the benefit of performing sacrifices of all descriptions and all kinds of beneficient works.*

The Raja Yoga, the strongest of its kind, in this case is sourced in the position of the Ascendant lord Mars in the 10th house. Mars gets friendly Rasi, Vargottama Navamsa, friendly Hora of the Sun, friendly Drekanna of Jupiter, own Chaturtamsa of Scorpio, own Saptamsa of Scorpio, friendly Dasamsa of Jupiter, exaltation in Dwadasamsa, friendly Shodasamsa of Pisces and friendly Trimsamsa of Jupiter in Sagittarius. In other words, he gets Vargottama Navamsa, one exaltation Varga, 2 own or Swavargas and 5 friendly or Mitravargas. Therefore, Mars as Ascendant lord attracting so many favourable Vargas becomes extremely potent to confer Raja Yoga in the 10th house.

Saturn Dasa, Venus Bhukti saw the senior Acharya voluntarily shed his body on September 26, 1954. The two planets in 6-8 positions led to the conferring of a full-fledged Raja Yoga on the Acharya with his succession to the pontificate on October 16, 1954. The natal Moon was under the influence of transit Saturn in Libra coming under *sadesathe*. The Acharya had enjoyed a strong bond with his master. The blow temporarily disturbed his composure (consistent with transit Saturn in Janma Rasi) which however the young Acharya soon regained.

Mars, the executive, in the 10th made the Acharya on excellent administrator whose dynamic vigour was infectious and soon made itself felt in many positive changes in the administration and management of the Math and its vast properties.

On September 21, 1989, in Ketu Dasa, Saturn Bhukti, the Acharya shed his mortal coils. Ketu in the 8th is a Maraka, aspected as he is by the 7th lord Venus. Saturn is not a strong Maraka by lordship or occupation but as Karaka for physical death can show the end.

BLEND OF DHARMA-MOKSHA TRIKONAS

The 1st, 5th and 9th houses are called Dharma Trikonas or the tripod of righteous inclinations. The 4th, 8th and 12th houses are described as Moksha Trikonas signifying spiritual propensities. Any relationship between the Dharma and Moksha Trikonas or their lords provides the needed impetus for spiritual growth and evolution of the native. Here, the 4th lord Saturn is in the 9th, the 8th lord Mercury is in the 1st and the 12th lord Venus in the 2nd gets connected to the 5th lord Jupiter by Parivartana creating the right planetary environment for the birth of a soul racing towards the Ultimate Goal. (*07.04*) ●

SCHIZOPHRENIC TENDENCIES AND LUNAR NODES — I

> 1. *Afflictions to the Moon from Rahu or Ketu tend to produce schizophrenic tendencies.*
> 2. *Afflictions to certain Nodal constellations generate similar tendencies.*
> 3. *The fourth house must also be similarly afflicted.*

RAMPANT CONDITION

OF ALL THE kinds of mental disorders that modern medical science has listed, pride of place goes to schizophrenia. Approximately one per cent of the total world population is said to suffer from it in any given year. In USA alone, more than 2 million people are said to suffer from it annually. And in Canada, one in every 12 hospital beds is used by one suffering from schizophrenia. Its incidence is not limited either geographically or racially but is rampant throughout the world. Another feature of this mental disorder is that almost all people suffer from it at some point of time in their lives at least momentarily. But what is cause for concern is not this group but those who fall victim to it in a chronic sense and for extended periods of time.

MOON AS PIVOTAL FACTOR

Schizophrenia can be a severe disabling mental disorder. The personality gets seriously disorganised and contact with reality is impaired although there may be no loss of intellectual functions. It has, on date, no known cure though partially effective medications are available. But their side effects are quite frightening. More important is community and family support to such individuals but the most important factor, the mind of the schizophrenic coming under the Moon, is beyond either and the product of one's own thought patterns and habits.

Many a time family members are baffled by changes in the behaviour of a person who has been known to be a normal loving person before. Such change in behaviour is not only confusing but also hard for others to accept. A person who has been sane in his interactions may all of a sudden exhibit unusual behaviour triggered by hallucinations and delusions which make it difficult to relate to him normally. Such a person could also suffer social isolation or withdrawal or speak and act in such a manner as to put off others.

When this happens, the focus of astrological examination must be the Moon, for it is the Moon that carries clues to the onset of such symptoms in two ways. Firstly, the Moon's position, housewise and sign-wise, and association by aspect and conjunction must be carefully scrutinized. Secondly, the Moon's longitude and thereby the Dasa running and the transits in operation when the behavioural changes occur must also be carefully examined.

Though modern medical science identifies the physical seat of the schizophrenic mind in the brain, its roots go much deeper and on which astrology can provide somewhat better insights.

Schizophrenia is difficult to identify from a distance and only those who have to interact closely with the person may realize all is not well. Even then, the illness itself is such, not much attention is paid to it by family members unless it assumes extreme proportions.

Schizophrenia may be chronic or a life time condition. Or it could show up once or twice in a life-time. In both kinds, it is the Moon that matters.

NODAL AFFLICTION

The most common symptoms of schizophrenia help in identifying the planet responsible for it. The symptoms can show up as hallucinations or delusions, both coming under Rahu who has the strength to eclipse the Moon and thereby, the mind. If the hallucinations and delusions can be traced to disturbance of sensory perceptions, the role of the Ascendant (physical senses) becomes significant. Such sensory mal-activity can take different forms. One may hear internal voices warning or advising or abusing one constantly. One may see people or images that others don't. One may begin to believe others (one or more) are out to harm them, poison them, hurt their reputation or scuttle their lives vocationally or otherwise. When the fear that someone is out to harm one takes over, it is basically the emotion of suspicion that gains unhealthy strength and control. Therefore, in all cases of schizophrenia, the most important affliction comes from Rahu or Ketu, the shadowy planets, that have a blurring effect on the planets involved and therefore, on their significations.

Chart 1: Born 23-2-1983 at 9h. 35m. at 13 N, 77 E 35 with a balance of 8 years 8 months of Rahu Dasa at birth.

VEN 8-9 MARS 6-24	ASCDT 3-18		RAHU 8-52 MOON 13-33
SUN 11-47	**Chart 1** **Rasi**		
MERC 19-25			
KETU 8-52	JUPT 17-6	SAT(R) 12-09	

	ASCDT		MERC KETU
	MOON	**Navamsa**	
	SUN SAT		MARS
	JUPT RAHU		VEN

A case of chronic schizophrenia, the native of Chart 1 has his Moon in Aridra, a Nodal constellation. The Moon is with Rahu, also in the same Nodal constellation ruled by himself. Mars aspects the Node-afflicted Moon. Given to bouts of uncontrollable anger which take the shape of violent shouting and also throwing things around, the native is a nightmare to his parents. The native is under medication and treatment in a premier mental institution of the country.

NODAL CONSTELLATIONS

The Moon in association with Rahu or Ketu predisposes a native to schizophrenia. Such association can also be due to the Moon occupying a Nodal constellation.

When the constellation is ruled by a Node, then it is usually more a case of the condition being mild and non-chronic. Nodal constellations are Aswini, Aridra, Makha, Swati, Moola and Satabhisha.

In this context, the classification of Nakshatras into Deva, Manusha and Rakshasa Ganas assumes importance. Deva Gana constellations are Punarvasu, Pushyami, Swati, Hasta, Sravana, Revati, Anuradha, Mrigasira and Aswini.

Manusha Gana Nakshatras are Rohini, Pubba, Poorvashada, Poorvabhadra, Bharani, Aridra, Uttara, Uttarashada and Uttarabhadra.

Rakshasa Gana constellations are Krittika, Aslesha, Makha, Chitta, Visakha, Jyeshta, Moola, Dhanishta and Satabhisha.

Makha, Moola and Satabhisha coming under Rakshasa Gana become dangerous. Aridra under Manusha Gana is relatively less vulnerable. Aswini and Swati coming under Deva Gana are slightly less prone to schizophrenic tendencies than the other Nodal constellations.

MILD CONDITION

A Nodal constellation free of sign-wise association with Rahu-Ketu and also not influenced by benefics causes schizophrenic tendencies of a mild type which aggravate under adverse transits and Dasas. The Dasas of the Moon and Rahu provide fertile soil for the tendencies to sprout. The Bhuktis of Rahu or Ketu or the Moon or Mars in the Dasas of related planets may also trigger the condition.

The periods when the Moon comes under the influence of Saturn's seven-and-a-half year cycle (*sadesathe*) when the 1st, 2nd and 12th houses from Janma Rasi (Moon-sign) are afflicted by transit Saturn's movement through them or when transit Rahu or Ketu touch the Janma Rasi aggravate the tendencies when the native may exhibit all the symptoms. He feels victimized or that he is persecuted by others and may suffer from paranoia and delusions.

A Nodal constellation free of Rahu-Ketu association by sign but aspected or conjoined by Jupiter or Venus destroys the schizophrenic tendencies it could otherwise produce but the natives are prone to mild degrees of fear and suspicion, not really justified by circumstances or people around them.

The Rakshasa Gana Nakshatras produce mindsets that are constantly stressed up making it hard for one to live with them. They can also produce *compulsive obsessive disorder*. They can be excessively demanding and dominating, this urge springing from a deep rooted inferiority complex that continually prompts them to say or do things that they believe will establish and prove they are superior to others.

CHRONIC CONDITION

If these constellations are afflicted by Rahu-Ketu by sign association the ground is laid for chronic schizophrenia resulting in behaviour that becomes increasingly threatening to peace at home involving family members or the marital spouse. Mars or Saturn or both influencing such constellations take the disorder to dangerous degrees.

The Moon is in Aswini, a Nodal constellation in Chart 2. The Moon is in sign association with Ketu, who is also in Aswini. The native is a schizophrenic who has been in medical institutions for treatment but with no marked improvement in her moods of extreme violence when she has inflicted injury on herself. Jupiter, though with the Moon, is separated by more than 28^0 from the latter. The

Chart 2: Born 26-1-1977 at 5h. 52m. at 13 N 05, 80 E 17 with a balance of 6 years 7 months 2 days of Ketu Dasa at birth.

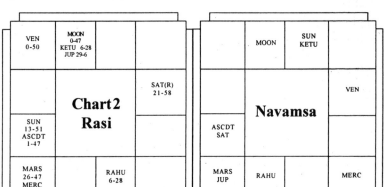

Moon is Vargottama but loses strength due to occupation of a cuspal point. The Lagna lord Saturn's retrogression makes his aspect on the Moon an affliction and does not help.

When it is sign association of Rahu-Ketu and the Moon the affliction is strong and produces chronic schizophrenia. It is this variety that needs to be guarded against in endorsing a chart for marital purposes.

If the Moon is the Manahkaraka or the natural significator of the mind, the 4th house is the Manahstana or the house ruling the mind. If the Nodal afflictions also involve the 4th house, then also there is a strong predisposition to schizophrenic tendencies. In most cases of schizophrenia, apart from the more compelling affliction to the Moon from the Nodal axis, the 4th house also suffers some kind of contamination from either Rahu or Ketu. The Nodes may be across the 4th or 10th houses or the 4th lord may be afflicted by either Node.

In Chart 1, the Moon-Rahu affliction spreads to the 4th house as well, the Moon in this case being the 4th lord. In Chart 2, the Node afflicted Moon occupies the 4th house. With reference to the Moon-sign, the Moon as 4th lord is again afflicted by Rahu.

A Rahu-Moon association produces delusions that take on specific themes based on the rest of the chart and the Moon's position and placement, sign and house-wise, as well as the associations he receives.

AXIS CONNECTION

Approximately one-third of those suffering from schizophrenia exhibit paranoid symptoms. They suffer from over suspiciousness, delusions of persecution or false and irrational beliefs that they are being cheated, conspired against, harassed, victimized or poisoned. And their fears may focus on one or more family member or colleagues depending upon the afflictions in the chart. It has been found in many cases, the person of focus in such cases usually has the schizophrenic's Nodal axis cutting across his own Ascendant. For example, if the Moon-Rahu combination is found in Aries, the focus of the native's suspicions could be a native with Aries or Libra as the Ascendant or Moon-sign. The focus of suspicion could also be one sharing the same sign for the Nodal axis as the schizophrenic. For example, if Rahu-Ketu or Ketu-Rahu occupy Cancer-Capricorn in one's chart, then the one with the afflicted Moon in Cancer-Capricorn could demonise the other with his unfounded suspicions.

Another variety of schizophrenia could produce delusions of grandeur that one is famous, holy, a celebrity or an important personality. All the actions and words of such a native reflect this deluded state of mind. However, the reality being very different, when the responses expected do not materialize from those around the schizophrenic, there can be an aggressive twist to one's behaviour in an attempt to produce the desired effect. This happens when Mars also enters the picture. If it is Saturn, the disappointment at not receiving the attention and importance one deludes oneself is rightfully one's, takes the form of extreme self-pity and withdrawal into a shell. The disorder then takes the form of deep depression. A schizophrenic can, apart from depressive moods, also exhibit extremes of elation. Throw Mercury into the picture and the explanation is clear. *(05.05)* ●

16

SCHIZOPHRENIC TENDENCIES AND LUNAR NODES — II

> 1. Afflictions to 5th house show nature of delusion, obsession or hallucination.
> 2. Jupiter, Venus or Ascendant lord influencing the Ascendant counters afflictions.
> 3. Moon well-placed or in favourable association diffuses schizophrenic tendencies.

POST ADOLESCENCE

SCHIZOPHRENIA SELDOM occurs before adolescence, though even children as young as 5 year olds can develop the disorder but this is rare. It is more common in the post adolescent stage when a person's identity as a male or female becomes distinctly and firmly established by changes in the body and the mind. When this happens one's psychological (and of course, physical) identification with the male or female sex determines one's cravings and urges, both of which come under the generic term *vasanas* coming under the rulership of the 5th house.

FIFTH HOUSE AFFLICTIONS

If the schizophrenic chart with Nodal affliction to the Moon suffers affliction to the 5th house from:-

   1. *Jupiter:* Delusions of scholarship, fame, spirituality and unearthly hankering for money and importance overtake the mind.

2. *Saturn:* Malice and excessive levels of jealousy can erupt due to self-pity springing from intolerance of another's looks, fame, learning, status, position, acquisitions or level of happiness. It can also spring from an extreme morbid pettiness that what one may be suffering from has not happened to someone else and from constantly wishing that the same adversity befall the other.

3. *Mars:* Avarice, vindictiveness and unrealistic levels of greed and a mad urge to dominate and control lead to violent rage and anger.

4. *Venus:* Sexual frustration due to disappointment, rejection or incapacity.

5. *Mercury:* Fear, cowardice and spinelessness leading to anxiety, depression and other morbid states of mind. It also helps fantasizing.

6. *Moon:* Lunacy, simple and plain.

Such afflicted Moon or Mercury or both the Moon and Mercury in the 5th house are often found in the charts of those suffering from hallucinations or hearing voices or seeing apparitions.

The afflictions to the planets influencing the 5th by aspect or occupation can be due to 8th house lordship, retrogression, combustion or association of malefics or a Papakartari Yoga.

When Mars afflicts the Nodal axis, there can be danger of violent behaviour — verbal or physical and it is most likely to be directed at family members. That is why those with schizophrenia can generally never be identified by outsiders; in other words, they may exhibit no abnormal behaviour but appear normal and sane to others while behaving abnormally with those against whom their anger or hate or fear is directed. Saturn's affliction can lead to violence against oneself.

Modern medicine knows of no single cause for schizophrenia and puts it down to a mix of heredity, behaviour and other factors. But, if astrology is made use of, schizophrenic tendencies can be spotted much before any damage to one's own life or another's is caused.

Those close to people with schizophrenia are often unsure of how to respond when such natives make statements that seem strange or are clearly false though for the natives themselves their bizarre beliefs and delusions seem quite real. Since the Moon in such cases is afflicted heavily, it means the native's perceptions are also severely distorted. Therefore as a palliative, instead of going along with the schizophrenic's delusions, one can clearly tell the native that one does not see things the same way or does not agree with the native's conclusions. Such a firm stand, is important and can, to an extent, help alleviate the schizophrenic condition.

STABILIZING INFLUENCE

The Moon though with Rahu or Ketu can still cease to produce schizophrenic behaviour when it receives stabilizing influences. The aspect or association of Jupiter is the best thing to have and counteracts the Nodal afflictions to the Moon. It goes without saying, the stronger the influence, the greater is the nullifying effect. Exalted Jupiter or Neechabhanga Jupiter or Vargottama Jupiter or an otherwise well-placed Jupiter totally erases the malefic effect of Rahu on the Moon.

The Moon if aspected by a favourable Saturn also gets relief from the Nodal affliction. But if Saturn himself be with the Moon and Rahu, it produces a very deep depressive maniac. Saturn's 3rd and 10th house aspects are good. The 7th house aspect of Saturn cannot rein in the affliction as Saturn himself could be afflicted by Ketu in that case.

Mars with the Moon-Rahu combine produces violent reactions — physical and verbal. However, if Mars is in the 10th from such a Moon, it is a balancing constructive influence that works against making the condition chronic. Mars in the 6th or the 7th from such a Moon cannot help but only aggravates the affliction by his adverse 8th house aspect and by his direct 7th house aspect.

Venus with the Node-afflicted Moon reduces the maleficence of the affliction. However, sexual delusions and fantasies could disturb the mind.

Mercury with the Moon under such affliction is no help for the former himself gets afflicted creating in addition Paisacha Yoga which is also a Yoga for mental sickness and distorted perceptions. Mercury in the 7th from the Moon-Rahu combine worsens the Yoga for Mercury too will be influenced by association with a Node. The Sun entering the picture in such a case brings the afflicted Moon into the New Moon or Full Moon phase which, in the absence of balancing factors, does not help mental health. But if Mercury is out of the picture, the Sun appears to be an exception in this context and foregoing his *Kraurya* or *Kruri* nature, strengthens the Moon and straightens him out knocking off the delusions and fears normally characteristic of such affliction. The solar influence on the Ketu-afflicted Moon generates spiritual ardour and evolution. If the Moon is Rahu-afflicted, the Sun is no help but sets the pitch for dementia.

ASPECT OF ASCENDANT LORD

The aspect of the Ascendant lord or the sign-dispositor on the Moon is a counterbalancing factor only so long as the Ascendant is strong or the Ascendant lord or the Moon-sign lord himself is not afflicted. In Chart 1*, the aspect of Mars as Ascendant lord does not help as being in the 12th from the Ascendant which in turn itself is afflicted by 11th lord Badhaka retrograde Saturn's aspect. He becomes incapable of countering the Nodal affliction to the Moon. Retrograde or combust planets influencing the Rahu-Ketu afflicted Moon aggravate the schizophrenic condition.

In Chart 3, the Rahu-Ketu axis is across the Ascendant and the Moon-sign. The 4th house from the Ascendant Scorpio is Aquarius which is free of Nodal affliction. The 4th house from the Moon is Leo which also is free of any Nodal connection. The native is in perfect mental health. The fact the Ascendant is strong aspected by its ruler Mars and the Moon is also fortified by virtue of his occupation of exaltation sign and own Nakshatra Rohini are factors that have contributed to the mental health of the native. The Moon as a strong

---

* See page 149 for Chart 1

Schizophrenic Tendencies and Lunar Nodes — II

Chart 3: Born 30-8-1975 at 14h. 03m. at 18 N 58, 72 E 50 with a balance of 3 years 4 months 24 days of Moon Dasa at birth.

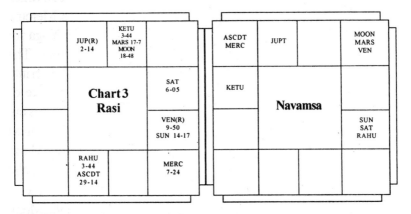

9th lord joining Ascendant lord Mars is also a factor that works against schizophrenic tendencies.

The combined aspect of Mars, Jupiter and Saturn is the best thing to have for a Rahu afflicted Moon. The 4th house must also be beneficially disposed. The suspicious nature and unfounded fears of the schizophrenic mind are then replaced by a mix of shrewdness, practicality, foresight and wisdom. Such a native is no naive fool but a careful judge of men and matters. Rahu here gives an uncanny intuition, not a morbid grandiose ego or unfounded fears making the native practical and endowed with vision and foresight.

LINKING SCIENCE TO ASTROLOGY

Modern science traces schizophrenia to different causes which seem to find astrological confirmation.

1. *Genetic Factors:* There is no clue as of now to understand how the gene for schizophrenic predisposition is transmitted. But astrologically, the Moon-Node combination has been known to recur in different generations and also in the extended family of any one generation.

2. *Chemical Activity in the Brain:* The astrological factor of Rahu (who rules all chemicals, potions and by extension, chemical

activity) and his association with the Moon who rules all body fluids, including brain fluid, is an important ingredient in combinations for schizophrenia.

3. *Abnormalities in Brain Structure:* Fluid filled cavities in the brain are known to be enlarged or certain sections of the brain are found to be of decreased size in schizophrenics. Rahu rules abnormality. Brain imaging done by modern techniques of those whose charts have afflicted Moon-Rahu-4th house features can perhaps show structural abnormalities confirming the astrological diagnosis.

A casual remark from a friend, an eminent cardiologist, set me thinking on the decisiveness nature of Rahu's role in schizophrenia. Referring to the pontiff of a deeply revered spiritual seat in the country, our friend eugolised on the previous pontiff and his efforts in revitalizing the organisational life of the pontificate at a time when it was in a shambles. "His own Guru" explained my friend, "developed schizophrenia and with him paying no attention to the spiritual seat and its well-being, a state of inept lethargy had set in. But his disciple was a very dynamic personality and worked hard to put the Math back on the rails".

SPIRITUAL STATE, NOT ABERRATION

We were baffled by the friend's statement. A man greatly respected in medical circles and who has held prestigious posts in the medical world, he would not have said anything so casually unless he knew what he was talking about. As a medical expert, his opinion could not be dismissed easily. But we knew for sure, as did countless devotees of the pontificate, of the great heights of spirituality the Guru had reached. And those devotees who had recognised his greatness were no mean credulous people. They were men of the world, several holding prestigious and responsible posts such as of Governors, Chief Justices of the Supreme Court and High Courts, High Court judges, leading legal luminaries, technocrats, scientists, bureaucrats, and of course, great philosophers, many of them from the west too. Surely, they could not all have been so naive as to be overawed and carried away by a schizophrenic as to consider him a spiritual giant and realized soul. His spiritual flights into the Supreme Consciousness, it was always known, could never fit into the corridors of reason. We had ingested the great soul's chart but the friend's remarks rankled us no end until we thought one more look at the chart and we would know for sure, whether he was a victim of schizophrenic delusion or in a state of superconsciousness or Nirvikalpa Samadhi. In the latter case "mystical experience, verbal expression, mental cognition and intellectual reasoning" are said to cease to function but in schizophrenia, all these are very much active but in an aberrational state.

Chart 4: Born 16-10-1892 at 7h.12m (LMT) at 13 N, 76 E with a balance of 1 year 9 months of Ketu Dasa at birth.

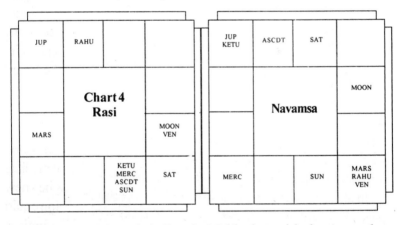

The sage's Moon is in Leo in Makha but with the Ascendant lord Venus (Chart 4). He is aspected by exalted 2nd and 7th lord Mars. Rahu-Ketu are nowhere near the Moon. The Moon is safe in every sense. But what about his occupation of the Node-ruled Nakshatra Makha? Makha comes under Rakshasa Gana. But this is parried by association with Venus, doubly favourable by virtue of his Ascendant lordship and exchange of signs with the sign-dispositor Sun. But Mars is aspecting the Moon. This is not an affliction except that it could have shown up as a quick temper in the early years of life and a fiery spirit of independence. The native was no schizophrenic but a spiritual master soaring in the skies of Advaita.

CONDITIONS

Summing up, schizophrenic tendencies are likely under the following astrological circumstances:

(a) The Moon is with Rahu or Ketu and the 4th house from the Ascendant or the Moon-sign also has Nodal affliction — *direct* or *indirect* — severe and chronic condition.

(b) The Moon is in a Nodal constellation with Rahu or Ketu and the 4th house from the Ascendant or the Moon-sign also has a Nodal affliction — *direct* or *indirect* — severe and chronic condition.

(c) The Moon is in a Nodal constellation and the 4th house from the Ascendent or the Moon-sign also has Nodal affliction — *direct* or *indirect* — less severe.

(d) The Ascendant or its lord has Nodal affliction. The 4th house from the Moon-sign or from the Ascendant has Nodal affliction — *direct* or *indirect* — less severe but recurring.

The term *direct* has been used for cases where the affliction is due to the Nodal axis occupying the 4th house either from the Ascendant or the Moon-sign. The term *indirect* refers to cases where the affliction is due to the Nodal axis afflicting the Ascendant lord or the 4th lord either from the Ascendant or the Moon-sign.

In all cases where the afflictions for schizophrenic tendencies are present, the following factors tend to diffuse the afflictions resulting in normal mental health.

(a) The Ascendant is occupied or aspected by its lord (unafflicted), Jupiter or Venus.

(b) The Moon is aspected or associated with Jupiter or Venus.

(c) The Moon is waxing or otherwise powerfully placed.

As always, it is best not to draw conclusions on isolated combinations but on the strength of the entire chart. (*06.05*) ●

SECTION II

METEOROLOGY AND SEISMOLOGY

SUN AND AGRICULTURAL ACTIVITY

1. *Solar movements influence terrestrial happenings.*
2. *Sun's entry into constellations changes weather patterns.*
3. *Solar ingress into sign has a bearing on crops.*

NO ROOM FOR EXPERIMENT

MODERN ASTRONOMY though recognised as a science is quite different from other recognised sciences and their methods in that there is practically no room for experiment in it which is one of the important criteria in defining what makes science, the others being observation, inference and verification. Astronomy is mostly, rather only, observation where all findings are derived from measurement and recording of radiation. Radiation, in turn, is not just light rays but is more sweeping in connotation and includes electromagnetic waves of all wave lengths — visible light, x-rays, gamma rays, ultraviolet and infrared rays, millimetre waves and radio waves. There may be many other kinds of radiation in the universe but for now, these are the different kinds of radiation that modern science has discovered and is therefore *limited* to in its understanding of the universe.

Astronomical studies that were limited to optical observations until only a few decades ago are now exploring new dimensions due to digital computers and satellite communications. The Hubble telescope launched by NASA and the Keck 10 metre telescope in Hawai have enlarged the window on the universe. New tools will be invented and new methods discovered, there is no doubt, in future by the scientist which will without question bring in more information on now unknown areas and levels of the pulsating universe to which we belong. Until then, let us be humble and not rule out phenomena in the universe, more particularly in the solar system currently baffling the modern intellect. To this realm of phenomena that is apparent, but not quite within the reach of the 21st century intellect, belongs Jyotisha or astrology, the science of correlations between human life and activity and celestial happenings. To dismiss this connection with arrogant scepticism as is being done in some quarters may serve no purpose except to pander to the puny human ego. On the other hand, every attempt, whether in tune with accepted methods of investigation or along innovative channels that may not have the sanction of orthodox science today would reflect an honesty of purpose and an open mind, the two true characteristics of a scientific intellect that could lead us closer to a better understanding of this connection.

SCIENCE MUST GROW, NOT STAGNATE

Science and with it thinking must grow and not stagnate. And for this what is required is an evolving intellect which has always been the characteristic of the ancient Indian thinker. This is equally true of the modern day genuine scientist though it may not apply universally to the scientific community. In ancient Europe, science evolved with old concepts and theories being replaced by new ones but the pace was extremely slow hampered as it was by the Church's dominance.

ANCIENT INDIAN TRUTH CONFIRMED

Aristotle, the Greek philosopher, thought that the earth was stationary and the Sun, Moon and stars revolved round it. This was in 240 B.C. Ptolemy in the second century A.D. improved on it and came up with a cosmological model. Later about 1514 A.D., Copernicus set aside these models and proposed one in which he put a stationary Sun in the centre and the earth and other planets revolving round it in circular orbits. Galileo and Kepler further worked on it. Unfortunately the former was put on the stake for his theories which at that time contradicted the theories endorsed by the Church. But Kepler's laws of planetary motion based on Tycho Brahe's work obtained respectability. Issac Newton then enunciated his universal law of gravitation explaining mathematically Kepler's laws. By now, the scientists had found the Sun was one of many such stars moving in orbits of their own and kept in place with their mutual gravitational pull. Once again, this discovery was only confirmation of the ancient Indian truth सप्त दिशा नाना सूर्या: (*there are many Suns in the several directions*).

JYOTISHA — STUDY OF RADIATION

Though these developments in astronomy let it grow in the West the growth was not really of an appreciable nature for these later day men of science failed to relate the earth and its denizens to what they discovered in the skies. They simply could not see the connection between man and his cosmic environment. It was the intellectual privilege of the ancient Indian to discover the equations between man and cosmos and call it Jyotisha. Jyotisha is the study of *Jyoti*, loosely translated as light or visible light rays but more aptly applying to radiation in general in all its forms, discovered or not so far by modern science and its impact on human life.

All of Nature, the ancient masters found, was in a state of constant and continual flux but which could be identified as coming under the three states of Srushti, Stithi and Samhara or creation, sustenance and destruction. And these changing moods of Nature, they found, were sourced in the Sun, the hub of the solar system inspiring them to pay homage to this golden orb with the well-known chant,

उदये ब्रह्मस्वरूपे मध्दाने तु महेश्वर: ।
अस्तमाने स्वयं विष्णु: त्रयी मूर्तिदिवाकर: ॥

Not only are these lines rich in poetry but also in scientific information for it is the Sun that is responsible for all life on the earth, its growth and destruction. Apart from such hoary scriptural references to this three-fold role of the Sun, the later day Indian astronomer cum savant of astrology Varahamihira who lived at least 2000 years ago also refers to the Sun the same way — लोकानां प्रत्योद्भवस्थिति विभु: — in his **Brihat Jataka**. This is a treatise on astrology dealing with that branch of Jyotisha known as Hora or predictive astrology. Varahamihira has also written two other encyclopaedic works **Panchasiddhantika** dealing with mathematics (spherical astronomy) and **Brihat Samhita** which covers mundane astrology. Varahamihira deals with different aspects of Jyotisha at a time when the West (largely read as the Greeks) was grappling to understand simple phenomena like the sunrise and sunset believing the Sun was a huge ball of fire suspended between the sea and the mountains.

Brihat Samhita deals with astronomical phenomena in connection with mass destinies and includes such subjects as weather, rainfall, agriculture, natural calamities — earthquakes, drought, volcanoes — prices, commodities and many other topics that have bearing a large groups of people and geographic regions. In many places of the work, Varahamihira frankly admits he is recording only what the ancients have discovered and enunciated indicating thereby the antiquity of the knowledge collected by ancient Indian thinkers.

SUN'S TRANSIT OF STARS

The movements of the Sun and stars, for example, were carefully studied and correlated with terrestrial phenomena by the Indian thinker or Rishi. Detailed observations of the rising and setting of particular stars coinciding with sunrise or sunset led to the discovery of certain clues to atmospheric conditions. They found that when the Sun traversed the star Krittika (*Pleiades*) the summer heat intensified. Krittika is associated with Agni, the Fire god in Vedic texts (कृत्तिका नक्षत्रमग्निर्देवता). Usually this passage of the Sun of the Zodiacal arc from $26^0\ 40'$ to 40^0 coincides roughly with the period between May 11th to May 25th when the Mercury shoots up to the highest each year. The Sun's conjunction with Aridra ($66^0 40'$ to 80^0 of the Zodiac) was seen to be accompanied by angry and strong winds. Aridra is said to be ruled by Rudra, the god of Fury (आर्द्रानक्षत्रम् रुद्रो देवता). The Sun's entry into Swati Nakshatra (*Arcturus*) which marks the Zodiacal arc from $186^0 40'$ to 200^0 was found to generate the most terrible cyclonic weather with winds ripping through coastal and adjoining areas devastating vast stretches of land. Swati is said to be ruled by Vayu, the Wind god (स्वाती नक्षत्रं वायुर्देवता). This is usually about the middle of October through most of November. Depending upon the other afflictions to which the Sun was subject to when transiting these asterisms, the degree and severity of the season was found to vary.

WEATHER CONDITIONS

The Sun and Saturn moving towards a conjunction show the winter that follows becomes extremely severe and in areas of snowfall, the temperatures dip dangerously low over an extended period. Likewise, when Mars moves to a conjunction with the Sun in the month of spring or just preceding it, the summer thereafter will be marked by frightening heat waves. If it is Jupiter who conjoins the Sun, dry weather prevails setting ready conditions for drought. In fact the combustion of Jupiter (July 10, 2002 to August 1, 2002) just as soon as it set foot into the solistial sign Cancer has already proved the connection right with near drought conditions prevailing in different parts of the country with delayed and scarce rains in these regions. Mercury with the Sun whips up windy but dry weather. With Venus, rainfall increases. Rahu makes for the severity of whichever season may be prevalent then while Ketu causes weather patterns to escalate wildly and frequently.

AGRICULTURAL CROPS

Agricultural crops are seen to respond to solar movements and influences.

According to Varahamihira,

वृश्चिकवृषप्रवेशे भानोर्ये बादरायणेनोक्ता: ।
ग्रीष्मशरत्सस्यानां सदसद्योगा: कृतास्त इमे ॥

XL-1 ॥

The good and bad Yogas, planetary configurations, that have been declared by Sage Badarayana for the growth of summer and autumnal crops, at the time of the Sun's entry into Scorpio and Taurus are explained here.

Scorpio and Taurus appear to have some unusual significance in affecting crops during the Sun's transit of these signs. The Sun's transit of Scorpio is said to affect summer crops while that of Taurus, autumnal crops. And the nature of influence on the crops is said to be determined by the positions of the other planets with reference to the Sun.

Favourable Conditions

भानोरलिप्रवेशे केन्द्रैस्तस्माच्छुभग्रहाक्रान्तै: ।
बलवद्धि: सौम्यैर्वा निरीक्षिते ग्रैष्मिकविवृद्धि: ॥

XL-2 ॥

If when the Sun enters Scorpio, benefics are in Kendras from him or conjoin him, it is said to be favourable for summer crops.

अर्कास्तिते द्वितीये दलाव्ल्यूरंलल्लल् युगपदेव वा स्थितयो: ।
व्ययगतयोरपि तद्ब्रिष्पत्तिरतीव गुरुएक्ष्टया ॥

XL-4 ॥

If Venus or Mercury (both of whom cannot occupy any Kendra other than the 1st from the Sun) are in the 12th from a Scorpio Sun, it is said to help summer crops. If such a Sun is also aspected by Jupiter, then farmers can look forward to a bumper harvest.

लाभहिबुकार्ययुक्तै: सूर्यादलिगात्सितेन्दुशशिपुत्रै: ।
सस्यस्य परा सम्पत् कर्मणि जीवे गवा: चाग्रया ॥

XL-6 ॥

Venus in the 11th, the Moon in the 4th and Mercury in the 2nd from the Sun show excellent crops. This becomes possible when Venus transits Virgo, Moon Aquarius and Mercury

Sagittarius at the Sun's ingress into Scorpio. *Such a combination additionally benefits cattle if at the same time Jupiter is in Leo in the 10th from the Sun.*

Unfavourable Conditions

कुम्भे गुरुर्गवि शशी सूर्योलिमुखे कुजार्कजौ मकरे ।
निष्पात्तिरस्ति महती पश्चात्परचक्रभयरोगम् ॥

XL-7 ॥

If the Sun's entry into Scorpio takes place when Jupiter is in Aquarius, the Moon is in Taurus (obviously, a waxing Moon with Pakshabala) and Mars and Saturn combine in Capricorn, though the crop itself will be good, there is danger of disease ruining it or destruction through enemies attacking.

मध्ये पापग्रहयो: सूर्य: सस्यं विनाशयत्यलिंग: ।
पाप: सप्तमराशौ जातं जातं विनाशयति ॥

XL-8 ॥

Likewise, if there is a malefic in the 7th from the Sun or if the Sun in Scorpio is surrounded by malefics, the result is destruction of the crops.

जामित्रकेन्द्रसंस्थौ क्रूरौ सूर्यस्य वृश्चिकस्यस्य ।
सस्य विपत्ति कुरुत: सौम्यैर्दृष्टौ न सर्वत्र ॥

XL-10 ॥

Malefics Mars and Saturn in the 7th and any other angle (Kendra) from the Sun in Scorpio will destroy the crops, and if they be aspected by benefics, the destruction would not be total or as widespread.

Applying these principles, the Sun's entry into Scorpio in 2000 would give us clues to the kind of summer crops in 2001.

Saturn was in Taurus at the solar ingress into Scorpio in November 2000 (Chart 1).

The year 2001 was indeed very bad for agriculture with many small farmers driven to desperation and suicide. Families in Orissa were reported to have been subsisting on a single meal a day, sometimes surviving on edible roots and greens from the forest. There were stories of families living on the poisonous rotten mango kernels, knowing full well its harmful effects but still callous to its dangers unable to bear the pangs of hunger. Jupiter too was in Taurus and though the plight of farmers in Orissa was pathetic, it was not so bad in other states, thanks to the Jupiterean presence in a Kendra from the Scorpio-Sun should which show destruction of crops.

Chart 1 : Solar Ingress into Scorpio : 14-11-2000 at 17h. 16m. at 28 N 39, 77 E 13.

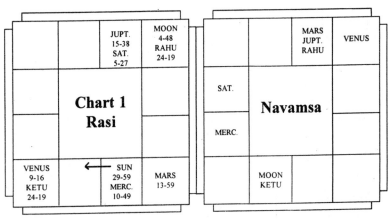

The 2001 solar ingress into Scorpio took place on 14-11-2001 (Chart 2). There is Saturn in Taurus in the 7th from the Sun which should show destruction of crops.

DISMAL - METEOROLOGY FAILURE

And how did the Scorpio-Sun of 2001 actually affect agriculture in 2002 in India? On July 24, 2002, the Union Agriculture Minister Ajit Singh officially admitted that the country was on the **"verge of the most widespread drought in 12 years"** with Rajasthan experiencing zero rainfall in **all of its districts**, Orissa with **28 out 30 districts** affected, Andhra Pradesh facing **49 per cent deficient rainfall**, Maharashtra reeling under a **17-day dry spell** delaying all sowing operations as also Tamil Nadu farmers facing **acute water problems**. Madhya Pradesh, Chattisgarh, Uttar Pradesh, Punjab, Haryana and to a lesser extent both Karnataka

Sun and Agricultural Activity

Chart 2 : Solar Ingress into Scorpio : 14-11-2001 at 23h. 30m. (IST) at 28 N 39, 77 E 13.

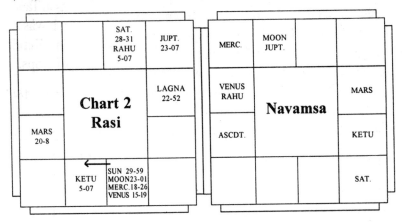

and Kerala were also facing drought-like conditions. **320 out of 524 districts monitored by the Agricutlure Ministry had insufficient rainfall.** It was clear Central, North and North-Western India as also parts of South India had been hit by a severe drought with the South-West monsoon playing truant with a few initial deceptive showers in June 2002. All attributable to the Scorpio Sun's affliction from Saturn.

Contrast the astrological factors and their results given by Varahamihira with what the India Meteorological Department (IMD) had to say with its prediction for 2002 of a "normal monsoon for the 14th successive year" and the actuality being witnessed across the land. The Department's long range forecast had said "the 2002 monsoon was likely to be around 101 per cent of its average value". It had predicted 104 per cent rainfall for North-East India which today is facing its worst drought. Yet the weather scientists would not accept this reality but continued to hold out hope describing the drought conditions "as a usual phenomenon" even as the situation worsened with each passing day. These assertions of the weatherman are said to be based on the *16 Parametric Model* of the IMD with 11 out of 16 parameters favouring a normal monsoon. Despite such an optimistic forecast, millions of farmers around the country continued to watch the dry skies day after day with practically little hope left with crops of cereals like bajra, jowar and maize and of pulses, oilseeds and paddy already damaged. A devastated farmer in Rajasthan with its blistering skies and parched earth summed up very aptly the IMD's performance, "Anyway what would they tell us that we do not already know. Donkeys do a better job of predicting monsoons than the army of weather scientists. They have an old saying in these parts that when a donkey's ears stand on end, rain is on the way. This year, they have barely flapped." *(10-02)*

AUTUMNAL CROPS

The solar ingress into Taurus and the influences that act on the Sun in this sign give a clue to the fate of autumnal crops. Benefics in Kendras (quadrants) from the Sun or the aspect or association of benefics with the Sun conduces to a good harvest (ग्रीष्मकसस्यविवृद्धिभवति). Likewise, when the Sun is in Taurus, if the Moon and Jupiter occupy Aquarius and Leo or *vice versa*, the autumnal crop prospers. When Venus or Mercury or both are in the 2nd or 12th, the autumnal crops grow well and if Jupiter also aspects such a Sun, a bumper crop can be expected. When Mercury and Venus flank Taurus with the Sun in this sign and Jupiter is in Scorpio, excellent crops are foreseen. The results will be good if, Venus is in Pisces, the Moon is in Leo and Mercury is in Gemini for a Taurus Sun.

Bad results implying destruction of crops are to be expected when malefics Mars and Saturn occupy the same positions given for benefics for a Taurus placed Sun. Mars and Saturn in the 7th or in a Kendra from a Taurus Sun destroy the crops. The aspect of benefics on the Sun may reduce the degree of destruction. Malefics Mars and Saturn in the 6th and 7th from the Sun though productive of good crops would make their prices slump.

The solar ingress into Taurus in 2002 occurred on 13-5-2002 (Chart 3). Malefics Mars and Saturn with Rahu are in Taurus. Additionally, benefics Venus and Mercury are also in Taurus. The Moon is in his sign of exaltation. The prospects for autumnal crops

Sun and Agricultural Activity

Chart 3 : Solar Ingress into Taurus : 13-5-2002 at 14h. 35m. at 28 N 39, 77 E 13.

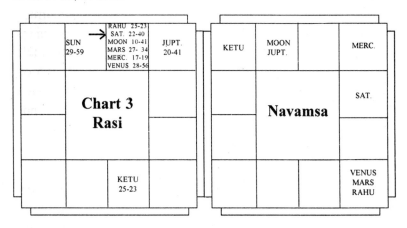

appear to be fairly good. But because of the presence of malefics, there may be destruction of crops in some parts due to disease or pests. The situation for autumnal crops therefore appears much better than for the summer crops in our country in 2002. (*11-02*) ●

SOLAR MOVEMENTS AND MUNDANE EVENTS

1. Sun's change of course disturbs political systems.
2. Sunspots trigger natural calamities.
3. Solar maxima and minima affect global weather patterns.

CHANGE OF COURSE

THE MOVEMENTS of the Sun are not confined to influencing atmospheric conditions and agriculture alone but also have a definite bearing on other terrestrial phenomena. According to Varahamihira, the Sun's Northern and Southern movements and variations in them which can be verified by actual observation (प्रत्यक्षपरीक्षणै:) are important too. He describes the results and consequences if the change in the Sun's course occurs premature to what had been observed during his time — the Southern course from the beginning of Cancer and the Northern from the initial point of Capricorn implying that sometimes, the Solistices could occur before touching these points.

If the Sun's change of course Northwards should occur before he reaches Capricorn, it implies destruction of countries in the west and south. If the change of course Southwards precedes the Sun's entry into Cancer, it would harm the countries in the east and west.

VARAHAMIHIRA ON SUNSPOTS

It fell to the credit of Varahamihira, perhaps for the first time in the world, to record in detail the phenomenon known as sunspots and solar activity. Though he does not refer to any particular instance of this phenomenon, he writes of it with the familiarity of one who has studied them and their results on humanity extensively. Nowhere in any other civilization of the world is the subject given such treatment as in Varahamihira's works. In contrast early descriptions featuring in European recordings are not later than the 12th century and apart from describing sunspots carry no other details. The Latin *Chronicle of John Worcester* talks of two sunspots seen on December 8, 1128 A.D. with a colourful drawing accompanying the description of two spots on the disc of the Sun. Chinese recordings predate these by many centuries but with no drawings until after 1400 A.D. All sunspot sightings were done with the naked eye depending upon favourable atmospheric conditions.

For example, one description says "a black vapour" was seen on the Sun. Medieval Arab astronomers too recorded sunspots between 840 and 1130 A.D. In all these ancient observations made outside of India, only the sightings were noted.

NUMBER AND RESULTS

Varahamihira, on the other hand, describes sunspots and their implications in quite some detail.

तामसकीलकसंज्ञा राहुसुता केतवस्त्रययस्त्रिशंत् ।
वर्णस्थानाकारैस्तान्दृष्ट्वोर्के फलं ब्रूयात् ॥ ७ ॥

He says there are 33 Ketus called Tamasakilakas or dark (shadowy) shafts which he calls the offspring of Rahu. And when they appear on the solar orb, their effects are to be declared according to their colour, position and shape.

तेषामुदये रूपाण्यम्भ: कलुषं रजोवृत व्योम ।
नगतरुशिखरामर्दो सशर्करो मारुतस्कन्ध: ॥ ९ ॥
ऋतुविपरीतास्तरवो दीप्ता मृगपक्षिणो दिशां दाहा: ।
निर्घातमहीकम्पादयो भवन्त्यत्र चोत्पाता: ॥१०॥

Varahamihira says their appearance on the solar disc presages evil (ते चार्कमण्डलगता: पापफला:....). Some of the results he attributes to the appearance of these shadowy shafts on the Sun are : *water turning turbid* or there is a rise in harmful organisms in water threatening the spread of water borne infections; *the sky being filled with dust* or the occurrence of dust storms and whirlwinds; *whipping winds devastating fields and breaking the tops of trees and mountains* — avalanches, cyclonic winds and storms that can ravage both cities and the countryside; *trees and creepers showing effects contrary to the seasons* or vegetation being adversely affected; *animals and birds getting affected by extreme heat* (or cold) *and viruses* or forest life as well migratory patterns of birds getting adversely affected; *the appearance of flares in the quarters* or volcanoes and outbreak of fires, especially forest fires; and the *occurrence* of *thunderbolts, earthquakes and other unusual phenomenon* or destructive rains, seismic disasters, sea storms and other natural calamities.

Briefly put all that Varahamihira is saying is that the appearance of sunspots or solar flares has a bearing on terrestrial affairs such as public health, animal and avian life as also other life forms and on the incidence of natural calamities and disasters.

REGIONS FACING SUN

Further on, Varahamihira describes the results of solar flares on regions facing the Sun when they are sighted. Such results include sufferings of kings, changes in mass psychology with great restlessness with its attendant evils overtaking people leading to revolutions and political upheavals, mass migrations, famine, drought, increase in crime and rivers and water sources drying up. Apart from these, depending upon the specific shape of the sunspots, results are spelled out. If it takes the shape of a rod, *death of a national leader*; if that of a truncated body, *outbreak of epidemics*; if of a crow, *increase in crime*; if of a nail or wedge, *famine and shortage of food*. If the sunspot takes the shape of an umbrella, it shows a *change of leadership at the country's helm* while if it is hazy and vaporous in shape, it can indicate *destruction of human life on a large scale* possibly due to war, bombing, genocide etc.

Depending upon the direction from which the shafts (spots) make an appearance, their colour, the season — rainy, summer, winter — and different categories of people are said to be affected. An interesting detail is provided where the result of a 12 year drought is correlated to the appearance of sunspots when the solar disc is deep blue (colour of the peacock's plume) in colour. Clearly a connection between sunspots and mundane happenings has been identified by Varahamihira.

MODERN ASTRONOMY ON SPOTS

What does modern astronomy say of sunspots? Sunspots are regions of the Sun that are a few thousand degrees cooler than the gas surrounding them. They, therefore, radiate less energy into space and appear darker. Astronomers have been recording the spots appearing on the Sun for more than 200 years now and have discovered a cyclic rise and fall with maxima and minima recurring about every 11 years. Though the sunspot cycle is of about 11 years, the interval from the maximum in the cycle to the next can be as low as 7 years or as large as 17 years. When a sunspot maxima occurs, the surface of the Sun is violently disturbed and particles and radiation of all wavelengths are emitted. Whenever there is a build-up and explosive release of magnetic energy in the solar atmosphere, there is a peak period in the sunspot cycle. These explosive outbursts of energy hurl particles and radiation into the solar system. These are called solar flares. For example, there was a series of powerful solar flares in August 1972. A spectacular eruption of luminous gas occurred on August 11 which rose to a height of 250, 000 kilometers above the solar surface in about 20 minutes arriving at the earth about 2 days later. Some of the charged particles in the solar wind penetrated the earth's magnetic field while others were repelled by it, both effects combining to create a major disturbance in the geomagnetic field tripping electric power lines in several places in Canada and the United States.

SUNSPOT CYCLE AND CLIMATE

There has been growing evidence of a correspondence or connection between the sunspot cycle and global climate. During a long period of solar inactivity known as the Maunder Minimum (1645 - 1745), the lowest temperatures were recorded on earth. In fact it was known as the *Little Ice Age* (1500 to 1850). In July 2000, a huge solar flare produced by a large sunspot group caused serious effects on earth that included radio blackouts on the sunlit side of the planet which happened to be the United States. Other effects included "single-event upsets, noise in imaging systems, permanent damage to exposed components and detectors and decrease of solar panel currents". These were noted no doubt but studies to trace the connection between solar activity and human life have been woefully negligible leading to a lack of proper understanding of the equation between the two.

MAXIMA, VIRUSES AND AVIAN LIFE

Scientists in NASA had recorded in June 2000 itself that the Sun was nearing the peak of its 11-year cycle of activity. This solar maximum is a two to three year period around peak when the solar activity is most turbulent buffeting the earth with powerful solar gusts. About the same time Indian newspapers reported that researchers were baffled by a new "worrisome" virus that could not be neutralised by existing vaccines. The *Indian Express* report said :

Work was on how to fight the virus which affects kidneys Indian Council of Medical Research (ICMR) Director General Prof. N. K. Ganguly said while addressing scientists at the fifth International Conference on "Molecular Epidemiology and Evolutionary Genetics of Infectious Diseases (MEEGID-5)" in Hyderabad. The ICMR chief also revealed that 11 new viruses had been discovered in India in the recent past. Efforts were on to develop vaccines for the new viruses. However, the discovery of new viruses and strains has underlined the need for scientists to continuously monitor infections, he said. Listing out some of the achievements of Indian scientists, particularly in molecular epidemiology, he said researchers have been able to indigenously solve the mystery behind the mass dying of vultures. Three viruses were initially identified as the cause behind these deaths and the Vigna virus was zeroed in on as the main cause of the death of nature's scavengers. Similarly, a Srinagar-based scientist had found a Hepatitis virus by employing epidemiological approach. The connection between cholera and global warming (El Nino) had also been firmly established by the Indian scientists by this approach, he said.

Indian scientists were baffled by the discovery of new viruses and the sudden dying of birds. Somehow, it does not appear to have occurred to them that there could indeed be a link between solar eruptions and terrestrial life and which Varahamihira has clearly enunciated in his **Samhita**. At the other end of the spectrum, Western astronomers are only now unravelling the fringe of the impact of heightened solar activity on global life and weather. For instance, scientist Claus Frohlich (June 2002) has shown in his paper *Solar Irradiance Variability and Climate* a direct correlation between solar maxima and drought. And according to him, sunspots affect the earth's atmosphere and air circulation as well as monsoon winds. A solar maxima year is almost always followed by drought the next year. In fact, the year 2001 was a solar maxima year and 2002 has seen the worst drought in 12 years in India. *(10-02)* ●

VARAHAMIHIRA'S LAW OF SUNSPOT ACTIVITY AND EVENTS ON EARTH

> 1. Russian research confirms Varahamihira's Law of Sunspot Activity and Terrestrial Life.
> 2. Political upheavals are linked to solar maxima.
> 3. Solar magnetic activity is influenced by heliocentric positions of planets.

SOLAR CYCLES AND EPIDEMICS

A RUSSIAN HISTORIAN Professor A. L. Chiszhevsky researched deeply into solar phenomena confirming Varahamihira's Law of Sunspot Activity and Terrestrial Life. Professor Chiszhevsky made a study of all the important epidemics and plagues since the last 500 years and found a close connection between their occurrence and the 11-year sunspot cycle. Briefly put, he discovered that epidemics such as influenza have an average periodicity of 11.3 years which is the same as the sunspot cycle. He found the first wave of the epidemic occurred about three years after every sunspot maxima and that the virulence of the micro-organisms varied in direct relation to the electrical tension in the atmosphere. He was able to establish a link between major political developments — revolutions, wars, agitations, political upheavals and migrations — and the sunspot cycle through correlation curves.

Dr. Chiszhevsky has also established an incidence of correlation between sunspot maxima and cardiovascular troubles. But unfortunately for Chiszhevsky, his findings only led to his being deported to the Siberian concentration camps by Stalin. The Russian dictator was furious that cosmic forces were being identified as being responsible for epochal events and which went against the Communist theory of class struggle and dialectical materialism as being the forces behind social revolution and upheavels. Later when Khruschev came to power, Chiszhevsky was brought back but by then he was too close to death to work anymore.

MAXIMA AND POLITICAL UPHEAVALS

If we examine the charts of sunspots and pay particular attention to the maxima which have occurred during the — first six decades of the last century, we will find that there have been six peaks of sunspot activity in the years 1905, 1917, 1927 and 1939-40, 1951-52 and 1962-63. The maxima which occurred in 1905-06 coincided with the revival of powerful democratic movements, wars and revolutions throughout the world.

The next great peak of sunspot activity occurred during the period of the years 1916, 1917 and 1918 which was the culmination of the First World War and which resulted in the great Bolshevic and Communist revolution which broke out in Russia and had great repercussions throughout Europe and the world, with attendant outbreaks in Germany and Hungary. Emperors and kings lost their thrones and great social disturbances were experienced everywhere. The third period of maximum sunspot activity occurred in 1927-29 and in England, a Socialist Government came to power while during the same period a great civil war raged in China and Gandhi's Civil Disobedience Campaign in India disturbed the hemisphere of Asia. The great period of unrest seemed to be largely centred on this occasion in the Far East.

"There seems to be some law at work here in that the main effect of the sunspot activities is to alternately disturb first Far Eastern countries and in the next maximum period Western countries. It will be observed that the 1905 maximum was largely felt in the Far East while the 1917 maximum was mainly centred upon the European scene. Then came the 1928 maximum which again affected the Far East and finally came the fourth maximum in 1939-40 when the Second World War broke out in Europe. This fourth maximum was certainly the most destructive and disturbing that Europe has experienced for centuries and the wholesale uprooting of populations and displacing of humanity has caused untold misery to millions of human beings. There is no doubt that humanity *en masse* is seized, as it were, by some malignant force of periodic occurrence, a force which at present seems entirely outside of human control for its origins are cosmic and no matter how all-powerful dictators and leaders of men may be, they, themselves, are as such the victims of this self-destroying and disturbing force as the common man.

"Statistics have also revealed that the most intense sunspot activity occurred in the following years : 1778, 1788, 1804, 1816, 1830, 1837, 1848, 1871, 1883, 1894, 1905, 1917, 1928, 1939 and 1951. Persistent activity was also observed during the years 1961-62. With these dates before us we could tabulate the more important events which history has recorded for us during these years. They are as follows :

"1778 - France declares war against Great Britain; 1788-89 - The French Revolution began; 1804 - Spain declares war against Great Britain; 1815-16 - Battle of Waterloo, Napoleon banished, Algiers bombarded; 1830 - Revolution in Paris, uprising in Warsaw; 1836-37 - Louis Napoleon attempts an uprising at Strasbourg; 1848 - General revolutionary movement throughout Europe; Riots at Milan, Messina, Munich, Paris; 1860 - Battle of Voluturno, French and British forces occupy Tienttin; 1871- Paris capitulates, Great Fire at Chicago; 1882-83 —Alexandria bombarded; 1894 - Japan declares war against China; 1904-05 - Russo - Japanese War commences; 1917 - First World in progress, Russian Revolution; 1928-29 - Earthquake in Greece, Vesuvius in eruption; 1937-40 - Second World War in progress; 1950-51 - Assam Earthquake, Korean War and America's humiliating debacles in Asia; and 1962-63 Chinese Invasion of India and Kennedy's assassination.

"For these facts in European history we are indebted to an American friend. Statistics are being collected to connect important happenings in Indian history with sunspot maxima. Can such an array of wars and revolutions, earthquakes and floods, the greatest and most devastating the world has ever known, be dismissed as coincidence? It will be noticed that the period quoted above covers almost 260 years and takes into account every one of the most intensive solar disturbances."[1]

BIRTH AND DEATH OF THE SUN

A high altitude solar-monitoring satellite orbiting Earth, the Solar Heliospheric Observatory (SOHO), recorded a large and novel event on the surface of the Sun — an eruption one million times the energy of Earth's most powerful earthquake on January 6, 1997. This solar storm threw an enormous fast travelling cloud of ionized (magnetically charged) gas in the direction of Earth, where scientists who were watching it, were held spellbound. Several days later on January 10 and 11, the cloud encountered our planet's magnetosphere, the protective aura that surrounds and shields Earth, "ringing it like a bell".

The solar event also had many interesting astrological ramifications as well.

The space storm totally destroyed a 200-million dollar Telstar communications satellite. On Earth, the Space Environment Center in Boulder, Calorado, U.S.A., issued a first-ever "Space storm alert". The actual storm, known as a coronal mass ejection, hurled on enormous cloud of magnetically-charged ionized gas, known as plasma, in the Earth's direction. Such clouds have the potential to affect the geomagnetic fields that surround and protect our planet

---

1. Planetary Influences on Human Affairs — Dr. B.V. Raman.

from cosmic rays and other forms of radiation. Similar storms in the past are known to have affected spacecraft in orbit, short-wave communications on Earth and electric power grids. In the "great geomagnetic storm" of March 13, 1989, for example, the entire North-east quadrant of North America was plunged into a blackout that caused voltage collapse and equipment malfunction proving clearly we are linked and susceptible to changes in space weather. For approximately twelve hours, the solar storm bashed earth, reversing the normal direction of the Earth's field.

In a *Science News* article, dated the exact day of the solar cloud's arrival at Earth, physicist Alexander Szalay of John Hopkins University reported that "Sound waves in the early universe may have helped orchestrate the striking pattern of galaxy clusters and huge voids seen in (space) today." Early in the universe's formation, acoustic oscillations — sound waves of specific frequencies — interacted with early forming atoms, "imparting their energy into density fluctuations that later developed into galaxies and galaxy clusters." According to *Science News*, these findings "propose that only acoustic waves with certain frequencies become part of galactic structure." Recent investigations have also shed light on the relationship between sound and the function of the Sun itself.

"To understand the Sun's cycles, we must look deep inside the star, to where its magnetism is generated... these oscillations which can be tens of kilometers high and travel a few hundred meters per second, arise from sounds that course through the solar interior.... when these sounds strike the Sun's surface and rebound back down, they disturb the gases there, causing them to rise and fall, slowly and rhythmically, with a period of about five minutes."

These sound waves evidently account for the rhythmic breath-like pulsations that the Sun exhibits. The Sun is now seen as a very dynamic and complex entity with cycles and rhythms of its own. Astrologically, this explains the symbolism of the Sun as ruler of Leo which rules the organ heart, the pump of the human body. If the heart is the centre of the physical body, the Sun is the centre of our solar system which again emphasises that without the Sun or the cosmic heart, earth would be rendered non-existent.

MAGNETIC ACTIVITY AND HELIOCENTRIC POSITIONS

There is mounting evidence that the magnetic activity of the Sun is linked to certain heliocentric positions of planets. John Nelson, a senior scientist with the Radio Corporation of America, in the 1940's found that when Venus, Earth, Mars, Jupiter and Saturn were almost in a straight line with the Sun or when they were at 90^0 angles from each other as seen from the Sun, conditions for radio reception and transmission were bad. He had been given the task of finding out ways to forecast the occurrence of increase in solar activity, since it was known that such increases caused disruption of radio communications. He also found that when the angles between these planets (as seen from the Sun) were 30^0, 60^0, 120^0, 150^0 conditions for radio reception were good.

Another scientist Paul Jose of the U.S. Air Force found that there was a link between maximum of solar activity and the movement of the Sun about the common mass of the center of the solar system.

Two other scientists, Jane B. Blizard and H. P. Sleeper, who undertook projects on solar activity prediction on behalf of the NASA (NASA was interested in such predictions because it was known severe activity on the Sun could damage sensitive communication satellites, so they wanted to avoid such activity when launching devices). Jane Blizard was able to show that when planets are in conjunction or opposition as seen from the Sun, then solar magnetic storms are very violent. Just as the Sun and Moon raise tides in the oceans, Blizard suggested that planets can also raise tides in the gases of the Sun which is called sunspot activity.

Changes in the sunspot activity or solar flares affect the earth's magnetic field. This is due to the solar wind which carries the corpuscular radiation (energy bursts from Sun) to the earth.

THEORY TO EXPLAIN ASTROLOGY

Therefore, using these facts, Dr. Percy Seymour[2], an astro-physicist from England, has a theory to explain astrology — the equation between man and planet.

(1) Planets affect the solar activity in specific ways. The heliocentric positions of planets affect solar gases just as the geocentric positions of the Moon cause tides and in other ways affect the human body.

(2) The solar cycle affects the geomagnetic field.

(3) Changes in the geomagnetic field affect life on earth (tides, weather patterns as also chemical activity in the brain and glandular secretions which, in turn, affect human behaviour).

(4) Therefore, there is a correlation between the Sun's radiation, planetary movements and human activity and life.

(5) The foetus at birth, points out Dr. Seymour, is phase-locked to planetary positions at that point of time due to resonance.

Arnold Mayer, a scientist and a member of the British Association for the Advancement of Science and the author of *The Circulation of Matter, Electrons and Stars,* explaining the correlation between planets and earth, writes : "So gradually do we become accustomed to these changes brought about by the tidal forces from day-to-day that they would perhaps escape our notice altogether, so far as the Sun is concerned, were it not for the fact that we are occasionally 'caught out' as it were by the action of the spring tides, which suddenly overflow and flood our public buildings at high tide on the Thames.

"The reason for this is that when the Sun and the Moon are in conjunction they are both concentrating their forces on the same part of the globe at the same time; this, added together, accounts for the abnormal conditions. Under normal conditions, there is always a high tide at London fifty minutes after the Moon has passed the meridian, *i.e.,* the position of the Sun occupies everyday at noon, Greenwich time.

---

2. The Scientific Basis of Astrology — Dr. Percey Leegnour

"Since astrology deals more particularly with the effects of heavenly bodies upon mankind, it does not require much imagination to appreciate the fact that this conjunction of the Sun and the Moon does definitely affect a child born during conditions of this nature. For, within our own bodies, we have innumerable glands whose work is the secretion of harmones. These are for ever adjusting themselves in harmony with our chemically changing environment without and are responsible for our emotions, desires, mental balance, rate of growth and length of life on this planet".

According to Dr. V. Gore, "It is but commonsense to say that the planetary positions of the Sun and the Moon which affect the sea-water causing tides are bound to affect all the store of fluids on the surface of the earth or contained in vegetable kingdom or in human beings.

"The blood is not only a fluid but contains the same salts that are dissolved in the ocean and that too practically in the same proportion. It contains nearly 80% sodium, 4% calcium and 4% potassium. The percentage with respect to magnetism varies. This similarity between the composition of salts in blood and in sea-water is not accidental. Life has its origin in the sea and the earth's early history is one of the sea life and as such it should be susceptible to the same influence of the Moon and the Sun.

"Hindu astrologers have given predictions for each day of the lunar month or Tithi. What is a Tithi ? It is nothing but the angular distance between the Sun and Moon in multiples of 12. For the eighth day, that is, when the Sun and the Moon are 90^0 apart they have said *Ashtamyam Vyadhinashastu or Ashtami Vyadhi Nashini*. That is, the eighth day removes the disease or cures the ailments. On this day the Sun and the Moon, being 90^0 apart, diminish each other's attraction on the fluids. The blood in the human beings remains thus comparatively in an undisturbed state from the outside influences and any medicine newly started on this day is bound to be more effective if it is properly chosen and that is why there is the importance of this day being *Vyadhinashini*."

If our activities, physiological and psychological, are regulated by glandular secretions which in their turn are conditioned by chemical changes occurring in Nature, then it follows that since these chemical changes are brought about by solar radiation and planetary alignments, these same forces affect man and earth.

Sunspots have been observed over many years and modern authorities conclude, as a result of researches, that "the existing abnormal changes which we call weather have their origin mainly in the variations of solar radiations." Many places on earth show more rainfall during sunspot maxima than during sunspot minima.

So long the Sun and what happens within him continue to intrigue the scientist on the why and how of it, so long will our understanding of the Universe remain veiled. And with it, our understanding of how astrology works. Until then, let us plod on slowly but surely in the path shown by ancient Indian masters on the workings of the Sun and his family and their impact on Earth and her inhabitants. Let us not, in arrogant conceit, refuse to use this body of knowledge to widen our intellectual horizons and alleviate human suffering by a foreknowledge of what is to occur. *(02-03)* ●

20

PLANETS AND SUMMER CROPS

> 1. *Sun's ingress into Scorpio affects summer crops.*
> 2. *Sun's ingress into Taurus affects autumnal crops.*
> 3. *Planets in Kendras from such a Sun determine drought or rain.*

SUPERIOR MERITS OF JYOTISHA

VARAHAMIHIRA begins his treatment of the subject of rainfall and weather in **Brihat Samhita** (XXI-1) with the Sloka

अन्नं जगत: प्राणा: प्रावृट्कालस्य चान्नमायत्तम् ।
यस्मादत: परीक्ष्य प्रावृट्काल: प्रयेत्नेन ॥

meaning, *as food forms the very life of living beings and as food is dependent on the monsoon, it should be investigated carefully.*

Never was the truth of this astrological maxim brought home more forcefully then in 2002 when the country faced its worst drought in nearly 12 years. With the monsoon failing and crops withering away in large parts of the land, the farmers had never had it so bad in recent memory. The Indian Meteorological Department set up precisely to forecast weather with heavy funding from the Central Government, as always, blundered with its prediction of a normal monsoon based on its *16 Parametric Model.* This was even as district after district in Central, North, North-west and South India reeled under blistering skies with no trace of rain. Even as the weather scientists stood baffled not knowing where their model had misled them, the student of Jyotisha was able to clearly understand the situation from principles of mundane astrology. Perhaps it was for such reasons that Varahamihira was prompted to ask *"Is there a science superior to this (astrology) by knowing which alone one gets the power of visualizing the past, present and the future even in this Kali Age which destroys all good things ?"* before beginning the discussion on the technical principles of weather forecasting in **Brihat Samhita** (XXI-4) when he said:

किं वात: परमन्यच्छास्त्रं ज्यायोऽस्ति यद्विदित्वैव ।
प्रध्वंसिन्यपि काले त्रिकालदर्शी कलौ भवति ॥

The aim of all sciences is to predict. Some predict with relative precision, some less so. Many fail in their predictions and only too often as is usually the case with meteorology and seismology. Yet there is not even a whimper of a protest against these failures which often mean, disastrous consequences for the population. Nor is there any condemnation of these white elephant sciences from any quarters. On the other hand, astrology, a science with much greater potential, is treated with derision. The reasons, of course, are only subjective. It attracts ostracism and resistance to even its mere description as science and entry into the comity of sciences. Despite such prejudiced treatment, in performance it excels many recognised sciences. The astrological forecast of the drought of 2002 is a case in point.

Down South, the drought last year brought in its wake tensions between Karnataka and the neighbouring state of Tamil Nadu with the Cauvery river reduced to almost a measly trickle. Frayed tempers, gimmicks like meaningless Padayatras and near total non-governance in Karnataka and angry protests from Tamil Nadu over the acute shortage of water made headlines day after day for over four months. The drought, the most acute in years, remained a burning issue throughout with the Tamil Nadu Government seeking additional release of the Cauvery waters. The matter was even taken before the Supreme Court. And the apex court's rap on the Karnataka

Government made it worse for an already beleagured State Government caught in several other mind boggling complicated issues. Now that again the days are getting hotter farmers everywhere are hoping things will not be as bad this year. Will 2003 be good, bad or worse than 2002 for the summer crops in Karnataka and Tamil Nadu ?

SOLAR INGRESS INTO TAURUS

The best clues to an answer to this question are to be found in solar movements which are closely interlinked with weather patterns and climatic changes which in turn affect agricultural crops. The Sun's ingress into Taurus is said to impact autumnal crops through changes in weather, pests and other forces. Likewise the Sun's entry into Scorpio is said to influence crops in the following summer. It was by using these clues that we were able to anticipate the drought of 2002 as early as in our editorial "World Trends and Tensions in 2002-2003" dated December 5, 2001, when we said, analysing the planetary factors for the lunar year Chitrabanu: "Worsening drought conditions in drought-prone areas, destructions of crops from pests ...." and specifically said "The Cauvery water tensions escalate" and which have since been proved by the tensions that rattled between the two States over the river waters.

OTHER FACTORS

The Sun is the most important factor in determining weather conditions. According to Varahamihira, the following planetary dispositions at the solar ingress into Scorpio are favourable for summer crops :-

1. Benefics occupy Kendras from the Sun;
2. Strong benefics aspect the Sun;
3. Strong benefics conjoin the Sun;

Here, the important factor, especially under *Condition 3*, is to ensure the benefic conjoining the Sun is strong. In other words, such a planet should not be combust when in the same sign as the

Sun. This applies specifically to the natural benefic Jupiter and not so much to the other two natural benefics Mercury and Venus whose distances from the Sun cannot go beyond a certain orb.

4. Jupiter and the Moon are in Aquarius or Leo jointly or severally;
5. Venus or Mercury is in the 2nd from the Sun;
6. Venus or Mercury is in the 12th from the Sun;
7. Venus and Mercury are both in the 2nd from the Sun;
8. Venus and Mercury are both in the 12th from the Sun;
9. Venus or Mercury is in the 2nd or 12th from the Sun who is aspected by Jupiter.
10. Venus and Mercury are in the 2nd and 12th from the Sun who is aspected by Jupiter.
11. Mercury and Venus flank Scorpio and Taurus is occupied by the Moon and Jupiter.
12. Jupiter is in the 2nd from the Sun.
13. Venus is in the 11th, the Moon is in the 4th and Mercury is in the 2nd from the Sun. That is Venus should be in Virgo, Moon in Aquarius and Mercury in Sagittarius.
14. Venus is in the 11th, the Moon in the 4th and Mercury in the 2nd with Jupiter in the 10th (Leo).

When these planetary conditions obtain with reference to the Sun, then crops will be good with conditions such as drought and shortage of water due to lack of rains being unlikely. These planetary conditions also protect the crop from destruction through pests and other forces which could include invading forces, plundering and pillage.

BUMPER CROPS AND BENEFICS

If Jupiter, Mercury and Venus as well as the Moon are all favourably placed fulfilling the conditions above, then it points to extremely good rainfall and bumper crops.

Apart from the solar ingress into Scorpio, the Sun's movement through Aries, Taurus or Gemini in conjunction with or aspected by benefics also helps crops.

Similarly when the Sun enters Scorpio, there are certain planetary dispositions which can lead to destruction of crops with shortage of water as the main reason.

The following planetary positions obtaining at the time of the solar ingress into Scorpio show destruction of crops with the weather gods playing traunt and destructive pests getting stimulated (restless) sufficiently to damage crops :

1. Jupiter in Aquarius, Moon in Taurus and Mars and Saturn in Capricorn;

2. Malefics on both sides of Scorpio, that is, malefics in Libra and Sagittarius. Such malefics can be Mars and Saturn.

3. A malefic, Saturn or Mars, in the 7th from Scorpio, that is, in Taurus.

4. A malefic such as Mars or Saturn in the 2nd from Scorpio in Sagittarius with no benefic aspects.

5. Mars and Saturn in a Kendra from Scorpio or in Aquarius, Taurus or Leo. The two malefics can occupy any of these signs either singly or jointly.

6. Mars in the 6th and Saturn in the 7th from Scorpio.

7. Saturn in the 6th and Mars in the 7th from Scorpio.

CONDITIONS FOR DROUGHT

The drought of 2002 was clearly reflected in the planetary pattern at the solar ingress into Scorpio in 2001 (Chart 1). Saturn is in the 7th from the Sun which is bad for the crops. Mercury and Venus in the 12th show good crops but Saturn in the 7th outweighs these influences to set the tone for the drought. According to **Brihat Samhita** (XL-8),

पाप: सप्तमराशौ जातं जातं विनाशयति ।

or, *a malefic in the 7th (from the Sun) destroys the crops.* This is exactly what happened in large parts of the two States.

The chart read with the Ascendant also taken into consideration can also help one understand the situation better. The Ascendant in Cancer is aspected powerfully by malefic, even if exalted, Mars.

Chart 1: Solar Ingress into Scorpio : 14-11-2001 at 23h. 20m. (IST) at 28 N 11, 77 E 13.

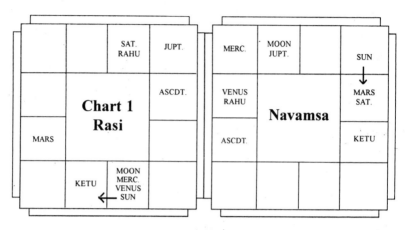

The Ascendant lord in the 4th is moving towards New Moon. The Tithi was Amavasya, a New Moon day, also unfavourable. The influence of Mars shows tensions and frustration which of course were evident throughout 2002 on the issue of water shortage.

GOOD MONSOON IN 2003

The solar ingress into Scorpio in 2002 has Mercury in Scorpio and Venus (R) in Libra (Chart 2). Jupiter in Cancer in exaltation aspects the Sun in Scorpio. According to **Brihat Samhita (XL-4)**,

अर्कात्सिते द्वितीये बुधेश्वा युगपदेव वा स्थितयो: ।
व्ययगतयोरपि तद्बिष्यत्तिरतीव गुरुद्दष्टया ॥

When Venus or Mercury or both be posited in the 2nd or the 12th from the Sun in Scorpio, summer crops will grow well. If, in addition, the Sun be aspected by Jupiter there would be bumper crops.

It is clear from this Sloka that Venus in the 12th from the Sun and Jupiter's aspect on the Sun from Cancer point to good summer crops in 2003. Mercury is in Scorpio itself and can be deemed favourably placed. But what about Ketu in Scorpio and Rahu in Taurus ? Can the Nodes be taken to operate as maleficsᅠ?

Chart 2: Solar Ingress into Scorpio : 15-11-2002 at 5h. 30m. (IST) at 13 N, 77 E 35.

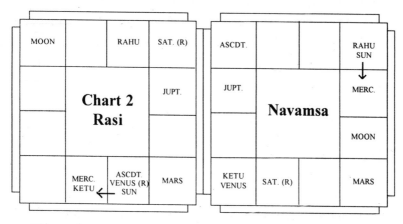

Throughout the chapter, Varahamihira takes cognisance only of the Sun, Moon, Mercury, Venus, Jupiter, Mars and Saturn and there is no reference whatsoever to the Nodes. Therefore, it may be redundant, at this stage of our understanding of these principles, to consider them as absolute malefics. However, it may not be a travesty of astrological logic to consider any planet associating with them as being afflicted and therefore, if benefic rendered slightly less so and if malefic, made worse.

In the chart in question, Mercury in Scorpio is with Ketu and can be hypothetically deemed to be blemished by such association. But at the same time since Mercury receives the aspect of exalted Jupiter, this blemish can be assumed to have been overcome. In contrast, Chart 1 has Saturn's maleficence aggravated by association with Rahu.

Therefore, in a broad sense, we can infer the summer crops of 2003 may not be threatened with destruction or damage through weather forces. One may recall that in 2002, tens of thousands of acres of standing crops in Tamil Nadu were destroyed due to acute water shortage. Going by Varahamihira's principles, the crops in Tamil Nadu and Karnataka come under favourable influences and therefore it may be logically deduced that rainfall could be normal.

Going a step further the Ascendant is a benefic sign Libra occupied by its ruler Venus and with exalted Jupiter in the 10th house. The Moon in the 6th is a waxing Moon with the Tithi being Sukla Ekadasi or the 11th lunar day of the bright half which are deemed favourable by general principles.

PANCHAMI CLUE

The weekdays, according to classical works, also have some bearing on crops and this is with reference to the weekday prevailing on the 5th lunar day after the dawn of the lunar new year or on Chaitra Sukla Panchami. If the 5th day of the lunar month of Chaitra falls on a Monday or Thursday there will be equitable distribution of rain throughout the year and crops will thrive; if Wednesday, it shows disturbed rains. If the 5th day of Chaitra coincides with Aridra, famine conditions prevail during most of the year accompanied by winds; Friday — destruction of crops; Saturday or Tuesday — want of rains and famine indications. But these clues are secondary to those obtained from the Scorpio solar ingress chart.

Chaitra Sukla Panchami in Swabanu is from 11h. 05m. on 6-4-2003 (Sunday) to 13h. 27m. on 7-4-2003 (Monday). Therefore Panchami coincides with a Monday which shows equitable distribution of rain in the lunar year (April 2003 to March 2004).

The Ascendant rising at Bangalore, capital city of Karnataka, is 17^0 56' Libra in Pisces Navamsa while that rising at Chennai (Tamil Nadu) is 20^0 26' Libra in Aries Navamsa. For both, the Ascendant Libra has its lord Venus in itself while exalted Jupiter is in the 10th house. Therefore, this is indicative of a far better year for both States. Karnataka may have sufficient rainfall and enough water to share with neighbouring Tamil Nadu, where also the rain gods may not frown this year. The indications for summer crops in both States are optimistic. *(06.03)* (*Written on 5-4-2003*). ●

TSUNAMI PREDICTION
— AN ASTROLOGICAL MODEL — I

> 1. *Planetary movements lead to increased solar activity.*
> 2. *Increased solar activity triggers geomagnetic disturbances. Geomagnetic disturbances affect the earth and its interiors.*
> 3. *Such disturbances can result in the shifting of tectonic plates.*

FIRST RECORDED TSUNAMI

IT WAS THE thirty-sixth year of Yudhistira's reign after the great Mahabharata war. The Yadava clan had destroyed itself in a mad drunken brawl. Lord Krishna had shed his mortal frame and the holy city of Dwaraka had suddenly become a mass grave. The sea which had been watching the tragedy of the Vrshni clan's self destruction could no longer hold itself back.

The sea, which had been beating against the shores, suddenly broke the boundary that was imposed on it by nature. The sea rushed into the city. It coursed through the streets of the beautiful city. The sea covered up everything. Even as they were all looking, Arjuna saw the beautiful buildings become submerged one by one. Arjuna took a last look at the mansion of Krishna. It was soon covered by the sea. In a matter of a few moments it was all over. The sea had now become as placid as a lake. There was no trace of the beautiful city which had been the favourite haunt of all the Pandavas. Dwaraka was just a name: just a memory.*

And with Lord Krishna gone, it was time for Adharma to move in. For Kali to take over. This transition which marks the onset of the age of moral decadence and is also of chronological significance has both scriptural and astronomical angles to it. The time cycle that began now was called Kali Yuga, the cycle of Kali and was defined by the conjunction of all the planets at the *First Point of Aries* or the initial point of the Zodiac. This definition of Kali Yuga is given in the **Surya Siddhanta** and also by the great mathematician Aryabhata I.

This conjunction would involve the major planets Saturn, Jupiter and Mars apart from the minor planets and the luminaries and it would be at the junctional point of the watery sign Pisces and the fiery sign Aries. Astrologically speaking, such a unique celestial event apart from its chronological importance, could have far reaching repercussions on terrestrial affairs. Seen in this light, the tragedy at Prabhasa and the sea rushing in and submerging the city of Dwarakapuri were nothing but the result of that rare *ashtagraha kuta* (8-planet conjunction) occurring in the *First Point of Aries*. The celestial event triggered powerful subterranean seismic activity in the Indian ocean in the region of the Arabian sea throwing up gigantic tidal waves that flooded the coastal city of Dwarakapuri submerging it under the seas. To the unbiased chronicler, this could be the first recorded *tsunami* in the history of India.

RELIABILITY OF ASTROLOGICAL MODEL

Tsunamis and other natural disasters have always succeeded in taking the geologist, the seismologist, the scientist, the met prophet, the oceanographer and the volcanologist by surprise. And this element of surprise has invariably proved terribly, terribly costly in

---

***Mahabharata** by Kamala Subramanian

terms of both human lives and suffering. **The astrological model, as on date, appears to be the only one that can provide any kind of clue to such a disaster, much before it strikes, and prepare a country to face the challenge.** Yet no attempt has been made in any quarter to take cognizance of planetary factors in the prediction of natural disasters. This obstinate reluctance to take note of the performance potential of astrology has no genuine reason behind it except a concealed contempt for it dictated by the intellectual fashion of the day. There is no spirit of inquiry, no scientific temper but only revolting levels of bias. No scientist in our country can be absolved at least in part of the moral responsibility for what happened on December 26, 2004 and its aftermath. If only the science community had taken note of astrological methods, the magnitude of suffering could definitely have been vastly reduced. Such grave calamities as the country saw on the Indian coastline, we hope, will prompt the real scientist in India to put aside his blinkers and approach this ancient discipline of Jyotisha to help reduce human suffering.

Tides, high and low, that sweep every day and produce waves, are caused by the gravitational pull of the Sun and the Moon. But tidal waves that assume dangerous proportions are said to result from an abrupt shifting of the sea floor and vertical displacement of the overlying water. Such waves known as *tsunami* are a common occurrence in Japan and the Pacific seas and have been several times anticipated in the pages of THE ASTROLOGICAL MAGAZINE in the past. But their occurrence in the junctional region of the Indian and Pacific oceans as to impact the Indian coastline is a rare event. However, for *tsunamis* to occur, it is necessary there should be severe seismic activity. Depending upon the epicentre of the earthquake, the *tsunami* may reach the coastline or could get diffused if occurring in mid-ocean. The first point to be emphasized in understanding the occurrence of a *tsunami* astrologically is to look for factors that are used to identify earthquakes.

Earthquake prediction has so far been evasive to seismology

though it offers theories which serve no useful purpose. According to the theory of the mechanism of plate tectonics, earthquakes are said to result primarily from the *heavings and groanings* of the earth's crust, although some of these are said to originate from deep within the mantle. Giant crustal plates (plate tectonics) are driven by convection currents on a hot plastic mantle. When they move past each other rubbing against each other in the process or move away at mid-ocean ridges, they allow hot magma to well-up from below leading to volcanoes, continental drifts and earthquakes.

WHY TECTONIC PLATES SHIFT

Original techniques of theoretically predicting powerful earthquakes are claimed by some Russian scientists. Studies of earthquakes of magnitude over 6 on the Richter scale have shown that at the moment of a quake, subsoil waters exhibit a sharp increase in the content of elements like helium, argon and uranium. But every time there is an increase in the content of these elements, an earthquake need not occur. But beyond such theories and years of research running into millions of dollars, there has been no progress in the matter of prediction either datewise or areawise with any degree of precision. Nor does seismology tell us why tectonic plates suddenly decide to shift. **Science will tell you there can be no effect without a cause but it will not tell you what causes tectonic plates to shift because it has no answer. Astrology provides the missing link with its parameters of planetary phenomena.**

Satellite observations have shown that due to the interaction between the magneto-sphere and the ionosphere, powerful currents are generated which constitute a single electrical system embracing the entire near earth space. Using the current system, the kinetic energy of the solar wind — the plasma flux ejected from the Sun — can be pumped into the thermal energy of the upper atmosphere. These processes lead to various geomagnetic disturbances which affect the earth and its beings as well as its interiors in different ways. They are also said to generate cyclonic and anticyclonic winds at the polar regions. The ejections and winds from the Sun and their intensity in turn are influenced by planetary movements. It is a commonly known fact that solar activity peaks up and down in a 11-year cycle which is closely related to Jupiterean movements. Jupiter, in turn, is influenced by forces generated by the endless orbitings of planets around the Sun forming different angles and aspects not only with the Sun but also with one another. This theory of planetary movements influencing earthquake activity finds mention in Varahamihira's **Brihat Samhita.**

PLANETARY INFLUENCES TRIGGER EARTHQUAKES

Varahamihira quotes others and their theories in Chapter 32, Sloka 1 when he says:

क्षितिकम्पमाहु रेके बूहदन्तर्जलनिवासिसत्वकुतम् ।
भूभारखित्रदिग्गजविश्रामसमुद्भवं चान्ये ॥

meaning, *some sages hold that an earthquake is brought about by huge animals living in the waters of the oceans (or, shall we say cyclonic forces) while others declare that it is the result of the heaving of the elephants of the quarters that are tired by the weight of the earth.*

The quarters are the directions or space and could imply disturbances in the atmosphere due to planetary forces (unknown, rather unseen). The use of the term *heaving* is remarkable because it fits in with the theory of tectonics where the huge plates are said to *groan and heave*. Their cause was attributed to powers (forces) from the quarters (diks) or space.

Sanskrit is a language that is not easy to comprehend except by those well-versed in it. So, its correct interpretation especially where ideas of science are involved is possible only by those who are proficient in both Sanskrit and science. And this is where the difficulty lies. Many brilliant scientific truths couched in allegorical expression are often missed and only the *puranic* significance retained.

In the next Sloka, Varahamihira says:

अनिलोऽनिलेन निहतः क्षितौ पतन सस्वनं करोत्यन्ये ।
केचित्त्वदृष्टकारितमिदमन्ये प्राहुराचार्याः ॥

meaning, *yet other sages like Vasistha declare that it is caused by the atmospheric wind (cosmic wind?) colliding with another and falling to the earth with a booming sound. There are still others like Vriddhagarga who maintain that it is occasioned by some unseen power.*

According to theories advanced by the Institute of Space Research of USSR Academy of Sciences, the solar energy impinging on the atmosphere results in geo-magnetic disturbances which affect the earth's equilibrium in different ways. And what can अनिलोनिलेन mean but this?

The Russians have also discovered that during earthquakes large-scale waves and inhomogeneities originate in the ionosphere. This is said to be due to the impact of acoustic waves on the ionosphere. They have also found that during the flight of spacecrafts near seismic regions, the onboard equipment registers specific electro-magnetic noise. Do we see a parallel in the lines क्षितौ पतन सस्वन (falling to the earth with a booming sound)?

According to Parasara,

आदिजमतः परं भयमपनयाम्यनिलानला म्बुपतिमदभिसष्ट कम्पाः कदाचिज्जगति ।
हिताहितवेदिनो भविष्यन्तीन्यर्कचन्द्र ग्रहणग्विकतचारजांश्च कम्पानाहुः ॥

meaning, *this shows that earthquakes are caused by eclipses of the luminaries, unnatural phenomena occurring in the planets and special movements of the heavenly bodies.*

It is therefore clear that earthquakes are triggered by planetary alignments, eclipses and major aspects and phenomena. (*03.05*) ●

TSUNAMI PREDICTION
— AN ASTROLOGICAL MODEL — II

1. *Planetary conditions for earthquakes precede tsunamis.*
2. *Heliocentric aspects too can be relevant.*
3. *Watery signs, watery Nakshatras and watery planets get stimulated.*

HELIOCENTRIC POSITIONS OF PLANETS

IN ORDER to understand the tsunami that struck the South Asian region in December 2004, we must take note of the fact that the year 2004 ended with one of the most unusual eruptions on the Sun. A gigantic coronal mass ejection (CME) originated from the solar surface where pent up magnetic energy was unleashed and flung into space as plasma (super heated gas). Recorded on instruments aboard the Solar and Heliocentric Observatory (SOHO) spacecraft, this burst of solar energy into space was visible to scientists over a nine-hour stretch. This event on the solar surface occurring at about the same time the earthquake-*tsunami* struck Asia assumes significance in our understanding of the phenomenon.

John Nelson[1] a senior scientist with the Radio Corporation of America, who had been entrusted with the task of determining changes in solar activity, as it was known such changes could affect radio reception, found as far back as in the 1940's that when Venus, Earth, Mars, Jupiter and Saturn were in almost straight line with the

Sun or when they were at 90^0 angles from each other as seen from the Sun, solar activity increased. He also found that when the angles between these planets (as seen from the Sun) were 30^0, 60^0, 120^0 or 150^0 solar activity was low and conditions for radio reception and transmission were good.

Two other scientists Jane B. Blizard[2] and H.P. Sleeper who undertook projects on solar activity prediction on behalf of the NASA also found that when planets are in opposition or conjunction as seen from the Sun, then solar magnetic storms are very violent. Blizard said just as the Sun and the Moon raise tides in the oceans, planets could also raise tides in the gases of the Sun. Changes in the sunspot activity result in coronal mass ejections (CME) which can affect the earth's magnetic field through the solar wind which carries the highly charged corpuscular radiation or energy bursts from the Sun to the earth. These charged particles in turn impinge on the magnetic field of the earth generating forces of extraordinary magnitude and intensity disturbing the earth's interiors (molten metal) resulting in subtarranean volcanoes and seismic activity. Based on this theory and planetary parameters including the October eclipses of 2004, we were able to anticipate in "World Trends and Tensions in 2004-2005" appearing in the THE ASTROLOGICAL MAGAZINE, January 2004, conditions that could "... tend to stimulate tidal waves, seismic tremors and subtarranean volcanoes in the Pacific seas and islands" which is what happened when the quake hit Sumatra on December 26, 2004 in the junctional region of the Indian and Pacific oceans. Mars and Venus were in exact heliocentric conjunction. Though it is the geocentric positions that are of the greatest importance in a study such as this, major heliocentric aspects occurring about the period defined by geocentric planetary parameters also assume relevance. What is attempted here is only a theory that has been further developed on DR. RAMAN's pioneering work on the subject.

The *Table* shows the heliocentric positions of planets at the time of occurrence[3] of severe earthquakes of magnitude 7 and above on the Richter scale in the region of the Indian ocean in the last 120 years. Charts 1 to 5, as always, show the geocentric planetary positions for these quakes.

ROLE OF HELIOCENTRIC MARS

Case 1
(a) Mars at 17^0 11' 03" Libra is in conjunction with Venus at 17^0 09' 14" Libra.

(b) Mars at 17^0 11' 03" Libra trines Earth at 12^0 06' 49" Gemini.

(c) Moon is at 12^0 06' 49" Gemini in *Aridra*.

Case 2
(a) Mars is at 18^0 22' 25" Capricorn in opposition to Venus at 26^0 30' 06" Cancer.

(b) Mars at 18^0 22' 25" Capricorn has no apparent aspect with Earth at 12^0 22' 46" Sagittarius but it is interesting to note Mars is in earthy Capricorn.

(c) Moon at 12^0 22' 46" Sagittarius is in *Moola*.

Case 3
(a) Mars at 16^0 42' 40" Gemini has no aspect with Venus at 19^0 15' 17" Scorpio. But Venus occupies a Martian sign.

(b) Mars at 16^0 42' 40" Gemini is conjunct Earth at 18^0 38' 40" Gemini.

(c) Moon is at 18^0 38' 40" Gemini in *Aridra*.

Case 4
(a) Mars at 19^0 29' 23" Sagittarius is conjunct Venus at 16^0 28' 53" Sagittarius.

(b) Mars at 19^0 29' 23" Sagittarius trines Earth at 27^0 37' 52" Leo.

(c) Moon is at 27^0 37' 52" Leo in *Uttaraphalguni*.

Case 5
(a) Mars at 13^0 02' 21" Leo has no apparent aspect with Venus at 22^0 03' 03" Cancer, but the two planets are in adjacent signs.

(b) Mars at 13^0 02' 22" Leo is square Earth at 23^0 24' 23" Taurus.

(c) Moon is at 23^0 24' 23" Taurus in *Rohini*.

These cases, though by no means exhaustive, appear to suggest a clear pattern involving Mars, Bhumikaraka (described in astrological texts as born of Earth) and Earth and Venus. Perhaps,

Heliocentric Longitudes of Planets

Case	Magnitude Richter Scale	Earth	Moon	Mars	Mercury	Jupiter	Venus	Saturn
1 26-12-2004	8.9	12° 06' 49" Gemini	12° 06' 49" Gemini	17° 11' 03" Libra	23° 36' 42" Leo	14° 02' 36" Virgo	17° 09' 14" Libra	0° 41' 45" Cancer
3 31-12-1881 Andaman Nicobar	8.1	12° 22' 46" Sagittarius	12° 22' 46" Sagittarius	18° 22' 25" Capricorn	29° 41' 13" Scorpio	10° 09'11" Taurus	26° 30' 06" Cancer	28° 10' 57" Aries
2 26-6-1941 Andaman Nicobar	7.4	18° 38' 40" Gemini	18° 38' 40" Gemini	16° 42' 40" Gemini	6° 18'30" Sagittarius	4° 39' 56" Taurus	19° 15' 17" Scorpio	20° 20' 18" Aries
4 9-3-1928 Indian Ocean	8.1	27° 37' 52" Leo	27° 37' 52" Leo	19° 29' 23" Sagittarius	8° 06' 19" Libra	22° 36' 01" Pisces	16° 28' 53" Sagittarius	21° 44' 04" Scorpio
5 12-8-1951 Indian Ocean	7.9	23° 24' 23" Taurus	23° 24' 23" Taurus	13° 02' 21" Leo	8° 03 06" Aries	23° 27' 50" Pisces	22° 3' 03" Cancer	16° 04' 01" Virgo

the heliocentric position of Mars could have a stimulating or exciting effect on the interiors of Earth, both Earth and Mars sharing astrological affinity. Also to be noted is the fact that the planets involved in the aspects, namely, Mars and Venus, are placed on either side of Earth's path round the Sun.

This pattern discernible in the heliocentric positions appears to have been known to our ancient masters when we look at Parasara's statement: *Arkachandra grahana graha vikrithachara jamscha kampana hayulu* meaning that *when the course of a planet is disturbed from the normal path owing to the force of attraction (gravitation) of the Sun, Moon and other planets, there is a shaking of the planet (Earth?).* Based on Parasara's observation, Dr. Raman has identified seven geocentric parameters for earthquake prediction after a careful study of over 200 earthquakes.

RAMAN THEORY OF EARTHQUAKES

1. Earthquakes generally, though not always, occur at the times of eclipses and near New and Full Moon days;

2. The time of occurrence will be near about midnight, midday or early morning;

3. The major planets Mars, Saturn, Rahu and Jupiter and the minor planets Mercury and the Moon will be in mutual angles (Kendras) or trines (Trikonas) and near the 10th or 4th house;

4. The Moon plays an important role and the Nakshatra ruling on that day gives a clue to the area of occurrence on the basis of the *Avakahada* arrangement;

5. Major planets generally occupy earthy or airy signs; and

6. The asterism of the day belongs to Prithvi or Vayu Mandala.

In the horoscope cast for the occurrence of the quake at Sumatra (Chart 1), the Ascendant is Capricorn, an earthy sign. Malefics Rahu, Saturn and Ketu are in quadrants. The Sun and Moon are in opposition, it being a Full Moon day. An interesting feature here is that Mars, a very important factor in studying any kind of terrestrial disaster, occupies Scorpio, a watery sign, and aspects the Moon in

Gemini. This quake impacted most the watery regions, rather than land masses. The impact was felt as far as the Andaman and Nicobar islands in the Indian ocean nearly 2000 kilometers away from the epicentre of the quake.

Case 1: Chart 1: December 26, 2004 at 6h. 28m (IST) at Sumatra (3 N 29, 75 E 77) with a balance of 5 months 13 days of Mars Dasa.

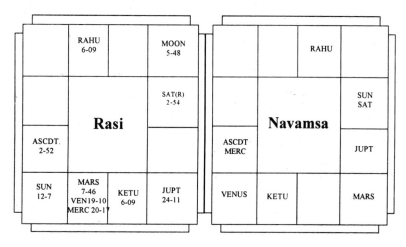

Five of the seven conditions given by Dr. RAMAN obtain here.
1. The day was a Full Moon day.
2. The time of occurrence was early morning.
3. (a) The major planets Saturn and Mars were in mutual trines.
   (b) Saturn, Rahu and Ketu were in mutual quadrants and also in quadrants from the Ascendant.
   (c) A Moon-Mercury opposition had taken place on 24-12-2004.
4. Jupiter was in Virgo, an earthy sign, and had moved into Chitta, a constellation ruled by Bhumikaraka Mars, on 18-12-2004.
5. The ruling Nakshatra was Mrigasira coming under Vayu Mandala.

Tsunamis have struck the Indian coastline including the Andaman and Nicobar islands on two earlier occasions too.

Case 2 : Chart 2: June 26, 1941 at 5h. 30m (IST) at 12 N 0, 92 E 05.

KETU 5-15 MARS 4-44		SAT 2-16 JUPT 15-24	SUN 12-24 MERC (R) 22-44 MOON 26-20 ASCDT 21-14
	Chart 2 **Rasi**		VEN 0-27
		RAHU 5-15	

	MERC ASCDT	MOON	
RAHU	**Navamsa**		VENUS
			MARS KETU
	SUN SAT		

On June 26, 1941 a severe earthquake of magnitude 8.1 (Chart 2) struck the Andaman and Nicobar islands and its destructive effect was felt marginally on the Indian coastline in Tamil Nadu. Earlier on 31-12-1881 also, a major quake of magnitude 8 (Chart 3) in the Indian ocean triggered gigantic waves that inundated the tip of the Indian peninsula.

Case 3 : Chart 3: December 31, 1881 at 5h. 30m (IST) at 12 N 10, 92 E 4.

	SAT (R) 14-49 JUPT(R) 25-35 MOON 27-37	KETU 16-34	MARS(R) 13-25
	Chart 3 **Rasi**		
VEN 6-16 SUN 18-45 ASCDT 16-02 MERC 14-46	RAHU 16-34		

		VENUS KETU	
MARS	**Navamsa**		
			MERC SAT
MOON	JUP RAHU		ASCDT SUN

Two other quakes of magnitude 8.1 (Chart 4) and 7.9 (Chart 5) are known to have occurred in the Indian ocean in March 1928 and August 1951 respectively.

Case 4: Chart 4: 9-3-1928 at 23h.35m (IST) at 2 S 05, 88 E 05.

JUPT 18-28		RAHU 22-36		SAT ASCDT		MARS	SUN
SUN 27-30 MERC 4-47	Chart 4 Rasi				Navamsa		RAHU
VEN 28-16 MARS 16-31				KETU			
	KETU 22-36 SAT 27-25 ASCDT 22-00	MOON 4-9		JUPT	MOON MERC		VENUS

SATURN AND MARS FACTORS

The charts for these quakes show some recurring planetary features.

In Chart 1, Saturn is square Rahu and Ketu.
In Chart 2, Mars is conjunct Ketu opposing Rahu.
In Chart 3, Mars and Saturn flank Ketu.
In Chart 4, Saturn is conjunct Ketu opposing Rahu.

In all these charts a recurring feature is that a Node, either Rahu or Ketu, gets influenced by Mars or Saturn.

In Chart 5, Jupiter is in opposition to Mars and Saturn. The Nodes do not figure directly in this case. The sign Pisces gets activated by Moon-Jupiter being in it and by the aspect of Mars and Saturn from Virgo, an earthy sign and from Hasta, a Nakshatra ruled by watery Moon. In all these charts but one where subtarranean earthquakes of high magnitude on the Richter scale have occurred, there is some kind of predominance of a watery sign connected with either Mars, Jupiter or Saturn but more particularly with Mars, triggering the natural event.

Case 5: Chart 5: August 12, 1951 at 9h. 44m (IST) at 34 S 00, 57 E 00.

MOON 24-05 JUPT 12-37				ASCDT		MARS	
RAHU 12-58	**Chart 5**			MOON SUN	**Navamsa**		MERC(R) KETU SAT
ASCDT 9-43	**Rasi**		KETU 12-58	RAHU			
MERC(R) 10-33	SUN 23-31	VENUS 8-27	MARS 16-08 SAT 21-17	VENUS		JUPT	

WATERY SIGNS, NAKSHATRAS AND MOON

Chart 1 has Mars in Scorpio, Saturn in Cancer — both watery signs.

Chart 2 has Mars with Ketu in watery Pisces.

Chart 3 has Rahu in watery Scorpio while Saturn (R) conjucts Jupiter joined by the watery Moon.

Chart 4 has Ketu-Saturn in watery Scorpio with Ketu. Ketu is known to act like Mars.

Chart 5 has Jupiter-Moon in Pisces and both the sign and its occupants are aspected jointly by Mars and Saturn.

In all these instances of earthquakes occurring in the Indian ocean, watery signs assume prominence under conditions occurring for earthquakes. Therefore, it may not be incorrect to surmise destructive *tsunamis* can be anticipated using the same parameters as for earthquakes but with the factors ruling *water* either in terms of sign, Nakshatra and the Moon assuming some unusual strength. Such planetary phenomena occurring can be expected to trigger *tsunamis*.

GEOGRAPHICAL ZONES

The approximate time frame based on eclipses and New and Full Moons can also be worked out. The approximate location of the *tsunami* strike is not easy to gauge. But if all the parameters relevant to earthquake *cum tsunami* can be identified for specific geographical zones, it may not be impossible to indicate the location with a fair degree of accuracy. If Indian seashores and the islands in the archipelago can be identified in terms of zones defined by latitudinal and longitudinal co-ordinates, if at least 5 of the parameters identified by Dr.Raman for earthquakes be present and in addition, watery signs get related to the major malefics and Mars also figures prominently influencing the Moon, watery signs or Moon-ruled Nakshatras, the possibility of a *tsunami* striking that region becomes high enough to warrant precautionary measures such as evacuation and other in coastal places.

Summing up, a *tsunami* can be anticipated when:-

(A) 1. Planetary conditions for earthquakes as identified by Dr.Raman occur.

2. Either Node — Rahu or Ketu — is influenced by Mars or Saturn.

3. Watery signs Cancer, Scorpio or Pisces get activated by Mars through occupation or aspect. If other malefics also influence these signs, the magnitude of the calamity may increase in severity.

(B) Heliocentric aspects involving the major planets, Mars, in particular occur under the conditions given under **(A)**.

It is a pity that the about 200 seismic observatories in our country coming under various organisations with nearly 58 seismic stations coming under the India Meterological Department alone had no inkling of the December 26, 2004 calamity and that, despite an army of scientists working precisely on this subject.

It is only the astrological model that can prepare a country to face such challenges. Yet, no effort seems to be forthcoming either from the community of scientists or the powers that be to take a serious look at the planetary parameters in disaster prediction. This fanatical bias against astrology is indeed a sad reflection on the scientific temper, rather the lack of it, in science circles of the country. There is no doubt it springs from a disdain for indigenous systems of knowledge rather than the professed spirit of inquiry or scientific temper. It is this attitude of bias that can be held partly responsible for the magnitude of the human tragedy consequent on the December 2004 natural disaster. (*04.05*) ●

---

1. John Nelson, "Shortwave Radio Propogation Correlation with Planetary Position" *RCA Review*, March 1951.

2. J.B. Blizard, "Long-range Solar Flare Predictions", *NASA Contractor Report*, CR 61316, 1969.

3. *Catalog of Significant Earthquakes* 2150 B.C. to 1991 A.D.

SECTION III
POLITICAL PREDICTIONS

23

LAGNA LORD'S BHUKTI AND RETURN TO POWER

1. *Rahu in the 11th confers Raja Yoga in his Dasa.*
2. *Bhukti of the Atmakaraka leads to Yogabhanga and loss of position.*
3. *Bhukti of the Lagna lord can revive and restore lost Raja Yogas.*

POWERFUL YOGAS

JAYALALITHAA'S CHART is an excellent illustration or dazzling Raja Yogas and their timing. In power, out of power, her political dalliances have never failed to evoke excited reactions from both admirers and opponents alike. That she enjoys a larger than life image and a presence that refuses to be ignored are indisputable. What is it in her chart that has helped her obtain this kind of a personality that never fails to draw attention. The Lagna? Is it its strength coming from powerful Kendras? Or, is it the luminous Moon shining with his digits full? Or, are the Raja Yogas so special in her chart that she has captivated the hearts of the Tamil Nadu masses like no other in recent times except perhaps her mentor and film-star-turned political leader the late M. G. Ramachandran? The Panchamahapurusha Yogas — Hamsa and Malavya — in powerful Kendras, the Lagna lord in the best trine, the 9th and the Moon with full digital strength partly answer this question. The rest of the answer lies in the entirety of the chart.

The Lagna in Jayalalithaa's horoscope is Gemini, an intellectual airy sign, rising in the 23rd degree in Punarvasu Nakshatra in Aries Navamsa. The 3rd Drekanna of Gemini rises which according to the revered Dr. B.V. Raman* shows one "rich in jewels, armed with bow, learned and peevish." These results, though not to be literally interpreted, have indeed made themselves felt in her persona.

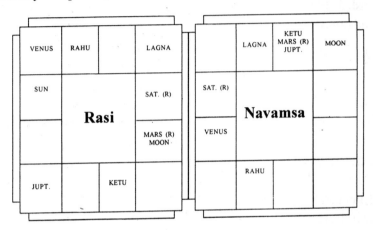

The Lagna lord Mercury is in the 9th, the best trine, in a friendly sign in retrograde motion. Though somewhat blighted by his association with the Sun, Mercury gains from the occupation of Dhanishta, a Mars-ruled Nakshatra and the aspect of Mars. His occupation of Aquarius, the Moolatrikona sign of a friendly Saturn, is also a *plus*-point which again gets somewhat watered down by sign-dispositor Saturn occupying the 6th therefrom. The retrogression of Mercury strengthens his Karakattwa of Buddhi or intellect making it sharp, refined and honed to a sensitive degree. Likewise, both the Lagna Gemini and the Lagna lord Mercury occupying airy signs give a decidedly intellectual orientation to the personality with its sights set on lofty altruistic ideals.

The Lagna lord Mercury is aspected by the 6th and 11th lord malefic retrograde Mars. This aspect further sharpens the intellect.

---

* Hindu Predictive Astrology.

Mars, being in the 3rd house, loses the sting of his functional maleficence and his power for evil is transmuted into a driving force that can know no let up once the target is defined. It not only gives an extremely analytical approach which gains in finesse as the Dasas progress but also endows the native with grit, surviving strength and courage and intrepidity against the heaviest of odds and an unshakable one-pointed determination that will stand no impediments and opposition, no matter how powerful.

WAXING MOON

The other planet influencing the Lagna lord Mercury is the 2nd lord Moon which, apart from contributing to a Dhana Yoga, also teaches the native the importance of Dharma (the 9th house being involved) in achieving the four-fold objectives of life or the Purusharthas defined in Sanatana Dharma. Political power is one such Purushartha coming under Kama. The Moon, more importantly, is the Manahkaraka ruling the central core of the native's personality, the mind. And how is the Moon placed? Situated in the royal, regal, authoritarian sign Leo, the mind displays all these traits in abundant measure. According to the revered Dr. Raman (*ibid*), Leo prominent in a chart makes the natives "majestic in appearance, broad shouldered, bilious in constitution, and bold and respectful in temperament. They possess the knack to adapt themselves to any condition in life. They are rather ambitious and sometimes avaricious too. They are independent thinkers. They stick to orthodoxical principles in religion but are perfectly tolerant towards others' precepts and practices. They are lovers of fine arts and literature and possess a certain amount of philosophical knowledge. They are voracious readers. If the Ascendant or the 10th house is afflicted, they may not succeed in life as much as they expect. They put forth much struggle. Their ambitions remain unfulfilled to some extent unless the horoscope has certain definite Raja Yogas. They are capable of non-attachment and contentment." Dignity and a rare aristocracy characterise such natives but the latter is heavily laced with authoritarianism.

MOON-MERCURY CONFLICTS

Jayalalithaa's birth having occurred on a Pournami, the Moon, Full and endowed with maximum digital strength, focusses sharply on Mercury, the Lagna lord and Buddhikaraka. This mutual aspect, though said to attract certain distinct disadvantages, also brings in a rare synergy between the Moon and Mercury or between the mind and the intellect. The element of detriment in the Moon and Mercury opposition remains and throws the native into constant conflict. She is torn between what is right and what is wrong, between what she would like to do and what she ought to do. This continuing tug of war though leading to much mental strain and several wrong decisions initially also opens up gradually a loftier spiritual side to the native with the change of Dasas.

The Moon also comes under the strong influence of Mars by conjunction. This produces a frenzied surge in the native to reach out for purely materialistic goals in the form of political ambition. But the Moon-Mercury involvement with Mars tends to generate simultaneous internal conflicts resulting ultimately in the thwarting of the desire for gain with love for what is right. Decisions are constantly the result of an endless internal churning process with infinite rounds of thinking and reviewing and re-thinking going on in the native's psyche. Against this picture of mental turbulence and intellectual conflict, there is a powerful Jupiter in the 7th house aspecting trinally the Moon or Manahkaraka. Jupiter represents the deeply spiritual urge in the innermost recesses of the human personality that characterises the yearnings of the soul for a fulfillment beyond the crass materialistic reaches of power and pelf. Jupiter aspects the Ascendant strengthening it while at the same time trining the Moon leading to a great longing for the refinement of the spirit and all things noble and sublime.

RAHU AND MUNDANE ASPIRATIONS

Even as the Moon-Jupiter trine makes the soul hearken upwards, Mars who rules the gross in the human heart tugs in the opposite direction forcing the Moon (Manas or mind) down to mundane aspirations. This continuing conflict is integrated into the native's personality and will be experienced most intensely in Rahu Dasa that is presently on. Rahu is in the 11th in a Martian sign and brings the Martian traits strongly to the fore. It was this facet of the chart that led us to say in THE ASTROLOGICAL MAGAZINE, April 2001 in an editorial dated February 16, 2001: "While the Hamsa and Malavya Yogas occurring in pivotal houses of the chart carry the potential for much achievement and a rare magnanimity and nobility of heart, the present Dasa of Rahu tends to act as a brake on both the spiritual and material potential of the chart.

"Rahu is in the 11th house, one of the best places for the Node to occupy. Rahu is aspected by 8th and 9th lord malefic Saturn(R) as well as 10th lord Jupiter. Rahu Dasa can, therefore, give good results too. The present Bhukti is of 8th and 9th lord Saturn(R). Saturn is in the 2nd and aspects the Dasa lord Rahu. As a malefic in a Maraka house, his aspect on Rahu shrinks Rahu's power for good. Worse, it makes the native vulnerable to offensives from quarters represented by Saturn. Saturn, as 8th lord and retrograde, aspecting the 8th, acts more as the 8th lord than the 9th lord. And one of the major significations of the 8th house is humiliation and defeat. Saturn, unfortunately, also happens to be the Atmakaraka by virtue of his having obtained the highest longitude in the sign of his occupation, Cancer. As a result, Saturn cannot help. Rather, he tends to prepare the ground for setbacks.

"Rahu reflects the results of both Saturn (शनिवद् राहु) and of his sign-dispositor Mars. Mars is a Yogakaraka from the Moon-sign which is quite powerful. The Moon is in Leo aspected by its own ruler Sun. Additionally, Mercury aspects it too. While this has its drawbacks, it is not all evil. The Full Moon's influence on Mars by conjunction, generates a strong Chandra Mangala Yoga which also gains from the trinal aspect of Jupiter. All these factors make Mars a strong Yoga-causing planet which influence is passed on to Rahu. **Therefore, Rahu's strength for Raja Yoga is indisputable. But** it is Saturn who throws a hammer in the spokes for two reasons. One, by his 8th lordship and two, by his obtaining the Chara Karakattwa of Atmakaraka. Saturn Bhukti, which is now on, will continue through the election month to about November 2001 and irrespective of which group joins her, will make the chief ministership elude her."

Saturn did show his power for evil even as he conferred victory on the party only to sabotage the leadership later. While the electorate showed it would simply not settle for anyone else, judicial reasons deprived Jayalalithaa of the seat of power. As Saturn Bhukti ended to make way for Mercury Bhukti, the Tamil Nadu High Court set aside the conviction that had led to barring her from contesting the elections in May 2001. Jayalalithaa is now in Mercury Bhukti (November 2001 to June 2004) of Rahu Dasa. Will she continue to pull the strings from behind the curtain or will she formally and officially assume the reins of the state ?

EARLY LIFE AND FILM CAREER

Before taking a critical look at the astrological factors for such a possibility, a brief review of Jayalalithaa's life against the planetary positions would not be out of place.

A bright student, thanks to the powerful disposition of the chart, the year 1964 brought in a major change in Jayalalithaa's life when she gave up her educational pursuits for a career in films. This shift which would change the entire course of life of the fiercely independent minded schoolgirl came about in Saturn Bhukti of Venus Dasa. Venus as 5th lord is exalted in the 10th — a position that shows a career related to art — films and dance in this case. Saturn as 8th and 9th lord is in a trine from Dasa lord Venus. This mutually favourable disposition of the Dasa-Bhukti lords resulted in a rather adverse situation where the native had to unwillingly give up academics for a film career. Though apparently the shift from school to the silver screen was easy and effortless, it must have led to a lot of heartburn for a youngster who loved books. Transit Saturn appropriately was in Aquarius afflicting natal Moon and showing much suffering and anguish. Venus, the Dasa lord, though exalted in the 10th, is caught in a Papakartari Yoga which tends to put one in circumstances over which one has little control and which one would normally want to get out of. Malefic Mars as 6th lord aspects the Dasa lord Venus adversely. Mercury, as the 4th lord, is aspected by a retrograde 6th and 11th lord Mars which could show an extremely dominating mother who decided what was what and imposed her own will and ambitions on the young native. Saturn, as 8th lord in the 2nd (Vidyastana), disrupted the native's scholastic pursuits.

Mercury as Lagna lord in the 9th gives proficiency in the Gandharva Vidyas of which classical dance is an important one. As Venus Dasa progressed with the 11th lord Mars aspecting him, the native's fame as a sensitive dancer and a leading film star kept growing. But Mars as 6th lord aspecting Kalatrakaraka Venus as Dasa lord brought in much frustration and made the native's personal life stormy and unhappy.

The next Dasa lord Sun, as 3rd lord joining the Lagna lord Mercury in the 9th in Bhagyastana, continued to help the native grow in stature in his period. The Moon Dasa too kept up the tempo, the Moon as 2nd lord being Full and aspecting the 9th house. Her film career flourished.

POLITICAL LIFE BEGINS

The next big event in Jayalalithaa's life was her entry into politics in 1982 when she joined the AIADMK under the guidance of her mentor. This came about in Moon Dasa, Saturn Bhukti. The Moon is aspected by the 10th lord Jupiter. Saturn, as 8th and 9th lord, in the 12th from Dasa lord brought in a major shift in her career. Transit Saturn was again active in Virgo bringing the chart under the last phase of *sadesathe* heralding new challenges and changes in life. The Dasa lord Moon, full and powerful in Leo, additionally strengthened by the aspect of his sign-dispositor Sun, brought the native the love of the people, of the public and of the masses even as the characteristic royal bearing that Leo conferred on her continued untouched. A favourable disposition of the Moon often leads to great popularity with the masses and which in this case led exactly to such a result.

Jayalalithaa was elected to the Rajya Sabha in 1984 in Ketu Bhukti. Ketu is in a Venusian sign and Venus is exalted in the 10th house. In 1984, events took a serious turn when the AIADMK leader's health began to give way. Jayalalithaa took up the mantle of her mentor on her young shoulders and steered the party and its ally to a massive victory in Venus Bhukti.

The period in December 1987 when the party leader and her mentor died coincided with the advent of the Dasa of malefic Mars. Mars is the planet of dissensions. Transit Saturn in Scorpio in the 4th from natal Moon saw the party split and the tensions continued into Mars Dasa, Rahu Bhukti. But Mars is at the same time powerfully placed with Vakrabala and is aspected by Lagna lord Vakra Mercury and sign-dispositor Sun. A Sasi Mangala Yoga is also present.

In January 1989 in Jupiter Bhukti, Jayalalithaa was elected to the Assembly and her unit of the party fared well. She became the first woman leader of the Opposition of the Tamil Nadu Assembly during this period. Under the same Bhukti, the split factions came together under her leadership and in the 1989 elections, she steered the party and its allies to a historic victory in the Lok Sabha elections.

Jayalalithaa assumed chief ministership of Tamil Nadu in June 1991 and completed her term after which she lost the state to the DMK in the next elections. Transit Saturn in the 7th and 8th from her natal Moon combining with the advent of Rahu Dasa, put her in political wilderness.

SWEEPING VICTORY *VERSUS* ATMAKARAKA

In May 2001, though the AIADMK swept the polls, Jayalalithaa was barred from contesting the elections on legal grounds. However, she was sworn in as the chief minister as leader of the party in the same month. The chief ministership was quashed by a Supreme Court order in September 2001 when she had to step down and a party designate assumed formal control. All these dramatic developments took place in Saturn Bhukti who as Atmakaraka did not help her retain her post. He conferred power on the native only to dislodge her consistent with his power for पदच्युति that is usually associated with the Atmakarakattva of a planet. However, about a month later, as Mercury Bhukti dawned, the High Court exonerated her of the conviction charges that had prevented her from contesting the elections.

The moot question now, whatever the intermediate developments *vis-a-vis* elections and the legal complications that may precede or follow the polls is, how effective are the Raja Yogas at this critical point in her career.

Transit Rahu is now in Gemini and moves backwards into Taurus about 14-3-2002 after which he begins to move towards a conjunction with Saturn around 11-7-2002. These transits involving Rahu could bring in an element of suspense and uncertainty and create difficulties and impediments in the Raja Yogas taking shape. However, the Dasa is of Rahu and of his capability to confer Yoga there is little doubt. The Bhukti now is of the favourable Lagna lord Mercury and can provide the necessary thrust to push the Raja Yogas through the adverse transits.* (*Written on 24-1-2002*). *(03-02)* ●

---

* Jayalalithaa was sworn in again as Chief Minister on 2-3-2002 vindicating the astrological anticipation.

LONGEVITY OF THE NDA GOVERNMENT AND MUHURTA PRINCIPLES

1. In Muhurta, the Moon in the 7th generates strokes of Balarishta.
2. Benefics in Kendras strengthen the chart.
3. Sun in the 11th is a formidable source of strength.

MUHURTA, ONLY DIFFERENCE

THE NDA Government was sworn in on October 13, 1999. Its term ends in October 2004 or, in another 28 months approximately. That is, if it survives till then. It has seen several high tension moments when the worst was feared but somehow the crises did not snowball into uncontrollable proportions. Everytime, even as things moved in adverse gear, other developments occurred which directly or indirectly worked to diffuse each crisis allowing the Government to breathe freely again. This time round, it was Gujarat which continued into most of the better part of 2002 until Musharaff's war psychosis took over the headlines and the attention of the country. This came at a rather inopportune time for the Opposition and its dynastic leader who were just beginning to believe that Gujarat could provide them the chance they had been waiting for after the 1999 fiasco of numbers. The Vajpayee Government had been brought down then by just one vote in an unbelievably politically infantile bid by the Congress leader for the prime-minister's *gaddi*. The elections that followed brought in the same Government with the same leader.

What is it that makes all the difference in the two Governments — pre October 1999 and post October 1999 — headed by the same prime-minister — with one going down before its time and the other crossing hurdle after hurdle and managing to stay afloat? The planetary conditions under which the Governments came into being can, to an extent, throw light on this political conundrum.

MOON AS WEAKENING FACTOR

Chart 1 fulfils most conditions required for a good Muhurta, except for the Moon in the 7th which is a Balarishta factor. Taurus rises in Aquarius Navamsa. Benefics Venus and Jupiter are in a Trikona (trine) and Kendra (quadrant) respectively. All the planets, except Rahu, occupy the visible half of the hemisphere strengthening the chart. The Lagna lord Venus in the best trine, the 9th, free of affliction is quite well-placed.

Chart 1 : BJP-led Government swearing in : 19-3-1998 at 9-33 a.m. (IST) at 28 N 38, 77 E 17.

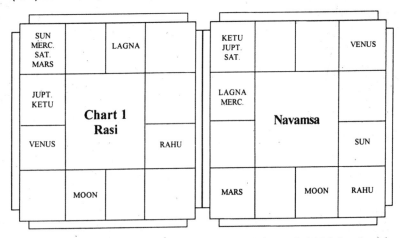

Jupiter occupies the best Kendra, the 10th, as the 11th lord with Ketu. All the malefics (natural) Sun, Mercury, Mars and Saturn are in an Upachaya in the 11th which is quite desirable. The 10th lord Saturn and the 11th lord Jupiter are involved in a Parivartana Yoga or an exchange of signs.

Longevity of the NDA Government and Muhurta Principles

The Moon is in the 7th which is not desirable in a Muhurta chart. The Moon occupies Anuradha, a Maha Nakshatra and gets Neechabhanga. The Neechabhanga is obtained by virtue of Jupiter, who gets exalted in a sign ruled by the Moon, being in a Kendra from the Lagna. The Moon in the 7th tends to generate strokes of Balarishta. But the Lagna lord Venus is in the 9th and the malefics are relegated to the 11th where they are supportive influences and cease to be baneful. The weekday is a Thursday (5), the Tithi being Krishna Shashti (21), the Zodiacal sign Taurus (2) and the Nakshatra Anuradha (17) with the Panchaka adding up favourably.

PARIVARTANA YOGA

An interesting feature that should draw the attention of the astrology student here is the Parivartana between the 10th and 11th lords Saturn and Jupiter respectively involving the 10th and 11th houses. Such a Yoga, in terms of results, tantamounts to the 10th lord being in the 10th and the 11th lord being in the 11th. In other words, the chart gets the benefit of the results that would acrue if the 10th lord Saturn were in the 10th and the 11th lord Jupiter were in the 11th.

The Government led by the BJP which took charge with Chart 1 was constantly rocked by the tantrums of some of its partners until the fateful day of 17-4-1999 when it lost the vote of confidence leading to the dissolution of the Lok Sabha. Fresh polls were announced when the efforts of the Opposition parties to form an alternative government came to nought.

The Moon in the 7th did show up his power for evil dealing a mortal blow to the Government. But the interesting fact is Chart 1 combined with Vajpayee's own chart was such that though the Government fell, the prime ministership remained intact.

WORKING OF BALARISHTA YOGA

The Balarishta factor caused by the 7th house Moon was to a great extent balanced by the 10th-11th lord exchange Yoga in Chart 1 and the Moon's Neechabhanga Raja Yoga in the Prime Minister's horoscope (Chart 3) analysing which we had said in THE ASTROLOGICAL MAGAZINE, October 1999 :

"Throughout the farcial exercise, the prime-ministership of Mr. Vajpayee endured, whether *de facto* or *dejure*, being immaterial, highlighting the Neechabhanga Raja Yoga under which his chart now functions. The voting out on 17-4-1999 and the dissolution of the Lok Sabha — one of the most severe Balarishta strokes (indicated in the swearing-in chart)— was also part of the package coming under the Neechabhanga Raja Yoga aided by the opposition of the Sun and Saturn with the highly malevolent retrograde Mars. The Neechattwa of the planets involved showed up in the sordid ganging up of the motley crowd of self-serving opportunists of the Opposition against the Government as also the shadow that fell on Rashtrapati Bhavan during those crucial days. Ultimately, that it ended as a futile exercise leaving the prime-ministership intact can be attributed only to the Neecha (debilitated) planet being checkmated by its Neechabhanga (cancellation of debility) strength.

"Astrology makes no claim of being able to identify every single specific detail in the unfolding of political or other events, but developments and situations can be indicated broadly with a fair degree of accuracy. A Neechabhanga Raja Yoga can cause what appears to be a fall but in reality only work to prepare the ground for a consolidation of the same Yoga."

If the Moon in the 7th in Chart 1 could be held responsible for the BJP led Government coming down in April 1999, the Parivartana between Saturn and Jupiter, the 10th and 11th lords, and the 10th lord Saturn acting as if in a Kendra can very well be deemed to have played a significant role in resurrecting the same Government in its new *avatar* as the NDA Government following the polls in October 1999.

The Ascendant Scorpio in Chart 2 is influenced by Neecha Moon from the Maha Nakshatra Anuradha just as in Chart 1. But while the Moon is in the 7th in Chart 1, he occupies the

Ascendant itself in Chart 2. Though Neecha or debilitated and therefore, lacking in strength initially, the Moon obtains Neechabhanga by reason of Venus, the ruler of his sign of exaltation, being in a Kendra both from the Ascendant and the Moon-sign, and therefore, becomes powerful.

Chart 2 : NDA Government swearing-in : 13-10-1999 at 10-30 a.m. at 28 N 39, 77 E 13.

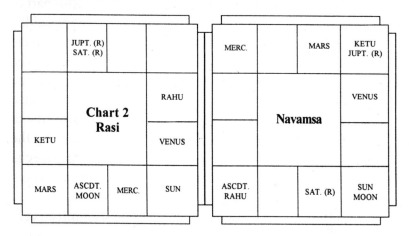

The Ascendant lord Mars in Chart 2 is in the 2nd exchanging signs with the 2nd lord Jupiter which helps to strengthen the Lagna. The trinal aspect of Jupiter on the 2nd which houses the Lagna lord Mars also strengthens the Lagna.

MOON IN LAGNA

As in Chart 1 where the Moon in the 7th is not a Muhurta-friendly factor, the presence of the Moon in the Ascendant itself in Chart 2 goes against basic tenets of Muhurta Sastra.

The Moon is described as changeable and the lunar influence on the Muhurta Lagna can work against its foundational strength. But this factor can be neutralised to a great extent by other more powerful Muhurta factors.

SUN'S SUPPORT

Some of the factors that can nullify such Doshas are the presence of Venus, Mercury or Jupiter in Kendras unafflicted, the Sun in the 11th house, an exalted planet in Lagna and Jupiter or Venus in a Kendra and malefics in the 3rd, 6th or 11th houses. And as Dr. RAMAN would always say "the most important question in Muhurta is the fortification of the Lagna and its lord."

According to **Kalaprakasika,**

यो दोषस्थान् निहन्त्येव यत्रेकादशग: शशी ।
दिवा सूर्ये निशा चन्द्रे शशी लग्नस्यैकादशास्थितं ॥
कोटिदोषा विनश्यन्ति गर्गस्य वचनं तथा ।

XXXIV - 111, 112

The Moon in the 11th from Lagna dispels all evils pertaining to an inauspicious time and to the Navamsa of malefics.

The Sun in the 11th from the rising sign during day and the Moon during night are powerful remedial forces, according to Sage Garga.

The Moon in the Ascendant can generate tremendous stresses and strains rocking the Government but as **Kalaprakasika,** says,

न तिथिर्न च नक्षत्रं च योगो न च चन्द्रमा: ।
सर्वमेव शुभं कार्ये रवावेकादशस्थिते ॥

XXXVI - 112, 113

The Sun in the 11th overcomes all Doshas or afflictions arising from Nakshatra, Yoga, lunar placement, planetary Yogas etc.

Here, the Sun is not only in the 11th but he is Vargottama and comes under a Subhakartari Yoga flanked as he is on either side by Venus and Mercury, both natural benefics.

Natural malefics Sun, Mars, Mercury, Saturn, Rahu and Ketu in the 3rd, 6th and 11th are also deemed favourable in Muhurta. In Chart 2, there is Ketu in the 3rd, Saturn in the 6th and the Sun in the 11th.

The lunar day being Sukla Chaturti (4) is not deemed auspicious. This, with the Nakshatra Anuradha (17), the rising sign Scorpio (8) and weekday Wednesday (4) adds up to 33 leaving the Chora

Panchaka of 6. The Moon and Jupiter are so placed as to show a Sakata Yoga. These factors work against Chart 2 but we must not overlook the fact, they are minor flaws. Not one of them is a Maha Dosha.

Chart 2 shares the same sign, as does Chart 1, as the prime minister's Janma Rasi (Chart 3) as its Ascendant which is a favourable factor. Otherwise, Scorpio Ascendant is generally not acceptable for a Muhurta Lagna. The Navamsa Lagna, unlike in Chart 1, is Sagittarius, ruled by the benefic Jupiter which eliminates Kunavamsa Dosha, a Maha Dosha.

In any case, Chart 2 is stronger than Chart 1. If the latter could help the Government survive elections and resurrect it in spite of Balarishta Moon in the 7th house, then, probably, would it be too much to expect the former chart with the Moon in Lagna to help the Government last full term?

IMPORTANCE OF LEADER'S CHART

The prime minister's horoscope (Chart 3) can provide some clues to the answer to this tricky question.

Rahu Dasa materialised the Neechabhanga Rajayoga caused by the debilitated Moon in the 2nd in Chart 3. Likewise, Rahu Dasa also helped the Sasa Mahapurusha Yoga generated by benefic Yogakaraka Saturn in Lagna to show up with Rahu deputising for the latter in accordance with the dictum *Sanivad Rahu*. Now that Rahu Dasa has ended and Jupiter Dasa has begun where will it all lead to ?

Jupiter conjoins the 11th lord Sun. Jupiter conjoins the 9th and 12th lord Mercury. Jupiter occupies Sagittarius, his Moolatrikona cum own sign in great strength, gaining even more fortification from his exaltation in Navamsa. Jupiter benefits from the aspect of exalted Yogakaraka Saturn. This being the case, Jupiter may not deprive the prime minister of his power. Jupiter also acquires extra strength by virtue of his very close conjunction with the Sun. Both Jupiter and the Sun are in Moola Nakshatra ruled by Ketu. Ketu, in turn, occupies Capricorn ruled by Saturn. Ketu, according to the dictum *Kujavad Ketu*, can act like Mars; he can also act like Saturn, his sign dispositor. And Saturn, we have seen, generates a strong Pancha Mahapurusha Yoga which acquires extra strength from his combined lordship of the 4th and the 5th houses for Libra Lagna and assumes special significance in this context by his aspect on the 10th house. The Ketu-Rahu axis influences the 10th house. So does Dasa lord Jupiter indirectly by virtue of his occupation of Moola.

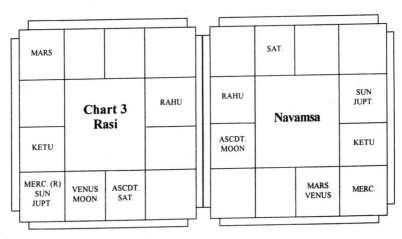

From Chandra Lagna, Jupiter is the 2nd and 5th lord conjoining 10th lord Sun and 8th and 11th lord Mercury. Jupiter also trinally aspects the 10th house Leo from the Moon. These would indicate Vajpayee's prime-ministership is not likely to be disturbed by political developments by Dasa lord Jupiter. But Jupiter though a benefic, yet as 2nd lord from the Moon in the 2nd, does not shed his Maraka power. We shall reserve a discussion on what role Maraka Jupiter will exactly play and in what way in Vajpayee's chart for a later date. But right now, suffice it for us to note that both Vajpayee's chart and the Muhurta chart when the NDA Government took charge appear to have a fair sprinkling of planetary factors that could help the Government carry on full term. (*Written on 18-6-02*) (*08-02*) ●

MUHURTA FACTORS AND NARENDRA MODI'S CHIEF MINISTERSHIP

1. Malefic Saturn in the 7th is a major drawback in a Muhurta chart.
2. The 8th house should be vacant.
3. Rahu and Ketu have no independent identity.

MEDIA ROLE FROM THIRD HOUSE

THE ELECTIONS in Gujarat in December 2002 saw the BJP come back to power with a stunning victory. The polls proved the voter had seen clearly through the country's oldest party's game of divide and rule and no longer trusted it rejecting it in unequivocal terms. And even as the media kept trying to tailor its bulletins to fit in, not with the fact of the landslide victory for the BJP, but its own wishes, repeating ad *nauseum* the elections had gone awry somewhere, the people of Gujarat were heaving a sigh of relief at the results they had produced through their votes. We hold no brief for any party — the BJP or the Congress or any other but there is no denying the fact, for anyone who can lay claim to even a modicum of objectivity, the way the media conducted itself over Gujarat brought it no credit but only dented its own credibility.

Gujarat has now moved into a new innings but with the same captain in control. The single main factor that sets apart the two Governments — pre and post Sabarmati Express tragedy and the Godhra carnage that followed — is the change in planetary positions when Narendra Modi assumed office for the second time as chief minister. Will this term also see a replay of the violence and tragedy the first term saw or will Gujarat move into some peace? Narendra Modi was sworn in as chief minister on December 22, 2002 (Chart 1).

Chart 1: Swearing-in: 22-12-2002 at 13h. 58m. (IST) at 23 N 02, 72 E 36.

	ASCDT. 4-13	MANDI 12-48 RAHU 16-07	SAT. (R) 2-45		MARS MANDI VENUS	ASCDT. RAHU	SUN
	Chart 1 Rasi		MOON 8-28 JUPT. (R) 25-14	JUPT.	**Navamsa**		
MERC. 27-06 SUN 7-52	KETU 16-07	MARS 20-55 VENUS 22-42		MERC.	KETU	SAT. (R)	MOON

The Lagna in Chart 1 is Aries with Mars and Venus in the 7th in a Kendra sign. The Moon is in the 4th also in a Kendra; so also exalted Jupiter. But the Muhurta suffers from Sagraha Chandra Dosha which is caused by the election Moon's association with another planet. It does not matter whether the planet so associating is a benefic or a malefic. The Moon joined by a benefic is frowned upon and deemed unfavourable by Muhurta principles. Its association with a malefic is treated as even worse. The 8th house is free of occupation, Rahu and Ketu having no independent identity in electional astrology.

An important angle to this study is the 3rd house and its disposition which will give a clue to the kind of media response the newly sworn in Narendra Modi Government will attract. The 3rd lord Mercury is Vargottama in the 9th which is a plus point but the 3rd itself is occupied by retrograde Saturn. Not a friendly media, but at least its hostility will be greatly toned down in this innings. Further, the 3rd and Lagna lords, Mercury and Mars respectively, are in mutually friendly Bhavas in the 3rd and 11th from each other. That indicates the press may gradually veer towards conducting itself with more responsibility and greater respect for truth, shedding some of its aversion for the incumbent. The 3rd lord Mercury in Uttarashada ruled by the Sun could even, at times, make it fawn on the Government.

Chart 2 : Swearing-in : 7-10-2001 at 11-00 (IST) at 23 N 2, 72 E 37.

		MOON 15-13 SAT. (R) 22-26	RAHU 8-28 JUPT. 22-07
	Chart 2 Rasi		
			VENUS 27-21
MARS 24-01 KETU 8-28	ASCDT. 20-03	MERC. (R) 5-24	SUN 21-34

	JUPT.	MOON	KETU
			SUN SAT.
	Navamsa		
ASCDT.			
VENUS RAHU	MARS MERC.		

The role the media played during the Sabarmati tragedy and its aftermath in Gujarat as also during the elections of December 2002 is clearly shown by Chart 2 cast for the time when Narendra Modi assumed office as chief minister the first time. The Lagna lord Mars and 3rd lord Saturn are in Shashtashtaka or mutually adverse positions. Saturn is retrograde. Saturn is with the deeply emotional Moon. The media went on a blitzkrieg of hostile and venomous criticism that was crudely one-sided and self-opinionated. It did everything but present facts honestly. Distortions and untruths became its weapons against the winning party as it refused to accept the people's verdict but tried to find ways and means to explain it away as not being the choice of the electorate, whatever that was supposed to mean. Such strong emotions and self-deception are possible only when the planet signifying the media is Vakra (or eccentric) or with Rahu when he becomes eclipsed and is influenced by watery factors by sign, constellation or planet such as the conjunction with the Moon and the occupation of a Moon-ruled Nakshatra Rohini as in this case.

SATURN'S POWER FOR EVIL

The Ascendant Scorpio in Chart 2 is aspected by the Moon and Saturn. Saturn, a malefic, in the 7th in a Kendra is a major drawback in a Muhurta chart. The Moon in the 7th is also undesirable while his association with Saturn brings the chart under the Maha Dosha of Sagraha Chandra Dosha.

Natural benefic Venus in the 10th is good. So also the Sun in the 11th which is a highly desirable factor.

The 7th and 8th houses are best vacant in Rajyabhisekham Muhurtas or elections for assuming political office. Both these Muhurta requirements have been flouted in Chart 2 damaging it severely. The Moon and Saturn are in the 7th. Jupiter (as also Rahu) is in the 8th.

CHORA PANCHAKA AND BREAKDOWN OF LAW

The weekday was Sunday (1), the Nakshatra was Rohini (4), the lunar day or Tithi was Panchami or the 5th day of the dark fortnight (15+5 = 20) and the Zodiacal sign was Scorpio (8). The Panchaka comes to 1 + 4 + 20 + 8 = 33. Dividing the result by 9, it gives a remainder of 6 which is Chora Panchaka or clearly indicative of trouble from marauders, rioters, outlaws and law-breakers. The Navamsa rising is of Capricorn ruled by Saturn, bringing the chart under the Maha Dosha of Kunavamsa.

Reassessing Chart 2 on general principles of prediction we find, not only does the Moon in the 7th generate a Balarishta Yoga but also Saturn there brings it under *sadesathe*, both factors that show infant mortality or early death in natal charts. Extending the same principle to Muhurta charts, such a disposition can show termination of the chief ministership much before its 5 year period. The Government did not survive beyond a few months.

Saturn who afflicts the chart powerfully is the 4th lord placed in the 7th and in this Kendra also points to failure of the venture begun or office assumed under his influence. This factor goes against Udayasta Suddhi or the Muhurta requirement of the Lagna and the 7th houses being strong, Saturn being a malefic. The 4th house rules vehicles and transport. Saturn as the 4th lord is in the 7th in Taurus (an earthly sign ruling roadways and railways) while joining the Moon (public) at the same time. The Gujarat Ministry came down following the violent frenzy that began with the burning of the ill-fated coaches of the Sabarmati Express and the mindless Godhra carnage thereafter vitiating the atmosphere of the state with raging emotions.

The Lagna lord Mars is in the 2nd with Ketu in a fiery sign and this is not a happy feature, especially when judged in the context of the Balarishta and Muhurta Doshas.

Jupiter's relegation to the 8th, the worst Dustana, in association with the incendiary Rahu shuts off any relief that the chart could otherwise have benefitted from. Against this background, the 8th house which shows destruction, becomes eminently capable of damaging the chief ministership through the instrumentality of violence. And as the sordid chain events have since proved, the killings led to the dissolution of the State Assembly. Elections followed belatedly with the CEC deciding on its timing for reasons best known to itself although similar and worse conditions did not come in the way of its announcing early elections in Kashmir.

Though Chart 1 does not suffer any Balarishta Yoga as does Chart 2 it too comes under Sagraha Chandra Dosha. Leaving aside Muhurta factors, what does a review on general principles point to?

JUPITER AS SAVIOUR

The Ascendant in Chart 1 aspected by its ruler Mars shows good organisational and leadership skills, Mars being the Karaka for management. This disposition also enables the chief minister to handle tricky and volatile situations with a near ruthless firmness.

Jupiter, the Karaka for religion, is well placed in his exaltation in the 4th sign from the Lagna. The communal weather in the State can be expected to be congenial. The Moon's association with the expansive planet Jupiter does not appear to endorse the apprehensions in certain quarters that the Gujarat experiment could harm true domestic values or threaten the country's secular and pluralist polity. It also assures the minorities of a fair deal from the Government for Jupiter is too noble, too magnanimous an element to generate an anti-minority mindset. Saturn who rules the backward and tribal sections of the population is in the 3rd aspected by 3rd lord Mercury who is Vargottama. The retrograde position of Saturn can excite some unrest in these sections but since as sign-dispositor Mercury aspects the former, the Government may be able to ensure these are ironed out quickly with no serious repercussions. The disposition of Mercury favours importance to educational opportunities, especially in backward and rural areas.

MRITYU PANCHAKA FOR DANGER OF ATTACKS

The weekday is again a Sunday (1), the Nakshatra is Pushyami (8), the Tithi or lunar day is Krishna Triteeya or the 3rd day of the dark half (15 + 3 = 18) and the Zodiacal sign is Aries (1). The total 1 + 8 + 18 + 1 works out to 28 leaving a Panchaka of 1 which is known as Mrityu Panchaka and which is far from desirable.

The Ascendant lord Mars shifts into the 8th Bhava; so also Jupiter who moves into the 5th Bhava from the 4th Rasi. These two factors make the chart vulnerable, especially that the Panchaka is Mrityu. The Lagna lord Mars is in the 3rd Drekanna of Libra which is described as Ayudha Drekanna. The 8th lord also being Mars, this assumes sinister significance. The Lagna itself is in the 1st Drekanna of Aries, an Ayudha Drekanna again. These factors could point to attacks of violence planned against the chief minister, against which suitable measures should be taken. Utmost vigil, if exercised in ensuring the incumbent's personal safety, can work towards diffusing and divitalizing these ominous indications from turning into painful actualities.

Aries, a militant sign, rises on the Ascendant aspected by Lagna lord Mars which does not rule out outbreak of sporadic violence in the State. However, the 4th lord Moon and 4th house Cancer benefit from the presence of exalted Jupiter which tends to contain the magnitude, frequency as well as severity of any such violent incidents. Venus is also in a Kendra and that could certainly indicate more peace and amity in the State. The influence of Jupiter on the 4th house by occupation as well as on the 8th house by aspect seems to insure the State against any devastation through natural calamity, not excluding destructive earthquakes. This is an important conclusion especially when one recalls the Gujarat earthquakes of 2001 and what the people suffered as a result. These same factors also rule out any serious terrorist attack or violence to the people. Jupiter's aspect on the 12th house as exalted 12th lord, public security benefits from new measures. A watery sign Cancer on the 4th house with the watery planet Moon there in waxing strength promises better irrigational projects and more attention to agriculture.

Whatever the fears of pseudo-secularists, the benefics in Kendras do not appear to support them. On the contrary, they point to more peace, stability and security for the people of Gujarat. *(Written on 6-2-2003) (04-03)* ●

PLANETS AND DYNASTIC AMBITIONS

> 1. The sign Cancer has a great affinity with India and her history.
> 2. The Ascendant, Sun and Moon in odd signs in a male chart and in even signs in female charts produce Mahabhagya Yoga.
> 3. Transit influences, even the best, cannot supercede natal influences.

CANCER AND INDIAN HISTORY

FOR NEARLY 37 years, in her 52 years of Independence, India has been under the sway of one family, the Nehru family — Mr. Jawaharlal Nehru, his daughter Mrs. Indira Gandhi and then her son, Mr. Rajiv Gandhi. All three were prime ministers of the world's largest democracy. And now again we have another member of the Nehru household, the daughter-in-law Mrs. Sonia Gandhi, on the political horizon of the country aspiring for the coveted prime ministership of the land.

Mrs. Sonia Gandhi does not have the Nehruvian magic which was a unique part of his personality and which was acquired through being in the thick of the freedom movement. Nor does she come anywhere near the kind of grooming Mrs. Indira Gandhi received, even from her childhood days, due to the closeness and proximity she and her family enjoyed with Mahatma Gandhi and other stalwarts of the freedom movement. Despite lacking these advantages

Mrs. Sonia Gandhi has the dynastic connection with the Nehru family and which gives her an inassailable advantage over all other aspirants to the post of prime minister in a land that has had the course of its political history swayed by a moribund, servile and sick infatuation for dynastic stock. While a democracy, especially such as ours, bars no citizen from harbouring prime ministerial ambitions, how far are they justified ? Not just on the basis of dynastic qualification, but more importantly, on the strength of one's horoscope?

We start with the most interesting part of Mrs. Sonia Gandhi's horoscope, the Ascendant Cancer. This sign, the 4th in the Zodiac, has a great affinity with India and her history. Of the many prime-ministers we have had, more of them have had Cancer rising on the Ascendant than any other sign — Mr. Jawaharlal Nehru, Mrs. Indira Gandhi, Mr. V. P. Singh and Mr. Devegowda. It is, therefore, that Mrs. Sonia Gandhi's horoscope assumes significance and merits an analysis in the context of the current political scene.

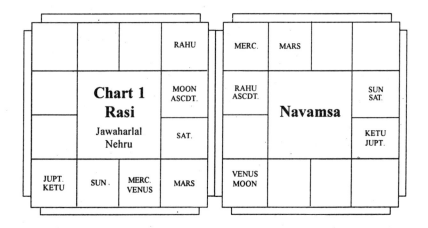

Mr. Jawaharlal Nehru (Chart 1) had the sign Cancer rising, occupied by its ruler Moon. Mrs. Indira Gandhi (Chart 2) had her Ascendant lord Moon in the 7th from it aspecting the Ascendant. Mr. Rajiv Gandhi's Ascendant Leo (Chart 3) had its ruler Sun in the 1st house itself.

Planets and Dynastic Ambitions

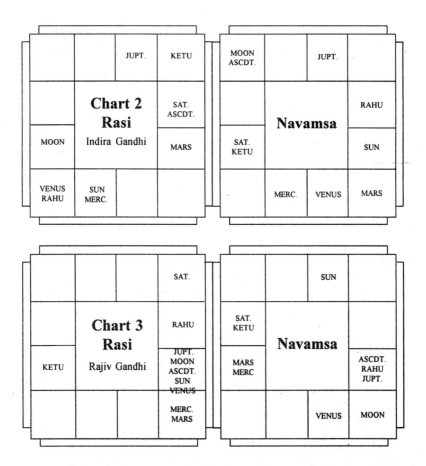

In all the three cases of the Nehru family, the Ascendant is fortified by the position of its ruler in the Lagna (Ascendant) which is also a Kendra. This disposition of the Ascendant and its ruler made the 1st house the center of the Raja Yogas in all the three charts.

In Mrs. Sonia Gandhi's case (Chart 4)*, in contrast, the Ascendant Cancer has its ruler Moon relegated to the 12th house. The Ascendant is occupied by retrograde 7th and 8th lord Saturn which changes the complexion of the entire chart in comparison to those of the other members of the Nehru family. The focus of the

---

* We cannot vouch for the correctness of the birth particulars.

		RAHU	MOON
HUS-BAND	Chart 4 Rasi Sonia Gandhi	SAT. (R) ASCDT.	
MARS	MERC. KETU SUN	JUPT. VENUS	

ASCDT.	MARS	JUPT. VENUS	RAHU
SUN	Navamsa		
MOON			MERC.
SAT. KETU			

chart shifts to Saturn and his 7th lordship instead of the Ascendant. This makes Saturn the convergent point of whatever Yogas the chart may have. In that sense, Mrs. Sonia Gandhi's chart becomes a good example of the **Streejataka** dictum found in classical works.

SEVENTH HOUSE FOR SPOUSE

According to **Jataka Parijata**, XVI-4,

स्त्रीणां जन्मफलं नृयोग्यमुदितं यत्तत्पतौ योजयेत् ।

meaning, *whatever effect may accrue from the horoscope of a woman which can be applied to men (only), should be ascribed to the husband.*

Therefore, taking Capricorn, the 7th house, as the Ascendant of the husband and reviewing the planetary map from this point of reference would give us better picture of the chart.

Saturn aspects Capricorn from the 7th where he gets Digbala as far as the husband is concerned. Rahu is in his sign of exaltation in the 5th, a trine, Venus, Yogakaraka *par excellence*, combining with Jupiter to the exact degree occupies the 10th house. The Sun, Mercury and Ketu are in the 11th house while the 11th lord Mars slips into the 12th house. This planetary arraignment made the spouse the prime minister of India's teeming millions. Of course, Mr. Rajiv Gandhi's own chart also had the requisite planetary material.

But what about Mrs. Sonia Gandhi's chart in terms of its own native *vis-a-vis* political office and power ? The Ascendant lord Moon is in the 12th which is an important horoscopic difference compared to the other three Nehru family charts where the Ascendant lords in the 1st house (a Kendra) conferred prime ministership on the natives simply by virtue of their birth in a particular family. Not only the Ascendant, but the Moon too in Charts 1, 2 and 3 occupies a Kendra in a state of dignity. In Chart 1, the Moon is in his own sign, in Chart 2 he is in the 7th aspected by its sign-dispositer Saturn and in Chart 3, in the 1st house in Leo with its sign-dispositer Sun joining it. But if their Ascendants or Moon-signs had not been fortified, the story would have been quite different but perhaps more congenial for the country.

EIGHTH HOUSE MOON AND SUDDEN DEATH

It is common knowledge that Mr. Sanjay Gandhi (Chart 5) * was being groomed to succeed Mrs. Indira Gandhi who had more or less decided he would be prime minister after her. But ironically, this did not happen. Mr. Sanjay Gandhi's horoscope has Capricorn rising Vargottama with Saturn (R) in the 7th aspecting the Ascendant and strengthening it. The 10th house has Venus and Jupiter in it. But what about the Moon ? He is in the 8th, the worst Dustana. Though Vargottama, he does not come under any strengthening benefic aspect or association. This disposition of the Moon in the 8th did not allow Sanjay Gandhi's prime ministerial ambitions to materialise and cut short his life in a violent air crash in June 1980. It was only after this tragedy that Mr. Rajiv Gandhi, who had not even in his wildest dreams ever nursed the ambition of ruling the land, was sucked into the murky arena of politics and made prime minister.

---

* The birth particulars interestingly, were sent by an erstwhile editor, a self-styled rationlist, of the now defunct *The Illustrated Weekly* to DR. RAMAN with a request for his analysis of the horoscope.

		RAHU	
	Chart 5		SAT. (R)
ASCDT.	**Rasi** Sanjay Gandhi		MOON
MARS	SUN MERC. KETU	JUPT. VENUS	

SUN		JUPT. MARS VENUS	RAHU
ASCDT.	**Navamsa**		MOON
SAT. (R) KETU			MERC.

MAHABHAGYA YOGA

The Ascendant lord Sun in Mr. Rajiv Gandhi's case in the 1st is in his own sign Leo which is also his Moolatrikona Rasi. The Moon also occupies the Lagna Kendra and both the luminaries benefit from a conjunction with Vargottama Jupiter. Venus also joins the Ascendant. The Ascendant, the Sun and the Moon being in the 1st in Lagna Kendra in a male sign Leo and the birth having occurred during daytime bring the chart under a Mahabhagya Yoga, a rare Yoga which confers unusually favourable results which, in this case, gravitated the native to the post of prime minister.

MULTIPLE PARIVARTANA YOGAS

Moving on to Mrs. Indira Gandhi's chart, its most striking feature is the sheer number of Parivartana Yogas it enjoys. Besides, every single planet has some kind of out-of-the ordinary strength.

The Ascendant lord Moon and the 7th lord Saturn have exchanged signs. Saturn, as the planet of the people, aspected by the amicable Moon, gave her a charisma that simply bowled over the masses. The Yogakaraka 4th lord (*cum* 10th lord) Mars has exchanged signs with the 2nd lord Sun. The 9th (*cum* 6th) lord Jupiter is not only retrograde and Vargottama but exchanges signs with 11th (*cum* 3rd) lord Venus. Rahu occupies the 6th, the best place for him. Ketu in the 12th is congenially placed. Mercury is Vargottama.

The Ascendant, the Sun and the Moon are the 3 pivotal centres of a chart and all of them are fortified here. The Ascendant Cancer is aspected by its lord Moon. The Moon itself in a Kendra in Capricorn is aspected by Vargottama Jupiter and his sign-dispositor Saturn. Further, the Ascendant, the Sun and the Moon falling in even signs in a night birth have constituted a Mahabhagya Yoga. With such a dazzling array of planets, it was not surprising Mrs. Indira Gandhi became one of the longest surviving and most powerful prime ministers of the country.

DANGER OF SATURN-RAHU PERIODS

It was in Saturn Bhukti of Jupiter Dasa that Mrs. Indira Gandhi became the Congress President. She became prime minister in Sun Bhukti of Jupiter Dasa. The Dasa lord is the 9th lord Vargottama in the 11th and a benefic *par excellence*. The Sun is the 2nd lord in exchange of signs with Yogakaraka Mars in a Kendra from the Dasa lord and in mutual aspect with him. Right through the rest of Jupiter Dasa and into Saturn Dasa, Mrs. Indira Gandhi continued to be in power, the planetary support from the duo helping her until she stepped into Venus Bhukti of Saturn Dasa.

Venus, the Bhukti lord, is in a Parivartana with the 6th lord Jupiter and associated with the Node Rahu. The Dasa lord Saturn in the Ascendant aspects the 10th house. Both Venus and Saturn are in mutually adverse positions. On June 28, 1975, Mrs. Gandhi clamped the infamous *Emergency* on the country paving the way for her electoral defeat on March 22, 1977. Venus and Saturn generate, in their mutual periods, unusual happenings and can even make rulers. But they are an intriguing pair and can also bring down rulers as it happened in Mrs. Indira Gandhi's case. But the same Dasa-Bhukti again propped her up until her Rahu Bhukti when she was shot dead by her own bodyguards on 31-10-1984. Of this we had indicated in THE ASTROLOGICAL MAGAZINE, September 1984 and also time and again in earlier issues that Mrs. Indira Gandhi would be vulnerable to danger of violence and her security measures should be beefed up thoroughly but the warnings went unheeded with tragic consequences.

Mrs. Indira Gandhi had Mars in the 8th from her Lagna lord Moon while Saturn was in the 7th from it, which led to her violent end.

AFFLICTION TO SEVENTH-EIGHTH HOUSES

Mrs. Sonia Gandhi shares some of the malevolent features involving the influence of Mars and Saturn on sensitive areas of her chart with Mrs. Indira Gandhi. She too has Mars in the 7th from her Lagna lord Moon with Saturn aspecting the 8th from it. Additionally, the Lagna lord Moon comes under heavy affliction from Rahu and Saturn flanking it. The Ascendant has retrograde Saturn with Mars aspecting it from the 6th house. Such planetary combinations are disquieting features and caution against vulnerability to danger of violence.

According to **Jataka Parijata**, XVI-29,

पुत्रेशेरिगते तनौ रिपुपतौ मृत्युर्भवेत् ।

If the 5th lord is in the 6th and the 6th lord is in Lagna, one faces mortal danger from an Ayudha or weapon.

Here, the 5th lord Mars is in the 6th and 6th lord Jupiter, though not in the Lagna, aspects the Lagna lord Moon. Though one cannot apply the results *adverbatim*, the indications should be taken note of and suitable measures initiated to prevent their materialisation. Applying the principle हेयं दुःखं अनागतम् or *of averting the danger that has not befallen* which is another way of handling adverse planetary indications the most rigid security measures must be ensured for Mrs. Sonia Gandhi to stave off these malefic influences.

The afflictions to the Ascendant are quite severe. According to **Brihat Parasara Hora**, 80-43,

लग्नचन्द्रगता पापकर्तरी यदि जन्मनि ।
तदा बाला कुलं पत्युर्नाशयेच्च पितुस्तथा ॥

which means, *if the Ascendant and the Moon are under a Papakartari Yoga, it acts adversely for both the parental and the marital family of the (female) native.*

Neither the results, nor the combinations, as always, can be taken too literally. Mrs. Sonia Gandhi's Ascendant, though not under a Papakartari, comes under a combined affliction from malefic Mars and Saturn. The Moon who is in the 12th comes under a Papakartari Yoga caused by Rahu and Saturn (R) on either side of it. This, therefore, can tend to make her pass through situations that carry extreme levels of despair and frustration. In the context of political figures as in this case, the native can also be drawn into a vortex of circumstances that could adversely affect the well-being of parties and people with whom the native gets involved deeply triggering over and over again events of great trial and tribulation that can lead to devastating effects at different levels.

But let us return to the question raging in the minds of most Indians — Will Mrs. Sonia Gandhi be the next prime minister of our country?

Mrs. Sonia Gandhi's entry into politics came formally on 14-3-1998 in Venus Bhukti of Mercury Dasa which began in March 1997 and will run upto January 2000. With her active entry into the Congress (I) party, it was claimed a rallying point had been found and factionalism, which had begun to eat into its vitals, was stemmed. The exodus amongst its members also was said to have been reined in. The party even fared better in the 1998 elections to some State Assemblies which revived its base to a degree. The credit for it was given to Mrs. Sonia Gandhi.

All these events broadly come under Venus Bhukti of Mercury Dasa. Venus is no benefic for Cancer Ascendant, but is rendered somewhat favourable by his association with the 9th lord Jupiter. There is a semblance again in this to Mrs. Indira Gandhi's chart which also enjoys a nexus between these two planets. While it was a Parivartana between Venus and Vargottama Jupiter in Taurus in Mrs. Indira Gandhi's case, here it is a close association between the two planets in the other Venusian sign Libra from where both planets aspect the 10th house. Venus Bhukti will cover the period of September - October 1999 when the elections will be held and the results announced. Will Venus confer the prime minister's post on Mrs. Sonia Gandhi?

TWO IMPORTANT ANGLES

In order to be able to answer this question, the chart has to be analysed on two fronts. One, if the basic strength of the chart warrants the Raja Yoga needed for political power and prime ministership. Two, if the Dasa in operation has any special features for such a high post.

The three pivotal points of the chart and their strength will answer most of the first question. The Ascendant has retrograde malefic Saturn in it which is more of an affliction than a strengthening factor. Incidentally, it gives an unfriendly forbidding appearance and demeanour. The Ascendant lord Moon who rules charisma is relegated to the 12th. These two factors involving the Ascendant refuse to invest Mrs. Sonia Gandhi with the kind of mass appeal and chemistry Mrs. Indira Gandhi possessed in abundance.

That apart, the Moon in the 12th is in a Dustana. He is aspected by the 6th and 9th lord Jupiter and Yogakaraka Mars. Considered from the Moon-sign, Mars is a malefic 6th and 11th lord and Jupiter is a Badhaka-cum-Kendradhipati, being the ruler of the 7th and 10th houses. Therefore, by position and association and aspect, the Moon has no particular strength. However, this is slightly compensated for by its digital strength or Paksha Bala, the Moon being full.

The Sun is in the 5th afflicted by Ketu and Mercury.

POTENTIAL LACKING FACTORS

These afflictions to the three central pillars of the horoscope draw away the much needed strength from the chart as a whole. They also tend to make the native difficult to deal with. Retrograde Saturn in the Ascendant makes one taciturn and tenacious, manipulative and capricious with a coldness that masks the intense mental activity that goes on inside one. The Moon is in Gemini a sign that brings in duplicity into one's thinking, especially that the Nakshatra involved is Aridra ruled by Rahu and which can rob one of foresight and blur one's power of judgement. The aspect of the Yogakaraka Mars (who, with reference to the Moon-sign is the malefic 6th lord) on the Manahkaraka Moon involving Dustanas — the 6th and the 12th — gives the native an obsessive love for power. The afflictions to the Sun give very little of substance to the overall personality. Not only that, it detracts from the political power potential of the chart.

NO YOGA FOR PRIME MINISTERSHIP

Coming to the Dasa, it is of the 3rd and 12th lord Mercury, who is placed in the 5th with exalted Ketu and the Sun, the 2nd lord. Mercury does not receive any stabilizing influence by aspect. His association with an eclipsed Sun cannot strengthen him but afflicts him making him a malefic. However, the Sun, as the political planet, associating with the Dasa lord Mercury has shown his flavour and drawn Mrs. Sonia Gandhi into political activity.

Going by the Moon-sign, Mercury as its ruler, becomes a little more supportive, but the affliction to him and his position in the 6th are greater drawbacks.

The only bright features operating during the election period would be transit Jupiter (in Aries) and Saturn in the 11th from the natal Moon. Transit influences, even if the best, cannot supercede natal influences which, here, are woefully inadequate to promise prime ministership. With such a weak planetary support system, Venus, the Bhukti lord, no matter how well-placed, cannot help. Additionally, Venus is the Atmakaraka and even shows, loss of position and fall from grace carrying within him the seeds of Yogabhanga of whatever meagre Yogas present in the chart. The Bhukti of the Atmakaraka planet, when the Dasa is not his own, rarely confers high office. Rather, it tends to pull one down. Therefore, though for the Congress (I), which refuses to look beyond the dynasty, the native may be its undisputed leader, horoscopic indications do not appear to promise anything beyond that. The prime ministership of the country may not be within the reach of Mrs. Sonia Gandhi. (*Written on 13-5-1999) (05-99)* ●

MARTIAN MOVEMENTS AND *JEHAD* AGAINST AMERICA

> 1. *In a national chart, the Ascendant lord aspecting the Ascendant makes for the political maturity of the country.*
> 2. *Mars-Rahu opposition on sensitive points presages great violence.*
> 3. *Dasa of 8th lord shows death, destruction and devastation.*

MARS AND BLACK TUESDAY

AS THE WORLD watched in stunned disbelief scenes that so far were only part of the fantasy world of movie and television stories, the twin towers of the 110-storeyed World Trade Centre in New York collapsed in a massive heap of burning dust. The world's sole Super Power, that strode the globe as a colossus, after the fall and break-up of the Soviet Union, was brought down to its knees by faceless villians in a surprising attack which caught the country unawares. And American invincibility suddenly seemed to have become myth. These diabolic trends were not anticipated, as the *Black Tuesday* of 11-9-2001 demonstrated, by even the most sophisticated intelligence agencies but were traced with a near amazing degree of accuracy by astrological methods. This is not a time to make out a brief for astrology and its immense potential as a tool of foreknowledge. But there can be no question after such a ghastly holocaust on the need to review the issue of astrology as an academic subject if only to equip oneself better to handle and may be, even prevent, human tragedies of such magnitude and proportion as have hit America. A careful back-tracking into the movements of Mars can provide vital clues to the when and how of such acts of barbaric insensitivity and how these transits work to rouse and precipitate the fires of hatred into diabolic designs.

FATEFUL MARS-RAHU OPPOSITION

Mars had already moved into an opposition with Saturn as the lunar new year Vishu began in March 2001 and this aspect continued until 23-8-2001 as the two planets transited Scorpio and Taurus respectively. The opposition was rendered worse by the retrogression of Mars in Scorpio. Mars reached a conjunction with Ketu on 14-9-2001 which meant he was in oppostion to Rahu on the same date involving Sagittarius, the natal Ascendant of the USA (Chart 1) and its ruler directly in a malevolent planetary pattern, which exposed the country to violent danger. Though the exact conjunction occurred only on the 14th, the Tuesday preceding it ruled by Mars set the mechanism for the attacks to occur. The Mars-Jupiter opposition on 3-10-2001 also involves the US Ascendant. These factors combined to bring the country under highly adverse

Chart 1 : USA : 4-7-1776 at 5-53 p.m. at 39 N 57, 75 W 09 with a balance of 15 years 7 months 22 days of Rahu Dasa at birth.

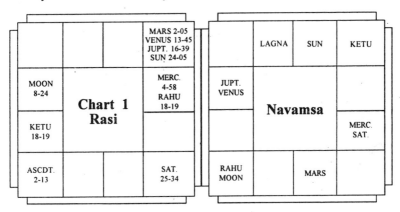

influences. The Mars-Ketu conjunction involved Moola, the constellation occupied by the Ascendant. All the planetary factors zeroing in to a highly sinister pattern led us to conclude as early as in November 2000 in THE ASTROLOGICAL MAGAZINE, January 2001, page 17 that "The retrogression of Mars in Scorpio warns against developments rousing the ire of the Arab world against the United States...." and "at least on two occasions, diabolic fundamentalist violence may be attempted." Unfortunately for both the country and the civilised world, these astrological warnings did not either reach those who could have made a difference or were not taken seriously and we know with what catastrophic results. That is not surprising considering the bias, hostility and misconceptions surrounding astrology and the angry efforts of many in official positions to stifle and kill its entry into the comity of sciences, blinded as they are by an arrogant sense of omniscience made worse by ignorance of its invaluable potential as a tool of foreknowledge.

Mars in his transits acts more as a trigger and catalyst but the explosive ammunition must already be present for the trigger to work. If it is not, Mars may only result in small scale attacks and tensions.

INBUILT AFFLICTION FROM MALEFICS

The powder keg in Chart 1 is provided by two powerful malefics Mars and Saturn spread over 2 powerful Kendras — the 7th and the 10th respectively in mutual aspect. As Jupiter, the Lagna lord, aspects the Lagna powerfully (the sign Sagittarius itself is an extraordinarily powerful and positive sign), the travails the country may come under may not generally be generated by home forces unlike in India where the absence of a direct Venusian aspect on the Ascendant as its lord opens up the country to all kinds of risks — internal and external. The external threats are obvious enough. It is the internal that are cause for concern and worry. And of these, India has had her ample share. Any crisis or disaster in the country has the tendency of provoking the reaction of trying to topple the party in power. There is no concerted effort by the political parties to express solidarity and to rally round the Government in the country's hour of crisis. But all effort is directed at doing everything possible to bring down the Government (Centre or State as the case may be) with the sole objective of grabbing power. In contrast, thanks to the Ascendant lord aspecting the Ascendant in Chart 1, though the Democrats and the Republicans fought one of the bitterest neck to neck electional battles for the Presidency, once the new President was sworn in, the Democrats who missed power by a hair's breadth immediately fell into place to work for the common cause of the country. And in this hour of crisis in American history when its people have been exposed to one of the most savage attacks of inhuman violence, not a single member of the Opposition party has so much as even whispered that Bush must step down, that Bush has failed the country and secretly bursting with glee thought that if not now, there can be no better golden opportunity (as our own Opposition leaders would have done) to bring him down. Such political maturity as one finds in the USA is the gift a powerful Ascendant lord aspecting the Ascendant can confer on a nation. But as Jupiter is joined by as many as 3 other planets and the sign he occupies is a common sign as is the Ascendant, it is a nation of multiplicity, the melting pot of different peoples. Yet the Jupiterean influence acts cohesively to cement the diverse peoples and their leaders into a commonality for whom nationhood, national concerns and national well-being are more important than vested interests. Contrast again with the US Ascendant Sagittarius the India Independence Ascendant Taurus, a fixed rigid sign standing for its hoary past of a single race. Its ruler Venus with as many as 4 other planets is a symbol of diversity in unity, of pluralism in a singularity that defies all logic. Yet the nation suffers from a serious pscyhological disorder of perennially shifting loyalties traceable to the occupation of a movable sign by Venus rendered worse by Rahu's presence in the Ascendant which infects it with the rabid virus of opportunism and vested interests.

Going back to the Mars-Saturn square in the United States' chart, it indicates a rulership role also while the natural maleficence of the planets involved gives a certain degree of ruthlessness. Mars in a predominant position in the chart and aspecting the Lagna Sagittarius to the exact degree, associating and colouring thereby its ruler Jupiter, influencing and controlling Venus and Sun as well as the 10th house and its occupant Saturn shows an assertive nature and a military might that tolerates little competition. Mars in Mrigasira is in his own Nakshatra which reinforces all the Martian traits in the national psyche.

CONGLOMERATE OF AFFLICTIONS

Mars, by himself, has moved through Sagittarius, the rising sign of the USA through its 10th house Virgo and also Gemini which houses a 4-planet cluster several times in the history of the nation; yet it was only now in September 2001 that he proved so explosive. Why did this transit prove so different? Transit Jupiter is in Gemini afflicted by Rahu resulting in a Guru-Chandala Yoga which not only divests natal Jupiter of his protective influence on the entire chart but also impairs transit Jupiter himself. Additionally, transit Ketu in Sagittarius afflicts the Ascendant, so does transit Mars. Not to be overlooked is that all the four eclipses of 2001 focus on Sagittarius (and Gemini), the ruling sign of the country. These transit influences read with natal directional influences and afflictions expose the country to severe catastrophes, both man made and natural.*

The Dasa is of the Moon, ruler of the 8th or the house of death, destruction and devastation. He occupies Aquarius, a sign that is closely associated with moslem powers. The Moon occupies Satbhisha ruled by Rahu who is symbolic of fanatical and fundamentalist moslem elements.

The Bhukti is of Saturn, ruler of the 2nd (finance and prosperity) in the 10th, which rules the seat of the Government and is aspected by Mars who rules the military powers of the state. The targets

---

* For more details, see THE ASTROLOGICAL MAGAZINE, January 2001.— **Editor**

clearly reflected these significations in the September 11th attacks. The Bhukti lord Saturn is in a mutually adverse position in Shashtashtaka (6-8) with the Dasa lord Moon.

With this natal planetary background, transit Saturn in the 4th from natal Moon brings the chart under Ashtama Sani making the country vulnerable to grave problems and setbacks.

AERIAL ASSAULTS AND GEMINI

The aerial assaults began with four hijacked commercial planes, loaded with aviation fuel, ramming into the heart of the financial and military centers of the United States. The first to take off was the United Airlines Flight 175 from Boston at 7-58 a.m. on that fateful day, followed quickly one after the other by other airborne bombs. The first take-off can be taken as the core Muhurta (Chart 2).

Chart 2: Take-off of UA Ft 175: 11-9-2001 at 7-58 a.m.(ZST) at Boston.

Chart 2 Rasi			
	SAT. 22-21	MOON 5-13 RAHU 9-50 JUPT. 19-07	
			VENUS 25-59
			SUN 26-24
KETU 9-50 MARS 8-58			ASCDT. 14-49 MERC. 21-49

Navamsa			
JUPT.		ASCDT.	KETU MARS
VENUS			SAT. MERC.
	RAHU	MOON SUN	

The Ascendant Virgo rises with its ruler Mercury in it pointing to the extraordinary brilliance and intelligence involved in both planning and executing the satanic attacks. The Moon is in Gemini, an airy sign, with Rahu-afflicted Jupiter. Jupiter, though a benefic, in this case acts as an affliction bringing the chart under Sagraha Chandra

Dosha, a Maha Dosha. The Kendras are occupied by powerful malefics — Mars and Ketu in the 4th and Rahu-afflicted Jupiter in the 10th. These are factors that do not make the time of take-off propitious for whatever mission the terrorists had in mind.

The Ascendant Virgo is strengthened by its ruler Mercury being in it. The initial round was successful (an interesting point for students of astrology here is the predominance of common signs and the presence of Mercury in a common sign Ascendant. While this can show twin or multiple births in a natal chart, in this particular instance of a Muhurta chart for a mundane mission, it has shown multiple assaults and targets. The heavy afflictions to the Moon not only show the diabolic intentions but also their self-destructive nature, both short and long term.

The rising sign Virgo (**6**), the Nakshatra Mrigasira (**5**), the weekday Tuesday (**3**) and the Tithi or lunar day Krishna Navami (**15 + 9** or the 9th lunar day of the dark fortnight) all add up to 38 which divided by 9 gives a Panchaka of 2 or Agni Panchaka. Except for the rising sign, none of the other factors is normally deemed Muhurtha-friendly.

This Muhurtha chart marking the first major offensive in the *jehad* against America is packed with self-destructive influences. Initial rounds of success may soon give way to a series of agonising but well deserved setbacks for the forces behind the September 11th attacks.

The United States is talking of war. Will it be a limited strike as when Sudan was hit in 1998 or earlier when a multi-national force chased Saddam Hussain out of Kuwait in 1991? Or, will a full-fledged war break out? Irrespective of the option the US may exercise frenzied preparations are already afoot for the war against global terrorism.

Saturn Bhukti runs upto January 2003. Saturn is in the 10th house of action in Chitta ruled by Mars. Mars, in turn, is in the 7th house of aggression in his own constellation. These factors clearly reflect the Amercian rhetoric for war. However, as Saturn is also the

Atmakaraka, it will not be easy for the US to build a coalition for these partners may put in conditional terms of a complex nature. At the same time, given the more complex nature of the terrorist networks and the need to take note of the economic, social and political implications of any step the US may take in its combat, the tactical challenges which Bhukti lord Saturn as an unhelpful Atmakaraka can generate for it may tend to delay war in the strict sense of the term.

A series of Martian aspects will take place in the coming months when terrorist attacks are likely to be met with swift military retaliatory action by the United States.

The Atmakaraka Saturn and the transits in 2001 are such as to frustrate the American efforts to hound out and nab the world's most wanted fundamentalist. Nor do these planetary patterns support the deliverance of Afghanistan from the Taliban and the restoring of the country to its former king. Any game-plan of the United States in this war against global terrorism would benefit vastly by taking cognizance of these astrological indications and exploring other alternatives more seriously.

MARS AND IMPULSIVE DECISIONS

The United States may not be able to effectively concretise its strategy on military operations in the year 2001. Though planetary influences, especially of Mars, may push leaders into impulsive decisions, the world is saved from a full-fledged war in 2001. What awaits the world in 2002 will be dealt with at a future date in these pages.

No terrorist act of violence, not even the most meticulously conceived, can be said to be beyond prevention where its foreknowledge is followed by human effort and faith in God. Such attacks have their genesis in human acts and follies of the past generated through freewill exercised wrongly — consciously or otherwise; it is this same force of freewill which if harnassed along right channels and timed astrologically can be used to handle and even prevent the escalation of human passions as shown by planetary

influences before they concretise into horrendous acts of carnage. The intelligence and other organs of the State would be ensuring the safety of its subjects if the inputs astrology as a science of tendencies can furnish are intelligently made use of to diffuse demonic forces from gathering strength and snowballing into deadly disasters as they did on the *Black Tuesday* of September 2001.
(Written on 26-09-2001) (11-01) ●